INSPIRE / PLAN / DISCOVER / EXPERIENCE

SAN FRANCISCO
AND THE BAY AREA

SAN FRANCISCO
AND THE BAY AREA

CONTENTS

DISCOVER 6

EXPERIENCE 58

NEED TO KNOW 252

Left: A rosy sunrise over Napa Valley vineyards
Previous page: View west from Jones Street

DISCOVER

The San Francisco skyline at sunrise

WELCOME TO
SAN FRANCISCO
AND THE BAY AREA

Iconic bridges and steep streets that slope down to the waterfront. Diverse neighborhoods, each adding a unique flavor to the city. Major museums and teeth-rattling cable cars. Whatever your dream trip to San Francisco includes, this DK Eyewitness Guide is the perfect companion.

1 A vintage cable car, making its way up one of the city's many hills.

2 PIER 39, still thronged with visitors at sunset.

3 The Bay Bridge, lit up at dusk as it stretches across the water to Oakland.

Fingers of fog drift beneath the Golden Gate Bridge, sliding over the hills and welcoming newcomers to the "City by the Bay," as they have since the days when fortune-seekers flocked here during the Gold Rush. But the fog can't hide San Francisco's beauty for long; from its seven steep hills, you'll find yourself confronted with stunning views at almost every turn.

"The City," as it's concisely known to locals, is a place of many nicknames – and many neighborhoods. Track down delicious Italian food in the vibrant North Beach area, or head to Chinatown to experience the spectacular Chinese New Year parade. For those in search of culture, the city's four principal museums – SFMOMA, the Asian, the Legion of Honor, and the De Young – will prove a highlight; if you're looking for nightlife, the buzzing Mission neighborhood is an excellent spot for bar-hopping.

Down on the water, two iconic bridges and a flotilla of ferries connect to lively bayfront cities such as Oakland and Berkeley. The lush vineyards of California Wine Country also lie within easy reach, while the coastal wonders of the Monterey Peninsula make for breezy weekend getaways.

From the Presidio to Alcatraz, we've broken San Francisco and the Bay Area into easily navigable adventures, with expert local knowledge, detailed itineraries, and colorful, comprehensive maps to help you plan the perfect visit. Whether you're staying for a week, a weekend, or longer, this guide will ensure that you see the very best that "Fog City" has to offer.

EXPLORE
SAN
FRANCISCO

This guide divides San Francisco into eight color-coded sightseeing areas, as shown on the map below. Find out more about each area on the following pages. For the Bay Area see p210.

Golden Gate Bridge

Fort Point

Pacific Ocean

Crissy Field

Palace of Fine Arts

San Francisco National Military Cemetery

The Walt Disney Family Museum

Presidio

Baker Beach

PRESIDIO

PRESIDIO AND THE RICHMOND DISTRICT
p60

Land's End

Lincoln Park

RICHMOND

Legion of Honor

Holy Virgin Cathedral

Sutro Heights Park

GOLDEN GATE PARK AND LAND'S END
p188

de Young Museum

California Academy of Sciences

Ocean Beach

Golden Gate Park

Mount Sutro

0 kilometers 1

0 miles 1

N

SUNSET

FOREST HILL

Twin Peaks

NORTH AMERICA

CANADA

USA

Seattle

• SAN FRANCISCO

Chicago • • Boston
• New York
Washington, DC •

• Los Angeles
Memphis •
• Atlanta

Houston •

MEXICO

Gulf of
Mexico

• Miami

Atlantic
Ocean

Pacific
Ocean

Alcatraz
Island

*San Francisco
Bay*

USS
Pampanito

PIER
39

FISHERMAN'S
WHARF

Fort
Mason

MARINA

FISHERMAN'S WHARF
AND NORTH BEACH
p90

• Coit Tower

Exploratorium

COW
HOLLOW

RUSSIAN
HILL

NORTH
BEACH

PACIFIC HEIGHTS
AND THE MARINA
p72

Cable Car
Museum

Transamerica
Pyramid

FINANCIAL
DISTRICT

Ferry
Building

PACIFIC
HEIGHTS

CHINATOWN
AND NOB HILL
p114

Old St Mary's
Cathedral

DOWNTOWN

Japantown

THEATER
DISTRICT

SFMOMA

St. Mary's
Cathedral

CIVIC
CENTER

Yerba Buena
Gardens

CIVIC CENTER
AND HAYES VALLEY
p158

City Hall

Asian Art
Museum

SOMA

DOWNTOWN
AND SOMA
p132

AT&T
Park

HAYES
VALLEY

MISSION
BAY

HAIGHT
ASHBURY

LOWER
HAIGHT

*Buena
Vista Park*

Mission Dolores

POTRERO

GLBT History
Museum

MISSION

HAIGHT ASHBURY
AND THE MISSION
p172

NOE
VALLEY

REASONS TO LOVE
SAN FRANCISCO
AND THE BAY AREA

Two iconic bridges glimmer above a city rich in history, multicultural neighborhoods, and world-famous eateries, while mild marine weather allows for waterfront fun. Here are some of our favorite reasons to visit.

1 WINE COUNTRY WEEKENDS

Take a balloon trip above the vineyards, taste the grape at welcoming wineries, and sink into a hot-springs spa in the Napa and Sonoma valleys.

FERRY BUILDING MARKETPLACE 2

Shop for treats at this soaring indoor food hall (p136), located at the foot of a landmark clock tower. On Saturdays, it expands into a lively outdoor farmer's market on the pier.

3 GOLDEN GATE BRIDGE

Every first-time visitor to San Francisco walks or bikes across the red-orange expanse of this suspension bridge (p64), a world-famous gateway to the vast bay and the Pacific Ocean.

4 HILLTOP VISTAS

Keep your camera close to hand as you wander the city. Legendary photo ops abound, from Pacific-side Land's End, to Coit Tower on Telegraph Hill, and the city skyline from the Marin Headlands.

CABLE-CAR TOURS 5

Climb aboard this National Historic Landmark for an open-air, rattling and bell-ringing ride, from Fisherman's Wharf, over Nob Hill, and down to Union Square in the heart of the city.

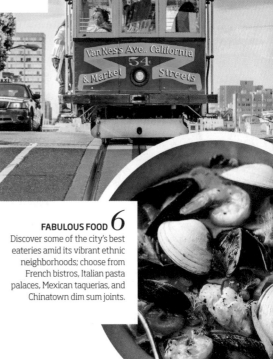

FABULOUS FOOD 6

Discover some of the city's best eateries amid its vibrant ethnic neighborhoods; choose from French bistros, Italian pasta palaces, Mexican taquerias, and Chinatown dim sum joints.

FIRST-RATE MUSEUMS 7

San Francisco offers a rich museum scene. The city's four major museums (SFMOMA, the Asian, the Legion of Honor, and the DeYoung) showcase ancient and modern art.

REDWOODS IN MUIR WOODS 8

These woods *(p218)* are one of the world's few remaining stands of old-growth coast redwood trees. For bird's-eye views, hike the Dipsea Trail.

9 PIER 39

A carousel, an arcade, an aquarium, and live outdoor entertainment lure fun-seekers to the most visited attraction in town *(p100)*, complete with exhibitionist sea lions only too ready to pose for photos.

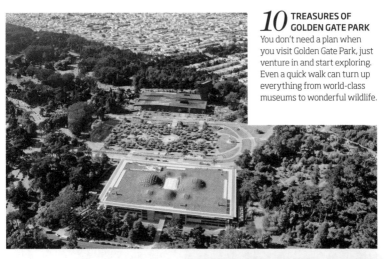

10 TREASURES OF GOLDEN GATE PARK

You don't need a plan when you visit Golden Gate Park, just venture in and start exploring. Even a quick walk can turn up everything from world-class museums to wonderful wildlife.

BEACH BLANKET BABYLON 11

This cult North Beach venue (p104) is the longest-running musical revue in live theater history. Head here for outrageous costumes and irreverent take-offs of celebs, royals, and politicos.

HISTORIC HOUSES 12

Having survived the 1906 earthquake, Painted Ladies *(p168)* line Alamo Square and parts of Broadway in Pacific Heights. Some houses can be toured; all can be admired.

GETTING TO KNOW
SAN FRANCISCO

Known for vibrant neighborhoods, major museums, and waterfront esplanades, San Francisco is the crowning city of the beautiful Bay Area. Visitors get around the seven steep hills by cable car and streetcar, but braving the city on foot can lead to hidden stairways that turn up pocket parks and stunning views. The wider Bay Area offers up even more cityscapes, picturesque towns and natural wonders to explore *(p208)*.

PAGE 60

PRESIDIO AND RICHMOND DISTRICT

Once the nation's premier army post, the Presidio is now a National Park bounded by beach, bluff, and stunning views. Thousands of people visit every year to enjoy a vibrant mix of museums, hiking trails, and recreational destinations. The adjacent Richmond district is a multicultural hub where a casual wander will turn up stunning architecture and restaurants serving cuisine from around the world.

Best for
History and outdoor recreation

Home to
Golden Gate Bridge

Experience
Exploring Fort Point and Crissy Field to find the perfect photo op of Golden Gate Bridge

PAGE 72

PACIFIC HEIGHTS AND THE MARINA

Kites fly and wind surfers skim the bay beyond the city's front lawn: Marina Green. Along the waterfront are busy yacht harbors and historic Fort Mason – now a top spot for art and dining. Heading away from the waterfront you'll find interesting spots like Japantown, as well as beautiful streets recalling past glories in their fantastic architecture.

Best for
Architecture and parks

Home to
Fort Mason and Japantown

Experience
A short walk around Pacific Heights to admire the architecture, crowned by the Queen Anne-style Haas-Lilienthal House

PAGE 90

FISHERMAN'S WHARF AND NORTH BEACH

One of the most famous spots in town, PIER 39 at Fisherman's Wharf is loaded with cafés, knick-knack stores, and legendary seafood restaurants, all to the background music of barking sea lions. The area's cultural history lives on in the Beat Museum and City Lights Bookstore, while iconic San Francisco sights like the Coit Tower, Lombard Street, and Alcatraz Island are irresistible photo ops.

Best for
Shopping and seafood

Home to
Alcatraz Island and Exporatorium

Experience
Hopping on a cruise from the wharf to explore the iconic Alcatraz Island

$\rightarrow$

PAGE 114

CHINATOWN AND NOB HILL

Between Stockton Street and Grant Avenue, the alleys of San Francisco's famous Chinatown are strung with red lanterns, and full of restaurants, Asian markets, and Chinese-inspired architecture. This is also the best place to see the city's historic cable cars trundling through the streets, as they take passengers high above downtown to Nob Hill. Rising above the city here are five iconic hostelries and a towering cathedral, as well as a charming park anchored by an elaborate replica of a 14th-century fountain.

Best for
History and views

Home to
Cable Car Museum and Stockton Street and Grant Avenue

Experience
A walk around Nob Hill to see millionaires' mansions, elegant hotels, architectural icons

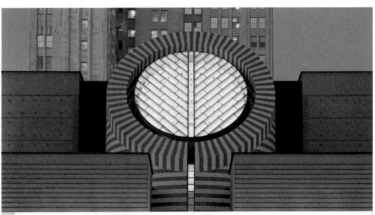

PAGE 132

DOWNTOWN AND SOMA

In downtown San Francisco you'll find the vast modern marvels of the financial district, like the Transamerica Pyramid and the Salesforce Tower. Nearby Union Square is the city's fashion center, encircled by department stores and shopping malls, and designer boutiques. To the south, SOMA (South of Market) is a hotspot for museum, galleries and nightlife.

Best for
Galleries, theater, and shopping

Home to
Ferry Building, SFMOMA, and Yerba Buena Gardens

Experience
Exploring the museums and galleries of SOMA, ending with a drink at Cityscape Bar & Lounge

CIVIC CENTER AND HAYES VALLEY

The buildings in the civic center are an outstanding example of the Beaux Arts style. It is perhaps the most ambitious and elaborate city center complex in the US and well worth an extended visit. The stunning architecture continues if you head up Fulton Street, which climbs gently to nearby Alamo Square where you'll find the iconic row of late Victorian houses known as the Painted Ladies.

Best for
Architecture and music venues

Home to
Asian Art Museum

Experience
A picnic at Alamo Square as you take in the amazing view of the modern city skyline behind old Victorian houses

→

HAIGHT AND THE MISSION

Vintage clothing, tattoo parlors, and record stores left over from the hippie-era Summer of Love comprise a colorful collage in the Haight Ashbury neighborhood. The oldest neighborhood, the Mission District, remains a multicultural area with a large Latin Amerian community, as reflected in the political and cutural murals that decorate the buildings.

Best for
Art and LGBT+ culture

Home to
Castro Street and Haight Ashbury

Experience
A walk down Castro Street, the heart of the city's world-famous LGBT+ hub

PAGE 188

GOLDEN GATE PARK AND LAND'S END

A masterpiece of 1890s landscaping, natural environments, and botanical gardens, Golden Gate Park sweeps to the Pacific. It encompasses three major museums, an outdoor concert plaza, biking and walking trails, and a lake where rowboats and pedal boats cruise. On the western edge of the city, Land's End offers miles of coastal footpaths, and the stunning Ocean Beach.

Best for
Nature and museums

Home to
California Academy of Sciences, de Young Museum and Legion of Honor

Experience
Warming up with a sunset bonfire on Ocean Beach

PAGE 208

THE BAY AREA

North of San Francisco is Marin County, covered in beautiful parks and forests. The cities of Oakland and Berkeley take up much of the East Bay area, while farther south along the peninsula are beautiful beaches and the exciting urban centers of Silicon Valley. Napa Valley and Sonoma County will be well known to wine lovers, while farther afield there are plenty of new places to discover, like the tiny town of Carmel-by-the-Sea and the delights of Old Town Sacramento.

Best for
Beaches and national parks

Home to
Santa Cruz Beach Boardwalk, Half Moon Bay, Napa Valley Wine Country, Healdsburg, and Monterey

Experience
A walk in the Marin Headlands to see the Golden Gate Bridge against the San Francisco skyline

←

① The Bay Bridge and downtown skyline, lit up at dusk.

② A solitary confinement cell in the infamous Alcatraz prison.

③ A vintage streetcar traveling through the city streets.

④ Visitor's at the fantastic SFMOMA gallery.

San Francisco is a treasure trove of things to see and do, and its compact size means that the city and its surrounding area can be easily explored. These itineraries will inspire you to make the most of your visit.

1 DAY

In San Francisco

Morning

Enjoy an all-American breakfast with a bay view at the Eagle Café *(PIER 39, Space A-201)*, before strolling through the famous pier's many shops and entertainments. Continue to Fisherman's Wharf, taking in steaming crab pots and fishermen unloading their catches at Pier 37, where you can clamber aboard the historic ships at the Maritime National Historical Park *(p102)*. From here, ferries depart for tours of Alcatraz Island *(p94)*, and cruise under the Golden Gate Bridge *(p64)* and around the bay. If you aren't inclined to set sail, hop on the rattling, clanging Powell-Hyde Cable Car for dizzying cityscape and ocean views up the steep streets.

Afternoon

In the historic Kimpton Sir Francis Drake Hotel, where uniformed "Beefeaters" greet guests and regale passersby, you can't get more San Francisco than lunch at Scala's Bistro *(432 Powell St)*, a dark-paneled brasserie famous for wood-oven-roasted meats, pizza, fresh pastas, and Italian wines. Afterwards, walk off your meal en route to Yerba Buena Gardens *(p142)*. Here you can view outdoor art installations, and the Martin Luther King, Jr. Memorial Waterfall. Across the street is the Contemporary Jewish Museum *(p148)* and the stunning SFMOMA *(p120)*, home to one of the world's most important collections of contemporary art.

Evening

As the glittering "Bay Lights" blink on across the Bay Bridge *(p224)*, ride a vintage streetcar down Market Street to the Embarcadero *(p144)*, a palm-tree-lined, waterfront promenade. Drop into the Exploratorium *(p98)* at Pier 15, an interactive museum that is open to adults only on Thursday evenings. At the nearby cruise ship terminal, multi-storied passenger liners are lit up at night like Christmas trees against the backdrop of the glowing Golden Gate Bridge. Head to the Slanted Door in the Ferry Building *(p136)* for a wonderful meal and amazing views of this sparkling nighttime display.

→

1 The sculpture garden of the de Young Museum.

2 A bowl of crab cioppino.

3 The pastel-coloured Painted Ladies.

4 Seals basking at the Point Lobos State Natural Reserve.

3 DAYS

In San Francisco, Monterey, and Carmel

Day 1

Morning Breakfast at the Beach Chalet (p204) and stroll along Ocean Beach (p202) before heading off to explore the greenery of Golden Gate Park (p206). On the same site, the de Young Museum (p194) is filled with treasures; you'll want to devote a couple of hours to browsing the exhibits here.

Afternoon Have lunch at the on-site Museum Café before making your way to PIER 39 to hop on a sightseeing cruise. Don't forget to bring your camera: out in the Bay you'll get spectacular close-up views of the Golden Gate Bridge and Alcatraz. Afterwards, walk up Columbus Avenue towards Coit Tower (p106) to take in vibrant 1930s-era frescoes at the tower's base, and dazzling views form the top.

Evening Nab a sidewalk table at Sotto Mare (552 Green St), famous for its cioppino and fresh oysters. As darkness falls, head to Beach Blanket Babylon, where costumed performers regale sold-out audiences with musical revues.

Day 2

Morning Breakfast at The Grove - Hayes (301 Hayes St) before strolling to the upscale boutiques and galleries of Hayes Valley (p166).

Afternoon Lunch and libations can be sought at the hip Absinthe Brasserie (398 Hayes St), known for its French-Italian cuisine and a lively bar scene. Walk to Alamo Square (p168) to see Victorian houses known as the Painted Ladies, then grab a cab to Mission Dolores (p182) in the Latino district to tour the oldest structure in the city. A stroll through the neighborhood's side streets turns up striking murals and the Mission Cultural Center for Latino Arts (p184).

Evening You'll probably need to queue up for dinner from La Taqueria (2889 Mission St), but their tacos area well worth the wait. End your evening by heading down the street to Foreign Cinema, where you can relax with creative cocktails and a vintage movie.

Day 3

Morning Drive south past the surfer's city of Santa Cruz to Monterey (p248) for some oceanfront fun. Get here early for the world-famous aquarium, a walking and biking trail by the water's edge, and shopping along Cannery Row, where John Steinbeck once roamed.

Afternoon Art-lovers should head for the leafy lanes of Carmel-by-the-Sea (p250), a century-old artist's colony of galleries and cottages. Don't miss the 16th-century Mission Carmel, and the Point Lobos State Natural Reserve, called the "greatest meeting of land and water in the world."

Evening A favorite sunset destination is cypress-fringed Carmel Beach, where you can drink in spectacular views across the Pacific. For dinner, aim for a historic eatery such as Mission Ranch (26270 Dolores St), located in an old farmhouse owned by Clint Eastwood.

7 DAYS

In San Francisco and the Bay Area

Day 1

Grab a cup of coffee and a pastry at HEYDAY *(555 Mission St)* and ascend to the 61st-floor skydeck of the new Salesforce Tower for jaw-dropping views. When back on the ground, wander through the downtown Financial District to Chinatown, where you can pick up lunch and do a bit of browsing. In the evening, go for a seafood dinner at Tadich Grill *(p147)* – the oldest continuously run restaurant in the state of California.

Day 2

From Pier 41, take a ferry across the Bay to Oakland *(p222)* for a waterfront breakfast on Jack London Square. Spend some time at the contemporary Oakland Museum of California, which showcases the state's art, history, and natural sciences. In the evening enjoy live music at the Greek Theatre on the Berkeley College

campus *(p226)*. Afterwards, famished foodies can head to the Shattuck Avenue "Gourmet Ghetto" for a wealth of excellent farm-to-table options.

Day 3

An early morning drive one hour north of San Francisco is rewarded with breakfast at Model Bakery *(644 1st St)* in Napa *(p241)*, where exotic food vendors, a brew pub, and oyster bar are all worth a lingering visit. Napa Valley Wine Country *(p238)* is the queen of California's wine regions and boasts over 400 wineries; call ahead to tour Castello di Amorosa, a massive, castle-like winery, or the Rubicon Estate Winery. Dinner is French fare at Napa's Angèle *(540 Main St)*, an old boathouse on the Napa River. From here, walk through the Old Town to catch a comedy show at the Uptown Theater.

1 Views from the Salesforce Tower.

2 Paper lanterns in Chinatown.

3 Fresh oysters, served throughout the region.

4 Bodega Bay at sunset.

5 A forest path through Muir Woods.

Day 4

In Sonoma Town *(p246)* grab breakfast at Sunflower Café *(421 1st St W)* on the historic Sonoma Plaza, then head straight to a tour of vine-covered Buena Vista, the state's oldest winery. Hop on the open-air tram through the vineyards at Benziger Family Winery to visit the Gloria Ferrer Champagne Caves *(p246)*. In the late afternoon, head up the road to the Jack London State Historic Park *(p247)*, before spending the night in a B&B on the Sonoma Coast.

Day 5

After breakfast at Willow Wood Café *(9020 Graton Rd)* in Graton, head to Bodega Bay *(p244)* for a spot of whale-watching. Warm up with a bowl of cracked Dungeness crab chowder at the tiny Spud Point Crab Company *(1910 Westshore Rd)*, then take a coastline drive along Highway 1 to the Armstrong Redwoods State Park *(p245)* to admire groves of ancient redwoods. End your day with dinner at Vintner's Inn *(4350 Barnes Rd)* in Santa Rosa, followed by a walk in the beautiful hotel grounds.

Day 6

Start your Marin County day trip with breakfast at the Dipsea Café *(200 Shoreline Hwy)* in Mill Valley. Then get an early start at Muir Woods and Beach *(p219)*, a wonderful hiking and cycling area and a haven for old-growth redwoods. Take a beach stroll or go waterfowl-watching, before heading to Sausalito's Cavallo Point Lodge *(601 Murray Cir)* – a former military base – for a comfortable dinner and cocktails.

Day 7

Houses cling to steep hillsides above the town of Sausalito on Richardson Bay *(p216)*, where kayaks, ferryboats, and sea lions share the choppy water. Breakfast at the Bayside Café *(1 Gate 6 Rd)*, then take the short ferry ride from Tiburon to Angel Island *(p217)* for dazzling Bay Area vistas, and a seafood lunch. When you've had your fill of exploring the island on its excellent walking and cycling trails, take the ferry back to San Francisco for an evening of gallery viewing and good food at Fort Mason *(p76)*.

A DRIVING TOUR
49-MILE DRIVE

Length 49 miles (79 km) **Stopping-off points** Hop out of the car at Fort Point for some fresh air and lovely Bay views **Signs** Follow the blue signs for the "49 Mile Scenic Drive"

Linking the city's most intriguing neighborhoods, fascinating sights, and spectacular views, the 49-Mile Scenic Drive is an official route that provides a splendid overview of the city of San Francisco for the determined motorist. Keeping to the well-marked route is simple enough – just follow the blue-and-white seagull signs. Some of these are hidden by overhanging vegetation or buildings, so you need to be alert. You should set aside a whole day for this trip; there are plenty of places to stop to take photographs or admire the views, and you may encounter slow city traffic.

*The **Palace of Fine Arts** (p68) stands near the wooded Presidio.*

*It's worth getting out at **Golden Gate Park** (p188) to explore some of the sights tucked away in the grounds.*

San Francisco Zoo and Gardens *is one of the best zoos in the US. Its attractions include Hearst Grizzly Gulch and the Primate Discovery Center.*

*From both summits of **Twin Peaks** (p184), the views over the city and bay are truly magnificent.*

INSIDER TIP
Know Before You Go

Avoid driving during rush hours: 7–10am and 4–7pm. Chinatown and Fisherman's Wharf are heavily pedestrianized, so take care in these areas. Watch out for foggy weather, which can obstruct views.

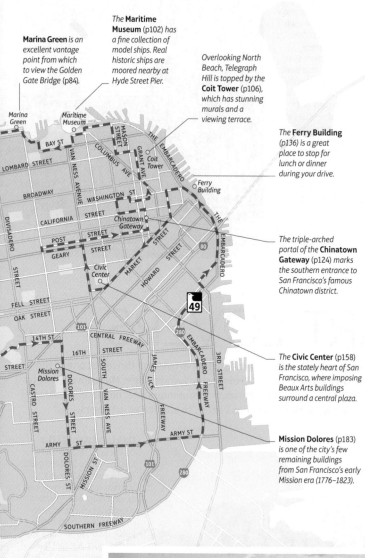

Marina Green is an excellent vantage point from which to view the Golden Gate Bridge (p84).

The **Maritime Museum** (p102) has a fine collection of model ships. Real historic ships are moored nearby at Hyde Street Pier.

Overlooking North Beach, Telegraph Hill is topped by the **Coit Tower** (p106), which has stunning murals and a viewing terrace.

The **Ferry Building** (p136) is a great place to stop for lunch or dinner during your drive.

The triple-arched portal of the **Chinatown Gateway** (p124) marks the southern entrance to San Francisco's famous Chinatown district.

The **Civic Center** (p158) is the stately heart of San Francisco, where imposing Beaux Arts buildings surround a central plaza.

Mission Dolores (p183) is one of the city's few remaining buildings from San Francisco's early Mission era (1776–1823).

→ A view of downtown San Francisco from the summit of Twin Peaks

Street Art

Rivaling Chicago and LA for public murals, San Francisco's street art enlivens the walls of its neighborhoods. The Mission district alone is emblazoned with more than 400 bright murals. This vast outdoor gallery includes the Carnaval Mural, which honors the area's Latin culture. In hotspots like Balmy Alley and Clarion Alley the murals come and go, while the 27 New Deal Social Realist murals in the Coit Tower *(p106)* are protected for posterity. Precita Eyes Muralists offers guided tours *(www. precitaeyes.org).*

→

Artists painting a mural in the Breakers Café in the Bay Area,

THE BAY AREA FOR
ART LOVERS

The Bay Area has long been a magnet for artists and thrives as one of the world's foremost art venues. From famous works at the Museum of Modern Art (SFMOMA) and de Young Museum to stunning street murals and Oakland's monthly art walk, the region has venues to enthrall all art lovers.

Oakland Art Walks

On the first Friday of the month, head to Oakland *(p222)* for the free Oakland Art Murmur Art Walk *(www. oak landart murmur.org).* About 50 galleries throughout the city open their doors to the public from 6 to 9pm and offer guided tours. A street festival is held downtown with food stalls and outdoor movies. Take time, too, to appreciate street art throughout the local neighborhoods. Many galleries also open on Saturday afternoons for artists' talks and the self-guided Saturday Stroll.

Street food stalls line Telegraph Avenue, as part of the Oakland First Fridays Festival

SFMOMA and De Young

The dynamic SFMOMA (San Francisco Museum of Modern Art) has an astounding collection of more than 32,000 modern and contemporary international artworks (p138). American painting and sculpture from the 17th century to today is the main focus of the de Young Museum (p194). It also has striking sculptural, textile, and photographic art from Africa and Oceania, including jaw-dropping Maori creations.

$\longrightarrow$

Bracket (1989) by Joan Mitchel on display at SFMOMA

Other Stellar Galleries

For French Impressionist masterpieces head to the Legion of Honor (p196). The Yerba Buena Center for the Arts (p142) showcases contemporary art and hosts the fascinating Museum of the African Diaspora, while the Asian Art Museum (p162) also has an outstanding collection. Across the Bay, the Art Museum at UC Berkeley (p226) has wide-ranging exhibits.

$\longleftarrow$

Exterior of the Yerba Buena Center for the Arts, an exciting venue for contemporary arts

Saks Fifth Avenue bordering an open air art market on Union Square ↑

SAN FRANCISCO FOR
SHOPPING

Shopping in San Francisco is much more than simply making a purchase, it's an experience that allows a glimpse into local culture, and an insight into the atmosphere of the various city districts - with fancy, glittering displays on Union Square to the vintage chic on offer in Haight Ashbury.

Chic Boutiques

Small business owners in San Francisco take much pride in bringing hand-crafted wares to their customers, and will often tell you the histories of these original items. Downtown's Financial District has long been the best place to go to check out local designers and craftspeople turning out high-quality, handmade products - a local tradition that includes Levi's jeans. Now other areas of the city are making names for themselves in the word of top-class design, including the Mission District - home of Heath Ceramics *(2900 18th St)*.

→

A showroom for Heath Ceramics, a world-class designer brand

Serious Shoppers

If you like to make time for a good, long shop in your vacation itinerary, be sure to spend a while exploring the blocks bordered by Sutter Street to the north and Market Street to the South, with Union Square as the centerpiece. Here luxurious shops mingle with inexpensive boutiques, and big brands sit next to exciting new labels. Most of San Francisco's major department stores are in or near Union Square, including Macy's and Saks Fifth Avenue. Fancy hotels, splendid restaurants, and colorful flower stalls all add to the posh atmosphere.

← Shoppers laden with big-brand purchases from the Union Square area

TOP 3 LOCAL MAKERS

Golden Gate Fortune Cookie Company
At 56 Ross Alley customers can taste samples before buying fortune cookies, which were a local invention (p124).

MAC
MAC (Modern Appealing Clothing) at 387 Grove Street sources one-third of its clothing (boths mens- and womenswear) from San Francisco designers.

Williams-Sonoma
Gourmet cooks dream of this famous brand's many kitchen gadgets and quality cookware, sold at 340 Post Street.

INSIDER TIP
Taxes

A sales tax of 8.5 per cent is added to all purchases made in San Francisco. Note that this is not refundable to overseas visitors, but you are exempt if your purchases are forwarded to any destination outside California.

The picturesque ↑ buildings and walkways of PIER 39

Marina District and North Beach

With the quaint and lively atmosphere of a small town main street, the Marina District section of Chestnut Street (p84) is a cute avenue which offers a little bit of everything. Whether you're a full-day shopper or just like to a quick look in the windows, there's plenty to see here, and lots of cafés and restaurants for breaks in between. In almost total contrast, PIER 39 (p100) is the place to go for souvenirs and candy stores. It may be a little tourist-centric, but it's also undeniably fun.

Michelin-Starred Menus

In San Francisco's SOMA district, Saison (*www.saisonsf.com*) and Coi (*www. coirestaurant.com*) are just a few of the Michelin-starred spots you can enjoy after a day exploring the area's fantastic art and entertainment venues. Farther afield in Oakland, chef James Syhabout's Commis *(p223)* showcases local ingredients with subtle flair, while shining brightly with three Michelin stars is The French Laundry *(p238)*, Thomas Keller's seasonally focused restaurant, tucked away in the tiny Napa Valley village of Yountville.

→

An elegeant torte served at Coi in the SOMA district

THE BAY AREA
LET'S EAT!

From fun food trucks to some of the world's most celebrated restaurants, the city's vibrant food scene should be a key part of any visit to the Bay Area. All the ingredients are here: the heady mix of cultural influences and flavors, and an abundance of fresh, high-quality local produce.

Farmers' Markets

Pottering around markets is a favorite weekend pastime for many San Franciscans, who take pride in the Bay Area's quality produce, like the fruit and veg sold at Alemany Farmers' Market *(100 Alemany Blvd)*. For local artisanal products, try the thrice-weekly Ferry Plaza Farmers' Market *(p136)*, which has a beautiful harbor-side setting.

→

Fresh produce on sale at the farmers' market by the Ferry Building

Mexican Fare

Some of the city's most celebrated cuisine is handed out through the tiny windows of hole-in-the-wall joints like Fistful of Tacos *(201 Harrison St)*, or delivered through hatches at El Norteño Taco Truck *(801 Bryant St)*. Don't let the settings fool you: with soft, freshly pressed tortillas, zingy vegetables and tender, marinated meat, these are some of the best tacos around. Mission District is the place for burritos, with La Taqueria *(2889 Mission St)* and Taqueria La Cumbre SF *(515 Valencia St)* among the local favorites.

← Tucking into a fully-laden, soft tortilla

ASIAN EXPERIENCE

San Francisco's Chinatown *(p122)* is the oldest in the US, established by immigrant railroad and farm workers in the 1860s. Today, the eight-by-six street blocks that make up the district are packed with dim-sum cafés, Asian bakeries and Szechuan seafood restaurants. Lesser known, but no less delicious, are the noodle, rice, and sushi dishes in the nation's oldest Japantown *(p78)*. Walk less than a mile east and you'll hit Little Saigon on Larkin Street, where the heady scents of fermented pickles and fragrant broth waft from tiny Vietnamese cafés.

↑ Fresh, locally sourced clams served at a San Francisco restaurant

Farm-to-Table Cuisine

Cooking with fresh, local, seasonal produce isn't just a trend in the Bay Area – it's a way of life. When the farms in question produce some of the most flavorsome and sought-after ingredients around, it's hard to think why it wouldn't end up on local tables first and foremost. Not just any table, mind you – many of the area's most beloved restaurants, from Sons & Daughters *(708 Bush St)* on Nob Hill to the venerable French Laundry *(p238)*, build their menus around ingredients sourced from local ranchers, farmers, and fishing crews.

Beautiful Beaux Arts

The Neo-Classical style of the Parisian École des Beaux Arts was favoured for major buildings following the 1906 earthquake. Opulent colonnades, sculptures, and pediments are typical of this lavish style. The most perfect illustration is the Palace of Fine Arts *(p68)* in the Marina District of San Francisco.

↑ The Palace of Fine Arts, built in 1915 for a world's fair

SAN FRANCISCO'S
ARCHITECTURE

San Francisco's hilly landscape means that this is one American city where its towering skyscrapers do not immediately capture the eye. Instead, the architectural highlights are woven throughout the fabric of the city streets.

Iconic Victorian

The city's most distinctive architecture is its array of Victorian houses, with their wooden frames and elaborate ornamentation. There are several different styles from this 55-year period *(p170)* and well-preserved Victorian buildings can be seen all over San Francisco, making a casual stroll along the city streets feel like walking through a colourful gallery. To see inside, head to Haas-Lilienthal House *(p83)* and Octagon House *(p83)*, which are open to the public.

←

Classic Stick style Victorian houses in the Haight Ashbury district

Arts and Crafts

A more rustic, down-to-earth style was adopted after the turn of the 20th century, inspired by the English Arts and Crafts movement. Architects used materials such as redwood and uncut stone, and borrowed decorative Japanese motifs to achieve a natural look. In the East Bay city of Berkeley (p226), the First Church of Christ, Scientist is a particularly fine example of the style, by architect Bernard Ralph Maybeck.

↑ First Church of Christ, Scientist in Berkeley, completed in 1910

The Evolving City

The Transbay redevelopment project downtown has changed the city's skyline. The project's centerpiece – the Salesforce Tower – is now the tallest skyscraper in San Francisco, and the tallest building in the western United States. As well as commercial and office space, the development will create thousands of much needed new homes in the city.

← The Salesforce Tower rising high over the San Francisco skyline

→ Mission San Francisco de Asís, or Mission Dolores, founded in 1776

RELIGIOUS ARCHITECTURE

The architectural diversity of the city is most apparent in its churches. Since the first simple missions, the city's churches have been built in an array of styles from Gothic to Baroque, with numerous hybrids in between. Many prominent churches reflect the traditions and styles of the countries from which their original congregations came.

Early San Francisco

From 1776 to 1823, Spanish missionaries employed labourers to construct seven missions and three fortresses. Seen at places like Mission Dolores (p183) the style is characterized by thick walls of rough adobe bricks, red tile roofs, and arcaded galleries surrounding courtyards. During the Gold Rush most buildings were only temporary but later fireproof brick was used; see the best survivors in the Jackson Square Historical District (p144).

The San Bruno Mountains south of San Francisco

Mountain Highs

Mountains dominate the Bay Area landscape, offering invigorating hikes and breathtaking views. The vistas from atop Mount Tamalpais are particularly stunning, especially at dusk. The San Bruno Mountains (south of San Francisco) and the East Bay Hills are laced with trails through the redwoods. At 3,849 ft (1,173 m), Mount Diablo is the highest mountain in the region; from its summit you can see the snow-capped Sierra Nevada.

THE BAY AREA'S
NATURAL
BEAUTY

From gorgeous beaches framed by rugged cliffs to redwood forests abundant with wildlife, the Bay Area is full of breathtaking natural beauty. San Francisco's rolling hills offer stellar views of the bay, ocean, and mountains. Experience nature's delights by hiking, sailing, biking, or scenic drives.

Golden Sands

Beach lovers are spoilt for choice in the Bay Area, which has around 250 km (150 miles) of coastline. Large waves make for great surfing. San Francisco's Baker Beach has stellar views of the Golden Gate Bridge, while Ocean Beach has nighttime bonfires. Farther afield, Stinson Beach is popular for its heaps of activities; Half Moon Bay has tide pools; and Santa Cruz is revered by surfers.

$\rightarrow$

Sunrise at Ocean Beach on the shores of the San Francisco Bay

EAT

Limewood Bar & Restaurant

In the Claremont Resort and Spa *(p225)*, nestled in the Berkeley Hills, Limewood offers sensational sweeping views of San Francisco, the Golden Gate Bridge, and the Bay. Sunsets from the veranda are sublime. Casual, contemporary and classy, it serves nouvelle California fare.

🏠 **41 Tunnel Rd, Berkeley** 🅦 **limewood restaurant.com**

💲💲💲

Fabulous Forests

Surprisingly close to San Francisco you can find great swathes of ancient California coast redwood forests, with their cool damp air and other-worldly serenity. The most famous is Muir Woods *(p219)*, which offers 6 miles (10 km) of easy trails. The glorious old-growth trees of Armstrong Redwoods State Park *(p245)* dwarf even those of Muir Woods, while Big Basin Redwoods State Park is an emerald gem in the Santa Cruz Mountains mere minutes from Silicon Valley.

→

Coast redwoods and a fallen tree *(inset)* in Big Basin Redwoods State Park

Wildlife Wonders

The Pacific waters and varied terrain of the Bay Area abound with wildlife. Migrating whales can be seen in winter from the cliffs of Point Reyes and from Santa Cruz pier, or year-round on trips to the Farallon Islands. Seals and sea lions sunbathe along the shore. Meadows and forests teem with mammals from deer to Tule elk. Those in luck may even spot mountain lion.

→

Elephant seals on a beach, Año Nuevo State Park

THE BAY AREA FOR
FAMILIES

The Bay Area is chock-full of kid-friendly activities and attractions, so you'll never be short of ways to keep the family entertained. Children of all ages will enjoy the gorgeous beaches, hands-on museums, fun educational experiences, and unique thrills like a ride on the clanging cable cars.

The Must Sees

No family vacation is complete without a visit to PIER 39 *(p100)*. Highlights include street entertainers, a carousel, the vast Aquarium of the Bay, and San Francisco's resident sea lions – just follow the sounds of barking and you'll find them lounging in a heap by the water. If you venture farther afield, the fantastic Monterey Bay Aquarium *(p248)* is a spectacular day out for the whole family. If it seems familiar, that's probably because it was used as inspiration for the aquarium in Disney's *Finding Dory* (2016).

→
The beautiful old-fashioned carousel on PIER 39 in Fisherman's Wharf

Full-Day Fun

If you have the whole day to fill, you can't go wrong with the California Academy of Sciences (p192). There's enough to keep kids fascinated for eons, including an aquarium, natural history museum, planetarium, and a domed, four-story rainforest with 40,000 live animals in three distinct ecosystems. For the ultimate day out at the seaside, head to Santa Cruz Beach Boardwalk (p230), a classic seaside amusement park with rides, games, and entertainment galore, while the beach itself is the perfect place for a picnic.

← Claude, an albino aligator at the California Academy of Sciences' Swamp exhibit

TOP 3 PLACES TO TAKE A BREAK

South Park
This oval oasis has play areas, a hummingbird garden, plus climbing structures and a sand pit (64 S Park St).

Alamo Square
While parents snap photos of the beautiful hilltop views, kids can enjoy the playground and Shoe Garden, which features cast-off footwear as art (p168).

Yerba Buena Gardens
A serene space in the heart of downtown, this garden makes a great stop to take a break between visits to the area's many museums (p142).

INSIDER TIP
Ride for Less

Make the journey part of the fun by including a combination of buses, streetcars, and cable cars as you travel the hilly streets of San Francisco. Under-5s travel free, and there are reduced fares for children aged 5 to 17.

An interactive maze at San Jose's Tech Museum of Innovation ↑

Hands-On Museums

Whether your children's interests tend towards art or science, you'll find scores of fun-filled museums that may spark a lifelong interest. If you're in Marin County to walk over the Golden Gate Bridge, don't miss the Bay Area Discovery Museum (p218), which has heaps of hands-on exhibits that are so fun your kids won't even realize they're learning. And if you venture out into San Jose (p234), your child (or the child within) can even build a robot at The Tech Museum of Innovation.

Club Scene

Like almost everything else in San Francisco, the city's nightlife is fairly casual, friendly, and low key, and even trendy venues like August Hall *(www.august hallsf.com)* may only be open one or two nights a week. If you want to sample an aspect of nightlife that is typically San Franciscan, try the stand-up comedy clubs or a cozy piano bar.

A DJ plays to a crowd of dancers letting off steam in a nightclub

THE BAY AREA
LIVE!

San Francisco has prided itself on being the cultural capital of the West Coast since the city first began to prosper in the 1850s. With a huge variety of entertainment options, it is one of the most enjoyable cities in the world, with big names in every branch of the arts performing here.

Popular Music Paradise

The Bay Area boasts the West Coast's best opera, ballet, and symphony orchestra, but popular music is where it really excels. Some of the city's quintessential sounds and venues are Dixieland jazz in the Gold Dust Lounge *(www.golddustsf.com)*, blues at Biscuits and Blues *(www.biscuitsandblues. com)*, and rock at The Fillmore *(www.thefillmore. com)*, the birthplace of psychedelic rock in the 1960s.

The Outside Lands Music Festival, held each summer in Golden Gate Park ↑

Fantastic Festivals

There are so many festivals across the whole spectrum of performing arts that it's definitely worth checking a Bay Area calendar of events while planning your trip. You may find that your visit coincides with the annual Comedy Day celebrations (www.comedyday.org) in Golden Gate Park, or a literary festival dedicated to Steinbeck or Shakespeare. Naturally, there are plenty of cool music festivals throughout the Bay Area, as well.

On Stage in San Francisco

The main Theater District (p151) plays host to major Broadway shows on tour, but it's really the alternative scene visitors should check out. The Mission District, in particular, is home to great venues such as The Marsh (www.themarsh.org) and Project Artaud (www.project artaud.org). The absolute must-see is the uniquely San Franciscan revue *Beach Blanket Babylon* (p104).

←

Gary Clark Jr. performing in San Francisco, and The Fox *(inset)* in Oakland

→

Geary Theatre, longtime home of the American Conservatory Theater

Sail the Bay

Sailing is synonymous with San Francisco Bay. On any sunny weekend, the waters are mottled with billowing sails. Cruising across the bay is a breathtaking sensation and offers stunning views of the City skyline and Golden Gate Bridge. The bay is one of the most challenging sailing environments in the world, due to lots of other vessels, strong currents, and the shifting winds that howl through the Golden Gate strait. Experienced sailors can charter yachts. Novices can take lessons with sailing schools and clubs, or you can choose a sailing excursion if you'd prefer to sit back and let someone else hoist the sails.

→

Sailboats navigating the choppy waters of San Francisco Bay

THE BAY AREA FOR
THRILL-SEEKERS

Bay Area inhabitants are famously active for good reason. Blessed with soaring mountains, a rugged coast, and a vast bay to choose from, there's no shortage of adventures to enjoy. The hills are laced with biking and hiking trails, and wind-whipped San Francisco Bay is nirvana for kite-surfing and yachting.

Mountain bike "Mount Tam"

Marin County is considered the Mecca of mountain biking, which was born in the 1970s on Mt. Tamalpais *(p218)*. The mountain summit is easily accessed via the Railroad Grade Fire Road (once the route of a scenic railroad), which begins in Mill Valley and snakes 7 km (4.5 miles) to the top, where you're rewarded with superlative views.

←

The beautiful Railroad Grade Fire Road on Mt. Tamalpais

ESCAPE FROM ALCATRAZ TRIATHLON

As punishing as a spell in the famous prison, this grueling triathlon draws 2000 Olympic champions, seasoned pros, and hardened amateur triathletes from around the globe each June. The grand-daddy of events is a 1.5-mile (2.4-km) swim from Alcatraz to San Francisco's Aquatic Park in biting-cold waters renowned for their ferocious currents. Next comes a brutal 18-mile (29-km) bike ride to Golden Gate Park and 8-mile (13-km) run to Baker Beach over varied terrain.

Motorbiking California's Coastal Highway

Few motorbike rides are as thrilling as that to Point Reyes Lighthouse (p218). The undulating, sinuous, and spectacularly scenic road along the coastal promontory combines everything that's fun about two-wheel touring. You'll sweep through lush rolling meadows and wind-scoured moorland and, finally, along a cliff-hugging ribbon snaking above crashing surf.

$\rightarrow$

Motorcyclist on the stunning Coastal Highway

Surf Mavericks

The Maverick's surf break, at Pillar Point off Half Moon Bay (p232), is world-renowned for ferocious waves that can top 20 m (66 ft). Big, scary and barreling ashore at 50 mph (80 km/h), these are for true experts only.

Nearby Santa Cruz (p230) is the capital of Bay Area surfing, with waves for every level, including Cowell's Beach for starters and Steamer Lane for savvy surfers. Wetsuits are de rigueur in the Bay.

$\leftarrow$

Courageous surfers riding monster waves at Pillar Point

Did You Know?

San Francisco's Theatre Rhino exclusively puts on plays by and about LGBT+ people.

SAN FRANCISCO'S
LGBT+
CULTURE

San Francisco's LGBT+ community dates back to the almost all-male populations of miners in the late 19th century. After the free-love movement of the 1960s, gay people began to come out and stand proud across the city, making it one of the best places in the world to be openly gay.

Community History

San Francisco isn't just called the world's gay capital because of the gay-friendly atmsophere and the cool Castro district. It's because the city is steeped in LGBT+ history, from the site of one of America's first LGBT+-related riots at 101 Taylor Street in 1966, to Pink Triangle Park, home to America's only memorial to the LGBT+ murdered during World War II. The GLBT Museum *(p182)* makes a great starting point for visitors interested in LGBT+ history. You could also catch Sunday service at the Glide Memorial United Methodist Church on 330 Ellis Street, which has been welcoming gay and transgender people since the 1960s.

↑ The choir at Glide Memorial United Methodist Church

San Francisco Pride

While there are LGBT+ festivals and events throughout the year, the highlight of the community calendar is definitely the "San Francisco Lesbian, Gay, Bisexual, and Transgender Pride Celebration", held at the end of June. There are performers on the main stage, marches, and a hugely popular parade on Sunday morning. While the focus is on fun, the event also aims to commemorate the highs and lows of LGBT+ history and to educate allies.

←

Performers in the world-famous San Francisco Pride parade

HARVEY MILK

With the rise of the gay Castro district, the LGBT+ community gained political force. In 1977, local business-owner Harvey Milk was elected to the Board of Supervisors, becoming the nation's first openly gay elected official. His tenure was cut short in 1978 when he and Mayor George Moscone were shot at City Hall by Dan White. The political movement was further fueled when White was found guilty only of man-slaughter and given a light sentence, and the city rioted in protest.

↑ City Hill illuminated in rainbow colors to celebrate San Francisco Pride

The Castro District

The Castro (p176) is San Francisco's main LGBT+ district. While a lot of places these days are gay-friendly, this area takes it to a whole new level, and the welcoming atmosphere here is just as much a draw for visitors as the many shops, clubs, cafés, and festivals all run with an LGBT+ clientele in mind. For a great intro to the area, join a local walking tour to learn about local history and sights (www.sfcityguides.org).

↑ A rainbow crosswalk heralding gay pride in the Castro district

Pianos in the Golden Gate Park

Every summer, the Golden Gate Park's Botanical Gardens tuck 12 pianos among the flower beds and invite visitors to play. Professional musicians are usually among those tinkling the ivories, and the gardens are often transformed into an alfresco concert hall. Pack a picnic, sit back, and enjoy the show.

A visitor playing a piano in the Botanical Gardens at Golden Gate Park

SAN FRANCISCO'S
HIDDEN GEMS

San Francisco's iconic landmarks are well known. But its lesser-known treasures are tucked away in neighborhood nooks and crannies or left forgotten among bigger attractions. Golden Gate Park, for example, is so large that many locals have never discovered everything it has to offer. Here are some of the city's best-kept secrets that are well worth seeking out.

 TOP 3 EAST BAY SECRETS

Niles Canyon Railway
Gold Rush-era steam trains and Pullman coaches run 90-minute journeys between Niles and Sunol (www. ncry.org).

Kaiser Center Rooftop Garden
Hidden atop a five-story parking garage beside Oakland's Lake Merritt (p222), this is one of the world's largest roof gardens.

Berkeley Rose Garden
Tucked away in the Berkeley Hills (p226), this serene garden is a riot of color in even the gloomiest weather.

Seaside Treasures

There are secrets to be discovered all around San Fransisco Bay. Three of the best include the Wave Organ, a huge acoustic sculpture played by the tide (p85); the Land's End Labyrinth, a rock maze of 11 concentric circles atop a cliff near the Legion of Honor (p196); and Sutro Baths (p205), the haunting ruins of what were once the world's largest swimming baths.

Secret Staircases

Hilly San Fransciso is home to some impressive hidden stairways. Head to 16th Avenue in Golden Gate Heights to scale the Moraga Tiled Steps. Mosaic tiles of animals and sealife cover this 163-step staircase. Fitness buffs should also seek out the Lyon Street Steps, a 288-step extravaganza, with views of the Presidio forest and the sparkling bay beyond.

→

Aileen Bar and Colette Crutcher's Moraga Tiled Steps; a detail *(inset)*

Peaceful Parks

Offering views equal to touristy Twin Peaks, Tank Hill Park – just below and north of its more famous neighbor – provides a great vista of the city and bay without the bustling crowds. For a more lively community feel, visit Duboce Park, in the Lower Haight. Here, kids will love the outdoor movie nights at the Harvey Milk Recreational Arts Center and will squeal with delight as they zoom down the Seward Street Slides (two long, steep, parallel concrete slides).

←

Eduardo Aguilera's amazing Land's End Labyrinth

→

Bench at Tank Hill with a spectacular view across the city

A YEAR IN
SAN FRANCISCO

JANUARY

△ **Golden Gate Kennel Club Dog Show** *(mid-Jan)* 2,000+ dogs and 175+ breeds vie for "Best in Show" at the Cow Palace.

FEBRUARY

Chinese New Year Celebration *(late Jan or early–mid Feb)* A parade in Chinatown.

△ **Giants Winter Fanfest** *(early Feb)* At AT&T Park, team members and alumni thrill fans with autographs and selfies.

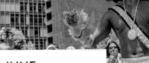

MAY

Cinco de Mayo *(May 5)* A big block party on Valencia Street in the Mission District, with plenty of music, food, and dance.

△ **Bay to Breakers** *(late May)* Tens of thousands of costumed walkers and serious runners join in the world's largest footrace, from the Ferry Building to Ocean Beach.

JUNE

San Francisco Jazz Festival (mid-Jun) For three decades, more than 30 live shows with world-famous headliners at SFJAZZ Center.

△ **San Francisco Pride** *(mid–late Jun)* The biggest event in the LGBT+ calendar. A colorful celebration and parade on Market Street with huge crowds of spectators.

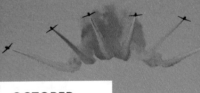

SEPTEMBER

Opera in the Park *(early Sep)* World famous opera stars perform in free concerts in Golden Gate Park.

△ **Folsom Street Fair** *(late Sep)* Music, comedy, crafts, drink, and dancing at the largest leather, alternative, and fetish street fair in the world.

OCTOBER

△ **Fleet Week** *(early Oct)* Honoring the US Navy and Marines, a breathtaking Blue Angels air show and ship tours on the Bay.

Castro Street Fair *(first Sun)* Arts, crafts, music and dancing at this ever-popular, gay-friendly street festival.

MARCH

△ **St. Patrick's Day Parade** *(mid-Mar)* Bars filled with green-clad patrons watch one of America's oldest parades down Market Street.

San Francisco International Ocean Film Festival *(mid-Mar)* Dozens of ocean-themed films are shown at Fort Mason.

APRIL

International Film Festival *(mid-Apr)* For two weeks there are screenings every day at the Kabuki and other theaters.

△ **Cherry Blossom Festival** *(mid–late Apr)* Japantown hosts a celebration of Japanese arts, crafts, food, and performers, and a colorful parade.

JULY

△ **Fourth of July** *(Jul 4)* Dazzling fireworks, local bands, food, arts, and crafts on PIER 39. The main fireworks extravaganza can be seen along the entire waterfront.

San Francisco Playwright's Festival *(late-Jul)* Readings, workshops, lectures, and performances of new works at the bay-side Fort Mason center.

AUGUST

Nihonmachi Street Fair *(early Aug)* A celebration of the Asian and Pacific communities held in Japantown.

△ **Outside Lands** *(mid-Aug)* A huge eco-friendly, activist-themed festival in Golden Gate Park, with music, food, and wine.

NOVEMBER

△ **Dia de los Muertos** *(Nov 2)* A Mexican celebration marked by a night-time procession through the Mission District, and the Festival of Altars, honoring deceased family members.

Illuminate SF *(late Nov)* Eco-friendly light-art installations throughout the city.

DECEMBER

△ **Union Square Christmas Windows** *(Nov–Dec)* Glittering, animated store windows around Union Square.

The Nutcracker *(mid–late Dec)* The San Francisco ballet company presents Tchaikovsky's beloved classic at the War Memorial Opera House.

A BRIEF
HISTORY

Tribes of Native Amercians roamed the misty hills above the sea for about 8,000 years before the arrival of Spanish explorers in 1769. On their heels came Mexican settlers, soldiers, and droves of gold seekers, giving the area a boomtown spirit that endures to this day.

The Early Years

Although European explorers sailed along the California coast in the 16th century, they all went past the Golden Gate strait without noticing the bay beyond it. It was not until 1769 that a party of Spanish explorers became the first non-natives to lay eyes on the bay. The Spanish quickly established missions and military forts, securing their foothold in the New World. Having broken away from Spain in 1821, Mexico opened California to foreign trade for the first time. In 1848 Alta California became a US state, and soon cries of "Gold!" rang out in the foothills, as miners rushed to the nearby Sierras to seek their fortunes.

1 A depiction of San Francisco in the mid-19th century.

2 The roadway being installed at the Golden Gate Bridge in 1937.

3 California Street, 1915.

4 City Hall, built in 1916 after the original was destroyed in 1906.

Timeline of events

1769

San Francisco Bay is discovered by a Spanish expedition led by Gaspar de Portola

1776

Mission San Francisco de Asís is founded by a Franciscan friar

1848

Treaty of Hildalgo ends the Mexican-American War, ceding California to the US

1849

Gold is discovered in the Sierras, setting off the Gold Rush; "'49ers" flock to settlements by the bay, which swell to boomtowns

1870

Golden Gate Park launches the westward expansion of the city

A Growing City

The riches of the Gold Rush attracted entrepreneurs from around the world, turning the city into an international hub of finance and innovation. Undaunted by a massive earthquake and fire in 1906 that destroyed much of the prosperous Victorian-era city, the ambitious residents rebuilt San Francisco; invented cable cars to conquer the steep hills; hosted the Panama-Pacific Exposition; and constructed bridges to connect the growing towns of the bay.

The Golden Age

Neither World War I, Prohibition nor the Great Depression could dampen the city's energy in the early 20th century, and the 1920s saw the creation of major arts venues and civic buildings. World War II brought industrial investment in the form of shipyards at Richmond and Sausalito. Fort Mason was the main supply base for the Pacific theater, and shipped out more than 1.5 million soldiers.

ROBBER BARONS

In the late 1800s, the "Big Four" railroad and Gold Rush tycoons – Huntington, Stanford, Hopkins, and Crocker – built palaces on Nob Hill, in a city based on the promise of sudden wealth. The founder of Stanford University *(p127)*, Leland Stanford drove the solid-gold "Last Spike," completing the First Trans-continental Railroad.

1873

First cable car is tested on Clay Street

1906

Measuring 8.25 on the Richter scale, an earthquake and a massive fire reduce much of San Francisco to rubble

1915

Panama-Pacific Exposition signals the city's revival and the completion of the Panama Canal

1936

Spanning the bay, the San Francisco-Oakland Bay Bridge opens

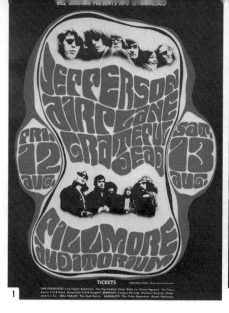

1 **2**

Fabulous Fifties amd Swinging Sixties

The anti-conformist "Beat Generation" kicked off an era of experimental art, recreational drugs, sexual freedom, and progressive ideas. During the Summer of Love in 1967, psychedelic rock music filled the Fillmore Auditorium and blasted Jefferson Airplane and the Grateful Dead into international fame. But along with the flower power there was unrest, as young people rebelled against wars and injustice. In 1969, Indians of All Tribes occupied Alcatraz to publicize Indian grievances, and througout the 1960s many San Franciscans protested against the war in Vietnam.

Highs and Lows

Although it was controversial in 1972, the 48-story, glass-and-aluminum Transamerica Pyramid ushered in an era of bold city development: a forest of gleaming skyscrapers, the BART subway connecting the towns of the Bay Area, and the massive Moscone Convention Center. Urban renewal saw blighted areas of the city torn down in favor of new developments, including the vast Embarcadero Center and the arts-and-entertainment

↑ Skyscrapers rising above Yerba Buena Gardens in downtown San Francisco

Timeline of events

1937
Golden Gate Bridge opens, connecting San Francisco with Marin County to the north

1967
During the Summer of Love, 100,000 people flock to the city to celebrate peace and free love

1972
The Golden Gate National Recreation Area is established in the city and the Marin Headlands

1945
The United Nations is founded at the San Francisco Conference

3

4

hub of Yerba Buena Gardens in the former SOMA warehouse district. But whilst the city skyline rose, the population suffered terrible losses when the mayor of San Francisco – George Moscone – and political activist Harvey Milk(p46) were murdered at City Hall in 1978. Further tragedies occurred during the AIDS epidemic of the 1980s, the Loma Pieta earthquake of 1989, and during a terrible fire that blazed across the Oakland hills in 1992.

San Francisco Today

Following the ups and downs of the dot-com boom at the turn of the century, San Francisco is once again an important international center of innovation and technology, with even more major companies thriving in Silicon Valley to the south. This new boom has made cities in the Bay Area some of the most expensive places to live in the US, but the high standard of living, and vibrant, progressive culture nevertheless attract more people every day. Museums and urban developments continue to open, with the new Salesforce Tower exemplifying a 21st-century boomtown spirit.

1 A 1967 poster for a concert at the Fillmore auditorium.

2 Transamerica Pyramid.

3 A baseball game at AT&T Park.

4 The San Francisco Pride parade.

Did You Know?

In 1961, city resident José Julio Sarria became the nation's first openly gay candidate for public office.

1978

Harvey Milk, the first openly gay elected official in California, is assassinated

1989

The Loma Prieta earthquake hits during a World Series baseball game, killing dozens in the Bay Area

2018

The Salesforce Tower, the second tallest building west of the Mississippi River, is opened

2014

San Francisco Giants win the World Series for the third time in five years

Clint Eastwood as the iconic titular character of *Dirty Harry* (1971)

A BRIEF HISTORY
ON SCREEN

Whether you retrace Clint Eastwood's steps in *Dirty Harry*, or relive memories of Robin Williams in *Mrs. Doubtfire*, movie and TV lovers of all ages will find a trip to San Francisco is like stepping into a film set.

While San Francisco doesn't turn out as many feature films as its high-profile neighbor, Los Angeles, it has nevertheless played a luminous supporting character in many of the world's most loved films. From classics like Alfred Hitchcock's *Vertigo* (1958), to more recent releases such as the Oscar-winning biopic *Milk* (2008), the city has given the big screen some of its most iconic sights and interesting tales. The city has also been the home of many famous TV characters, including the Tanners of *Full House* and a cartoon version of Jackie Chan.

↑ James Stewart and Kim Novak in Alfred Hitchcock's *Vertigo* (1958)

On Screen Guide

1958
Vertigo

1968
Bullitt

1971
Dirty Harry

1987-1995
Full House

1941
The Maltese Falcon

1978
Invasion of the Body Snatchers

1979
Escape from Alcatraz

1986
Star Trek IV: The Voyage Home

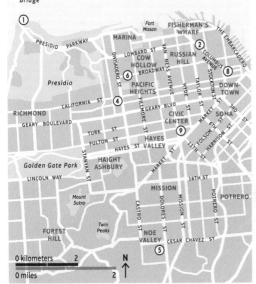

San Francisco Bay

Golden Gate Bridge

Alcatraz Island

FILMING LOCATIONS

① *Vertigo*, Fort Point

② *Dirty Harry*, Saints Peter and Paul Church

③ *Escape from Alcatraz*, Alcatraz Island

④ *Full House*, 1709 Broderick Street, Pacific Heights

⑤ *Sister Act*, St. Paul's Catholic Church, 221 Valley St, Noe Valley

⑥ *Mrs. Doubtfire*, 2640 Steiner Street, Pacific Heights

⑦ *The Rock*, Alcatraz Island

⑧ *Zodiac*, Transamerica Pyramid

⑨ *Milk*, City Hall

FULL HOUSE

The opening credits of the iconic American sitcom *Full House* show a Victorian home that is not one of the Painted Ladies (p168), as many viewers believe. The facade of the Tanner family home actually belongs to 1709 Broderick Street in Pacific Heights. The show's ongoing sequel, *Fuller House*, is also set here. The creator of the series, Jeff Franklin, bought the property in 2016, driven by the same sentimentality that lures fans here every day.

↑ Robin Williams masquerading as a nanny in *Mrs. Doubtfire* (1993)

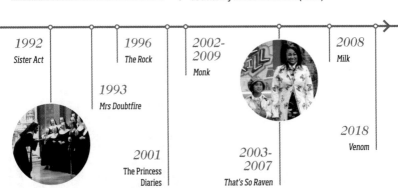

1992
Sister Act

1996
The Rock

2002-2009
Monk

2008
Milk

1993
Mrs Doubtfire

2001
The Princess Diaries

2003-2007
That's So Raven

2018
Venom

EXPERIENCE

Golden Gate Bridge towering above the Bay

PRESIDIO AND THE RICHMOND DISTRICT

Despite being neighbors, the Presidio area and the Richmond district have very different histories. The Presidio was originally a Spanish fort established in 1776, which fell under Mexican control when the nation became independent from Spain in 1821. It was taken over again by the US military during the Mexican-American War (1846–48), and continued to play a role in American military endeavors in the Pacific until 1995.

The Richmond district, meanwhile, has been a green, tranquil, and sophisticated neighborhood since the mid-19th century, and has long had a highly multicultural population of Irish-, Russian- and particularly Chinese-Americans.

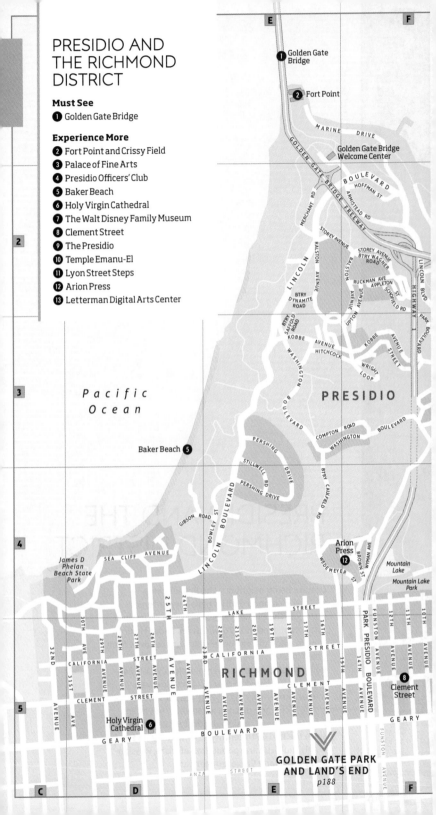

PRESIDIO AND THE RICHMOND DISTRICT

Must See

1 Golden Gate Bridge

Experience More

2 Fort Point and Crissy Field
3 Palace of Fine Arts
4 Presidio Officers' Club
5 Baker Beach
6 Holy Virgin Cathedral
7 The Walt Disney Family Museum
8 Clement Street
9 The Presidio
10 Temple Emanu-El
11 Lyon Street Steps
12 Arion Press
13 Letterman Digital Arts Center

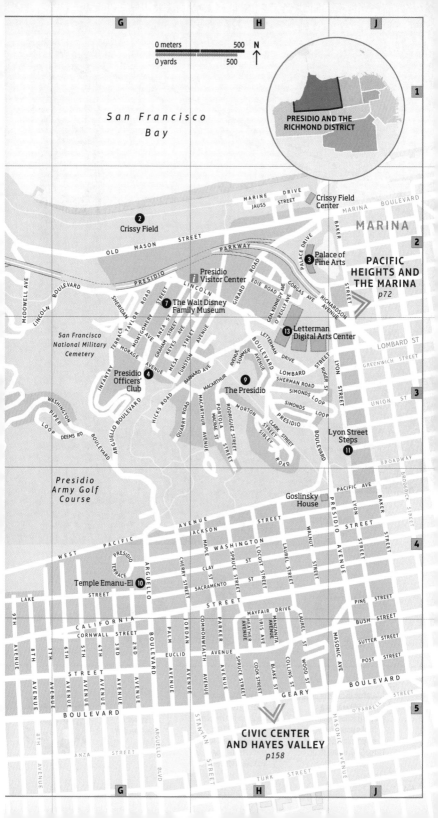

San Francisco Bay

PRESIDIO AND THE RICHMOND DISTRICT

Crissy Field Center

MARINE DRIVE
JAUSS STREET

MARINA BOULEVARD

MARINA

2 Crissy Field

OLD MASON STREET

PARKWAY

PRESIDIO

BAKER STREET

PALACE DRIVE

3 Palace of Fine Arts

PACIFIC HEIGHTS AND THE MARINA
p72

McDOWELL AVE

LINCOLN BOULEVARD

LINCOLN

Presidio Visitor Center

GIRARD ROAD

EDIE ROAD

GORGAS AVE

RICHARDSON AVENUE

San Francisco National Military Cemetery

SHERIDAN AVENUE

TAYLOR ROAD

MORAGE

MONTGOMERY STREET

ANZA AVE

GRAHAM STREET

KEYES AVE

MESA

7 The Walt Disney Family Museum

GEN KENNEDY AVE

O'REILLY AVE

13 Letterman Digital Arts Center

LOMBARD ST

GREENWICH STREET

INFANTRY TERRACE

AVENUE

FUNSTON AVENUE

BARNARD AVE

AVENUE

LETTERMAN BOULEVARD

SUMMER AVENUE

DRIVE

RUGER ST

LYON STREET

UNION ST

4 Presidio Officers' Club

HICKS ROAD

QUARRY ROAD

MACARTHUR AVENUE

MACARTHUR

9 The Presidio

PORTOLA STREET

RODRIGUEZ STREET

MACRAE ST

MORTON STREET

LOMBARD

SHERMAN ROAD

SIMONDS LOOP

SIMONDS LOOP

PRESIDIO BOULEVARD

ARGUELLO BOULEVARD

WASHINGTON

PIPER LOOP

DEEMS RD

BOULEVARD

CLARK STREET

SIBLEY ROAD

11 Lyon Street Steps

BROADWAY

Presidio Army Golf Course

Goslinsky House

PACIFIC AVE

PRESIDIO AVENUE

LYON STREET

BAKER STREET

BRODERICK STREET

PACIFIC AVENUE

WEST

PRESIDIO TERRACE

ARGUELLO

JACKSON STREET

WASHINGTON STREET

CHERRY STREET

MAPLE STREET

SPRUCE STREET

LOCUST STREET

LAUREL STREET

WALNUT STREET

10 Temple Emanu-El

CLAY ST

SACRAMENTO ST

STREET

PINE STREET

LAKE STREET

9TH AVENUE

8TH AVENUE

7TH AVENUE

6TH AVENUE

5TH AVENUE

4TH AVENUE

3RD AVENUE

2ND AVENUE

CALIFORNIA STREET

CORNWALL STREET

ARGUELLO BOULEVARD

PALM AVENUE

JORDAN AVENUE

EUCLID AVENUE

COMMONWEALTH AVENUE

PARKER AVENUE

MAYFAIR DRIVE

HEATHER AVENUE

IRIS AVE

MANZANITA AVENUE

SPRUCE STREET

COOK STREET

BLAKE ST

COLLINS ST

WOOD ST

LAUREL ST

MASONIC AVE

BUSH STREET

SUTTER STREET

POST STREET

BOULEVARD

STREET

BOULEVARD

GEARY

O'FARRELL STREET

MASONIC AVENUE

CIVIC CENTER AND HAYES VALLEY
p158

8TH AVENUE

ANZA STREET

ARGUELLO BLVD

STANYAN STREET

TURK STREET

→
The Golden Gate
Bridge against the
San Francisco skyline

Timeline

*Jan 5,
1933*

Construction
officially
begins

Dec 1933

▽ Repairs begin
after the same
trestle is damaged
in a storm

Aug 11, 1930

▲ After decades of debate
and deliberation a
construction permit is
finally issued for a
suspension bridge over
the Golden Gate strait

Feb 26, 1933

▲ The official ground-
breaking ceremony takes
places - a festive event
with over 100,000
attendees eager to
celebrate the long-
awaited bridge project

*Aug 14,
1933*

▲ Part of the
access trestle
is destroyed by
a ship

GOLDEN GATE BRIDGE

♦ E1 🚌 2, 28, 76 🕐 Times vary, check website 🌐 goldengate.org

You may expect such a famous city landmark to feel familiar, but visitors to the Golden Gate Bridge are sure to find themselves in awe when they see it in person. Whether you journey across or just view it from the shore, this iconic bridge is sure to capture your imagination and get your fingers itching for a stunning photo of your own.

Named for the entrance to the Strait of San Francisco Bay called "Golden Gate" by John Fremont in 1846, the bridge opened in 1937, connecting San Francisco with Marin County (p216). Breathtaking views are offered from this world-famous landmark, which has six lanes for vehicles, plus a pedestrian and bicycle path. It is the world's ninth-largest suspension bridge but it was the world's longest one when it was built.

Cars driving southbound from the Marin County side toward San Francisco must pay a toll, and pedestrians and cyclists are only permitted on the eastern sidewalk.

 INSIDER TIP
Before You Go

Check the bridge's website for a few top tips so you don't get caught out on your visit (goldengatebridge.org/bikesbridge/bikes.php).

The Opening of the Bridge

The bridge that most people said could never be built was completed on time and under budget in the midst of the Great Depression, under chief engineer, Josph Strauss. On May 27, 1937, Golden Gate Bridge opened only for pedestrians, and an estimated 200,000 people came to be the first to walk across. The roadway opened the next day, and an official convoy of Cadillacs and Packards were the first vehicles to cross the bridge.

→
The first pedestrians on the Golden Gate Bridge, May 27, 1937

THE BRIDGE IN FIGURES

Crossing the Bridge
Every year approximately 41 million vehicles cross the bridge (about 112,000 a day).

Incredible Cables
The two great 7,650-ft (2,332-m) main cables are more than 3 ft (1 m) thick, and contain 80,000 miles (128,744 km) of steel wire, enough to encircle the earth at the equator three times.

The Concrete
The volume of concrete poured into the piers and anchorages during the bridge's construction would be enough to lay a 5 ft (1.5 m) wide sidewalk stretching from New York to San Francisco.

Built to Last
The bridge was designed to withstand 100 mph (160 km/h) winds. Each pier has to withstand a tidal flow of more than 60 mph (97 km/h), while supporting a 22,000-ton steel tower.

Jun 1935

The south tower (closest to San Francisco) is completed

Timeline

Jun 1934

△ The north tower (near the Marin County end of the Bridge) is completed, although some records claim it was finished in November

TOP 3 VIEWS OF THE BRIDGE

Baker Beach
The city's biggest and most popular beach isn't ideal for swimming, but it makes up for it with stunning views *(p69)*.

Fort Point
The northernmost point of San Francisco offers angles that really highlight the incredible scale of the bridge *(p68)*.

Vista Point
Head to this popular spot on Marin County side to get a photo of Golden Gate Bridge with a San Francisco backdrop *(p220)*.

↑ Photographers setting up to capture the Golden Gate Bridge from Baker Beach

Apr 27, 1937
▽ Joseph B. Strauss leads dignitaries to the center span with a final gold rivet

Jun 1936
△ With the last suspender rope in place since March, work begins on the roadway that will connect San Francisco and Marin County

Feb 17, 1937
10 workers are killed when a safety net fails

May 27, 1937
△ Opening day. Every siren and church bell in San Francisco and Marin sounds in unison as part of a huge celebration. The following day, President Roosevelt holds a dedication ceremony via telegraph

EXPERIENCE MORE

Fort Point and Crissy Field

♀ E1 **⌂ Marine Drive**
☎ 556-1693 **⏰ 10am–5pm Thu–Tue (Fri–Sun only in winter)**

Completed by the US Army in 1861, this fort was built partly to protect San Francisco Bay from any attack, and partly to defend ships carrying gold from California mines. It is the most prominent of the many fortifications constructed on the coast, and is a classic example of a pre-Civil War brick fortress. The building soon became obsolete, as its 10-ft- (3-m-) thick brick walls could not stand up to powerful modern weaponry. It was closed in 1900, never having come under attack.

The brickwork vaulting is unusual for San Francisco, where the ready availability of good timber encouraged wood-frame constructions. This may have saved the fort from collapse in the 1906 earthquake. It was nearly demolished in the 1930s to make way for the Golden Gate Bridge, but it survived and is now a good place from which to view the bridge. National

Did You Know?

A popular walking path winds through Crissy Field from the Marina to Fort Point.

Park Service rangers in Civil War costume conduct guided tours. A tidal marsh once covered the area called Crissy Field. After two centuries of military use, the Field was transformed into a waterfront park for recreation and education. The Crissy Field Center offers a rich array of programs, including many geared toward kids, from wildlife treks to kite-flying.

Palace of Fine Arts

♀ H2 **⌂ 3601 Lyon St, Marina District** **🚌 22, 28, 29, 30, 41, 43, 45** **⏰ For events only** **🌐 palaceoffinearts.com**

One of San Francisco's most prominent pieces of architecture, the Palace of Fine Arts is the sole survivor of the many grandiose monuments built as part of the 1915 Panama-Pacific International Exposition, a world fair celebrating San Francisco's recovery after the 1906 earthquake. The building has been restored and is now a space for theater, music, and dance.

Presidio Officers' Club

♀ G3 **⌂ 50 Moraga Ave** **🚌 29, 43** **⏰ 10am–5pm Tue–Sun** **🌐 presidio.gov**

The Officers' Club overlooks the parade grounds of the Presidio and the 19th-century barracks. Built in the Spanish Mission style (p36) in the 1930s, it incorporates the adobe (sun-dried brick) remains of the original 18th-century Spanish fort and hosts events and exhibits on California history.

Baker Beach

♀ D3 **⏰ Dawn–dusk daily**

Baker Beach is the largest and most popular stretch of sand

The grandiose Palace of Fine Arts, an events and performance space ↑

in the city and is often crowded with sunbathers. The chilly water and strong currents make it a dangerous place to swim, but it is a fine place to go for a walk. Fishing is also good here. There are forests of pine and cypress on the bluffs above the beach, where visitors can explore Battery Chamberlin, a gun emplacement from 1904. On the first weekend of each month rangers show the "disappearing gun," a heavy rifle that can be lowered behind a thick wall to protect it from enemy fire, and then raised again to be fired.

Mickey Mouse memorabilia and exhibits at the Walt Disney Family Museum

6

Holy Virgin Cathedral

📍D5 🏠6210 Geary Blvd 🚌29, 38, 38L 🕐8am-6pm daily 🌐sfsobor.com

Shining gold onion-shaped domes crown the Russian Orthodox Holy Virgin Cathedral of the Russian Church in Exile, a startling landmark in the suburban Richmond District. It was designed by Oleg N. Ivanitsky and built in the early 1960s. In contrast to those of many other Christian

denominations, the services here are conducted with the congregation standing, so there are no pews or seats.

The cathedral and the many Russian-owned businesses nearby, such as the lively, long-established Russian Renaissance restaurant, are situated at the heart of San Francisco's extensive Russian community. This has flourished since the 1820s, but expanded greatly when more immigrants arrived after the Russian Revolution of 1917, and especially in the late 1950s and late 1980s.

7

The Walt Disney Family Museum

📍G2 🏠104 Montgomery St 🚌28, 43 🕐10am-6pm Wed-Mon 🌐waltdisney.org

Opened in 2009, this superb museum documents the life and amazing career of Walt Disney (1901–66). A must for Disney fans, the museum has ten interactive galleries with film clips, storyboards, photographs, movies, and original artwork, such as early drawings of Mickey Mouse.

Did You Know?

Presidio is the Spanish word for a fortified military base, built to protect against pirates and other enemies.

8

Clement Street

📍 F5 🚌 2, 29, 44

This is the bustling main thoroughfare of the otherwise rather sleepy Richmond District. Bookstores and small boutiques flourish here, and the inhabitants of the neighborhood meet together in a lively mix of bars, fast-food cafés, and ethnic restaurants. Most of these are patronized more by locals than by tourists. Clement Street is surrounded by a district known as New Chinatown, home to more than one third of the Chinese population of San Francisco. As a result, some of the city's best Chinese restaurants can be found here, and the emphasis in general is on East Asian cuisine. However, the area is known for the diversity of its restaurants, and Peruvian, Russian, and French establishments, among many others, also flourish here. The street stretches from Arguello Boulevard to the north–south cross-streets which are known as "The Avenues."

9

Presidio

📍 E3 🚹 210 Lincoln Blvd, on the Main Post; Open 10am–5pm daily
🌐 presidio.gov

The Presidio is a national park and former military fort. The site has a long military history. It has played a key role in San Francisco's growth, and has been occupied longer than any other part of the city. Remnants of its military past, including barracks, can be seen everywhere. There are 24 miles (39 km) of hiking trails, cycle paths, and beaches. A free shuttle, the PresidiGo bus, operates within the park, stopping at over 40 destinations. Golden Gate Bridge crosses the bay from the northwest corner of the Presidio. The Visitor Center is a good place to get your bearings and find out what events are on; there are regular ranger walks, live music, and family activities.

The steeply descending Lyon Street Steps, with their beautiful views over the bay

10 🎵

Temple Emanu-El

📍 G4 🏛 Lake St and Arguello Blvd 🚌 1, 2, 33, 38 🕐 By appointment
🌐 emanuelsf.org

After World War I hundreds of Jews from Russia and Eastern Europe moved into the Richmond District and built religious centers, many of which are still major landmarks. Among these is the Temple Emanu-El, its dome inspired by that of the 6th-century Santa Sophia in Istanbul. The temple is a majestic piece of architecture. It was built in 1925 for the city's longest-established Jewish congregation (which was founded in 1850). The architect was Arthur Brown, who also designed San Francisco's City Hall *(p166)*. With its red-tiled dome, Emanu-El is a Californian architectural hybrid, combining the local Mission style *(p36)* with Byzantine ornament and Romanesque arcades. Its interior, which holds nearly 2,000 worshippers,

Former military housing in the Presidio, with the Golden Gate Bridge beyond ↑

is especially fine when bright sunlight shines through the earth-toned stained glass.

---

11 Lyon Street Steps

 J3 🏛 Lyon St and Broadway 🚌 3, 41, 43, 45

A real gem hiding in plain sight, the Lyon Street Steps consist of 332 steps and offer jaw-dropping views of the city and the bay for those who brave the climb. Given their location within the Richmond neighborhood, they can easily be worked into walks extending from the Presidio to Pacific Heights, or from the Panhandle to the Marina. As you climb (or even better, descend) the steep steps, you'll see the Presidio forests to the west and Billionaires Row to the east. Because of the area's beauty, the homes in this area tend to be owned by the seriously wealthy. Residents include United State Senator Dianne Feinstein, oil heir Gordon Getty, and Oracle founder Larry Ellison.

---

12 Arion Press

📍 F4 🏛 1802 Hays St 🚌 1, 2, 28, 38 🕙 10am–5pm Mon–Fri 🌐 arionpress.com

Considered one of the nation's leading publishers of fine-press books, Arion Press produces highly sought-after books, prized by collectors for their quality and rarity. With titles ranging from classic literature to commissioned new works, the texts that the Press creates are famous for their sense of erudition and diversity. Its authors include Ovid, Shakespeare, Laurence Sterne, Herman Melville, Emily Dickinson, Gertrude Stein, Sigmund Freud, Allen Ginsberg, and David Mamet. Visiting their free gallery will give you a sense of San Francisco's contribution to literary history, as well as the city's tradition of producing high-quality handmade items. Situated in the gorgeous Presidio, the gallery is well worth a visit in between touring Outer Richmond and Baker Beach. Guided tours

require advanced reservations and are available every Thursday at 3:30pm.

---

13 Letterman Digital Arts Center

 H3 🏛 Chestnut St and Lyon St 🚌 28, 43 🕙 9am–5pm Mon–Fri 🌐 presidio.gov/places/letterman-digital-arts-center

A pilgrimage spot for *Star Wars* fans, the Letterman Digital Arts Center was founded by filmmaker George Lucas and the Presidio Trust in 2005 to house Industrial Light and Magic, Lucasfilm Ltd, and other companies. The sprawling campus includes landscaped grounds, a natural lagoon, and photo-worthy views of the Golden Gate Bridge and the Palace of Fine Arts. Aside from the beautiful views, the other draw is the life-size statue of Yoda, the wise *Star Wars* character. Take a peek in the lobby to see more life-size figures and other movie memorabilia.

The Wave Organ, designed by Peter Richards and George Gonzalez

PACIFIC HEIGHTS AND THE MARINA

Pacific Heights is an exclusive neighborhood that clings to a hillside rising 300 ft (100 m) above the city. The area was developed in the 1880s, after cable cars linking it with the city center were introduced. With its magnificent views, it quickly became a desirable place to live, and elegant Victorian houses still line its tree-shaded streets.

To the north of Broadway, the streets drop steeply to the Marina District, ending at San Francisco Bay. The houses here are built on a once-marshy site that was cleared and drained for the Panama-Pacific Exposition, and the ambience is that of a wealthy seaside resort, with boutiques, lively cafés, and two prestigious yacht clubs.

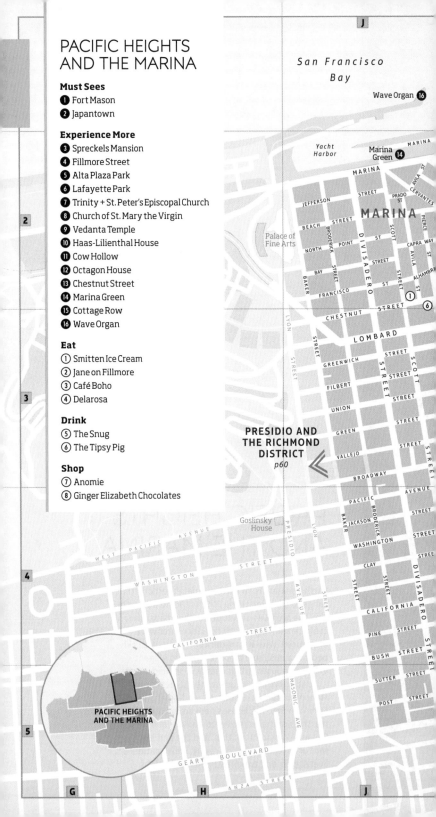

PACIFIC HEIGHTS AND THE MARINA

Must Sees
1 Fort Mason
2 Japantown

Experience More
3 Spreckels Mansion
4 Fillmore Street
5 Alta Plaza Park
6 Lafayette Park
7 Trinity + St. Peter's Episcopal Church
8 Church of St. Mary the Virgin
9 Vedanta Temple
10 Haas-Lilienthal House
11 Cow Hollow
12 Octagon House
13 Chestnut Street
14 Marina Green
15 Cottage Row
16 Wave Organ

Eat
① Smitten Ice Cream
② Jane on Fillmore
③ Café Boho
④ Delarosa

Drink
⑤ The Snug
⑥ The Tipsy Pig

Shop
⑦ Anomie
⑧ Ginger Elizabeth Chocolates

San Francisco Bay

Wave Organ **16**

Yacht Harbor

Marina Green **14**

MARINA

Palace of Fine Arts

1

6

PRESIDIO AND THE RICHMOND DISTRICT
p60

Goslinsky House

PACIFIC HEIGHTS AND THE MARINA

① 🍴 💻 🛍

FORT MASON

📍 E1 ⛺ 2 Marina Blvd 🚌 22, 28, 30, 30X, 43, 49 🕐 9am–5pm Mon–Fri
🌐 fortmason.org

Once a military base, Fort Mason is now a cool and vibrant arts and culture center, and a definite hot-spot for foodies.

Fort Mason reflects the military history of San Francisco. The original buildings were private houses, erected in the late 1850s, which were confiscated by the US Government when the site was taken over by the US army during the American Civil War (1861–5). The Fort remained an army command post until the 1890s, and also housed refugees left homeless by the 1906 earthquake. During World War II, Fort Mason Army Base was the point of embarkation for around 1.6 million soldiers.

Fort Mason was converted to peaceful use in 1972. The original barracks and the old

↑ Guests at a fine art exhibition in the Fort Mason Center for Arts and Culture

hospital – which serves as a Visitor Center and headquarters of the Golden Gate National Recreation Area (GGNRA) – are both open to the public. Fort Mason has some of the city's finest views, looking across the bay toward Golden Gate Bridge and Alcatraz.

Fort Mason Center for Arts and Culture

Part of the Fort is now occupied by one of San Francisco's prime art complexes. Fort Mason Center for Arts and Culture is home to over 25 cultural organizations, art galleries, museums, and theaters. Particular highlights include the SFMOMA Artists Gallery, which offers artworks from Northern Californian artists for sale or rent, while Italian and Italian-American artists display their works at the Museo Italo Americano. The Mexican Museum has a unique collection of over 12,000 objects representing thousands of years of Mexican history. Among the many places to eat at Fort Mason Center is Greens, one of the city's best vegetarian restaurants. Hours vary for each venue, so check the website to learn more about each one. Thousands of events occur at Fort Mason Center every year, as well, so be sure to check the events calendar during your trip.

↑ The buildings of the Fort Mason complex on the piers in the Marina District

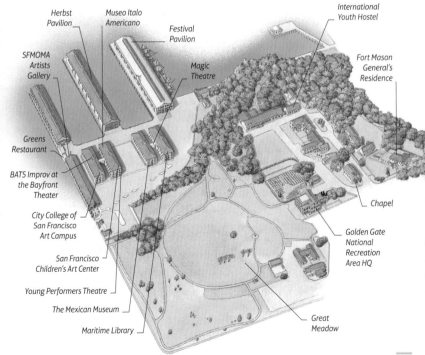

Herbst Pavilion

Museo Italo Americano

Festival Pavilion

SFMOMA Artists Gallery

Magic Theatre

International Youth Hostel

Fort Mason General's Residence

Greens Restaurant

BATS Improv at the Bayfront Theater

City College of San Francisco Art Campus

San Francisco Children's Art Center

Young Performers Theatre

The Mexican Museum

Maritime Library

Chapel

Golden Gate National Recreation Area HQ

Great Meadow

② ⊕ ⊖ ⊕

JAPANTOWN

📍 E4 🚌 2, 3, 22, 31, 38 🌐 sfjapantown.org

It may be smaller than San Francisco's famous Chinatown, but visitors should make sure not to overlook the city's Japantown district. Full of fun shops, great food, and cultural experiences, the buildings of the Peace Plaza make you feel like you've stepped off the streets of San Francisco and right into urban Japan.

Japantown has a full calendar of cultural events from spring to fall, and even without any traditional festivals in winter it's an unmissable place for foodies, shoppers, and Japanophiles at any time of year. Many of the restaurants come complete with plastic food displays in the window, just like you'd find in Tokyo. And shops selling traditional clothing and homeware are interspersed with modern stores selling anime merchandise, beauty products, and all things *kawaii* (cute).

Historic Japantown

At one time in the early 20th century, this area had one of the largest populations of Japanese people in the western world. Also known as "Nihonmachi" (the Japanese translation for "Japantown"), the area was the heart of the local Japanese-American community, and had the look and feel of downtown Tokyo. That changed when those of Japanese birth or descent were tragically interned during World War II. It wasn't until the 1960s when the area regained some of its historic character, that the original Japan Center shopping complex was built as part of a scheme to revitalize the Fillmore District. At the heart of the complex, and centered upon a five-tiered, 75-ft (22-m) concrete pagoda, is the Peace Pagoda Garden.

Did You Know?

This is one of only three Japantowns in the US, all of which are in California.

↑ Ceramic bowls decorated with traditional designs, on sale in Japantown

Festival Seasons Calendar

Spring

▽ The Japanese tradition of cherry blossom is enjoyed here in April, along with festive food and performances

Summer

▲ The Anime Festival and Cosplay takes place in July, when fans of Japanese animation dress up like their favourite characters

Fall

▲ In September the Sumo Champions Exhibit takes place outside in the Peace Plaza

←

The Peace Pagoda at the heart of Japantown, a gift from San Francisco's sister city, Osaka

↑ Fillmore Street, with its attractive array of boutiques, cafés, and restaurants

EXPERIENCE MORE

③
Spreckels Mansion

L3 🏠2080 Washington St 🚌1, 3, 10, 47, 49 🕐To the public

Dominating the north side of Lafayette Park, this imposing Beaux Arts mansion (p36) is sometimes known as the "Parthenon of the West" on account of its Classical-style columned facade. It was built in 1912 for the flamboyant Alma de Bretteville Spreckels and her husband Adolph, who was heir to the sugar fortune of Claus Spreckels. Alma filled the house with antiques bought on trips to Europe and was renowned for her lavish parties. The house is now owned by novelist Danielle Steel. It occupies a block on Octavia Street, which is landscaped in the style of Lombard Street (p103). The mansion's architect was George Applegarth, who in 1916 designed the Legion of Honor (p196) to house Alma Spreckels' burgeoning collection of fine art.

④
Fillmore Street

K4 🚌1, 2, 3, 10, 22, 24

Fillmore Street survived the devastating 1906 earthquake virtually intact, and for several years afterward served as the civic heart of the city. Government departments, as well as private businesses, were housed in the district's shops, homes, and even churches. Today the main commercial district of Pacific Heights is located here, from Jackson Street to Japantown around Bush Street. This area boasts an abundance of bookstores, restaurants, and boutiques.

⑤
Alta Plaza Park

K4 🚌1, 3, 10, 22, 24

Situated in the center of Pacific Heights, Alta Plaza is a beautifully landscaped urban park, where San Francisco's elite come to relax. There are stone steps (offering great city views) rising up from Clay Street on the south side of the park. These steps may be familiar from films – Barbra Streisand drove down them in What's Up, Doc? From the north side you can see several splendid mansions, including Gibbs House at 2622 Jackson Street, built by Willis Polk in 1894. Covering nearly 12 acres (4.8 ha), Alta Plaza was the site of a quarry when it was purchased by the city of San Francisco in 1877. It was another 20 years, however, before landscaping works began. The area served as a campsite for victims of the 1906 earthquake and fire.

Did You Know?

Trinity Episcopal Church is the second oldest congregation in the city of San Francisco.

6 Lafayette Park

📍 L4 🚌 1, 10, 47, 49

One of San Francisco's prettiest hilltop gardens, this is a leafy green haven of pine and eucalyptus trees, although its present tranquillity belies its turbulent history. Along with Alta Plaza Park and Alamo Square, the land was set aside in 1855 as city-owned open space, but squatters and others, including a former City Attorney, laid claim to the land and built houses on it. The largest of the houses stood at the center of the hilltop park until 1936, as the squatter who had built it refused to move. It was finally torn down after the city authorities agreed to swap it for land on Gough Street. Steep stairways now lead to the park's summit and its delightful views. In the surrounding streets are scores of palatial buildings, with particularly ornate examples along Broadway, Jackson Street, and Pacific Avenue going east–west, and on Gough and Octavia streets north–south.

7 Trinity + St. Peter's Episcopal Church

📍 L4 🏠 1620 Gough St 🚌 1, 2, 3, 10, 19, 22, 38, 47, 49
🌐 trinity-stpeters.org

This dramatic edifice is modeled on Durham Cathedral in northern England, arguably one of the finest examples of Norman architecture in the world. The oldest Episcopal church on the Pacific coast, Trinity dates back to 1849 and Sunday services are still held in the main sanctuary. Its colorful stained-glass windows were designed by a pupil of John La Farge, a leading figure in the New York art scene during the late 19th century. The high altar displays the 1894 jewel-encrusted Trinity Cross, presented as a gift on Trinity Sunday by the women of the parish. The church also has a strong musical tradition; it has a fine pipe organ and is home to the award-winning male-voice choir Chanticleer, who regularly perform here.

DRINK

The Snug
Classic cocktails are given a fresh update in this bright, stylish spot. The hip clientele lounge on comfy leather sofas to sip raspberry negronis or bourbon sours with Chinese plum.

📍 K4 🏠 2301 Fillmore St
🌐 thesnugsf.com

The Tipsy Pig
Low lighting and polished wood surfaces give this bar a warm, old-fashioned feel, but the cocktails - shaken and muddled with fresh fruit, herbs, and house-made syrups - are thoroughly modern.

📍 J2 🏠 2231 Chestnut St
🌐 thetipsypigsf.com

The grand and historic ↑ Trinity + St. Peter's Episcopal Church

8

Church of St. Mary the Virgin

📍K3 🏠2325 Union St 🚌22, 41, 45 ⏰8:30am-4pm Mon-Thu 🌐smvsf.org

Evoking the more rural early 19th-century years of Cow Hollow, this rustic, wooden-shingled Episcopal church stands at the west end of what is now the busy Union Street shopping area.

One of the natural springs that provided water for the Cow Hollow dairy herds still bubbles up in the grounds, now largely hidden from the view of passersby on the street by the church's original lych-gate and hedge.

The small, plain building is an early example of the Arts and Crafts style *(p32)* later used in more prominent Bay Area churches. Below the

steeply sloping roof, the walls are faced with "shingles," which are strips of redwood nailed in overlapping rows onto the building's wooden frame. Part of the building was remodeled in the 1950s, when the main entrance was moved from Steiner Street to the opposite end of the building; however, the fabric has been well preserved.

9

Vedanta Temple

📍K3 🏠2963 Webster St 🚌22, 41, 45 🔒To the public 🌐sfvedanta.org

One of the bay area's most unusual structures, the Vedanta Temple is an eclectic combination of a host of divergent decorative traditions. The roof is crowned by a rusty red onion-shaped dome similar to those seen on Russian Orthodox churches. It also has a tower resembling a crenellated European castle, and an octagonal Hindu temple cupola.

Other architectural features include highly decorated Moorish arches, medieval parapets and elements of Queen Anne *(p36)* and Colonial styles. It was built in

SHOP

Anomie
Stand-out fashion, handcrafted jewellery and quirky homeware line the shelves of this boutique, with a focus on items designed and made in the city

📍K3 🏠2149 Union St ⏰11am-7pm daily 🌐shopanomie.com

Ginger Elizabeth Chocolates
The sugar-pink walls and embellished counters give this shop the look of a lavish dressing room. Its sweet treats, from rainbow macarons to chocolate bark, are just as pretty (and indulgent).

📍K3 🏠3108 Fillmore St ⏰11am-8pm Wed-Sat (to 6pm Sun) 🌐gingerelizabeth.com

an old-fashioned air to the district, in stark contrast to the sophistication of the merchandise on display. It's a popular place for brunch and has some fine coffee shops.

---

⑫ Octagon House

📍 J2 🏠 2645 Gough St
🚌 28, 45, 47, 49 🕐 Noon–3pm on second Sun of month, and second and fourth Thu of the month
🚫 Jan 🌐 nscda-ca.org/octagon-house

Built in 1861, the Octagon House is an eight-sided wooden building. It houses a small, but engaging, collection of decorative arts and historic documents of the Colonial and Federal periods. Included are furniture, paintings, Revolutionary playing cards and signatures of 54 of the 56 signers of the Declaration of Independence. Entry to the house is free, though a donation is suggested.

↑ The handsome Octagon House, now a fine decorative arts museum

---

1905 by the architect Joseph A. Leonard, working closely with the Northern California Vedanta Society minister, Swami Trigunatitananda.

Vedanta is the highest of the six schools of Hinduism, and the building symbolizes the Vedanta concept that every religion is just a different way of reaching one god. The Temple is now a monastery, but it is worth a visit just to marvel at this bizarre building from the outside.

---

 ⑩ (♿)(Ⓜ)(🏛)

Haas-Lilienthal House

📍 L3 🏠 2007 Franklin St
🚌 1, 12, 19, 27, 47, 49 🕐 For guided tours only: noon–2:30pm Wed & Sat, 11am–3:30pm Sun 🌐 haas-lilienthalhouse.org

This exuberant mansion in Queen Anne style *(p32)* was built for the rich merchant William Haas in 1886. Alice Lilienthal, his daughter, lived there until 1972, when it was given to the Foundation for San Francisco's Architectural Heritage. It is the only intact private home of the period open as a museum, and is

←

The striking Vedanta Temple, built in an unusual mix of architectural styles

---

↑ One of the rooms in the Haas Lilienthal, with its authentic decor and furniture

complete with authentic furniture. A fine example of an upper-middle-class Victorian dwelling, the house has very decorative gables, a circular corner tower, and highly elaborate ornamentation.

A display of photographs describes the history of the building and reveals that this grandiose house was modest in comparison with some of those destroyed in the earthquake and fire of 1906.

---

⑪ Cow Hollow

📍 K2 🚌 22, 28, 30, 30X, 41, 43, 45, 49

Cow Hollow, an attractive, upmarket shopping district along Union Street, is so called because it was used as grazing land for the city's dairy cows up until the 1860s. It was then taken over for development as a residential neighborhood. In the 1950s the area became fashionable, and chic boutiques, antiques shops, and art galleries took over the old neighborhood shops. Many of these are housed in restored 19th-century buildings, lending

← Relaxed alfresco dining on Chestnut Street, the Marina District's main hub

Chestnut Street

📍 K2 🚌 22, 28, 30, 30X, 43

The main shopping and nightlife center of the Marina District, Chestnut Street has a varied mix of movie theaters, markets, cafés, coffee houses, and restaurants. It's a great place to stop for a meal and people-watch, having a much more low-key and local feel than you'll find in the busier tourist areas. The commercial strip stretches just a few blocks from Fillmore Street west to Divisadero Street, after which the neighborhood becomes predominantly residential in character.

INSIDER TIP
Flicks on Chestnut Street

After shopping or as a prelude to a night out, head to one of the old-school movie theaters a block apart on Chestnut Street. The Presidio and the Marina theaters both screen new releases and offer an intimate movie-watching experience.

Marina Green

📍 J2 🚌 22, 28, 30, 30X, 43

A long thin strip of lawn running the length of the Marina District, Marina Green is popular with kite-flyers and for picnics, especially on July 4, when the city's largest fire-work show can be seen from here (p51). Paths along the waterfront are the city's prime spots for cyclists, joggers, and roller-skaters. Golden Gate Promenade leads from the west end of the green to Fort Point, or you can turn east to the Wave Organ at the harbor jetty.

Cottage Row

📍 K4 🚌 2, 3, 8AX, 8BX, 22, 38

One of the few surviving remnants of working-class Victorian San Francisco, this short stretch of flat-fronted cottages was built in 1882, at the end of the Pacific Heights building boom. Unusual for San Francisco, the cottages share dividing walls, like terr-aced houses in Europe. Their

utter lack of ornament, and their location on what was a dark and crowded back alley, emphasize their lower-class status. The Cottage Row houses were saved from dest-ruction during the process of slum clearance in the 1960s. A program organized by Justin Herman awarded grants to

help people restore their existing houses, rather than replace them. All but one have now been restored; they face a small attractive park.

Wave Organ

 J1 🚌 30, 30X

Sitting at the tip of the breakwater that protects the Marina is what has to be the world's most peculiar musical instrument. Built by scientists from the Exploratorium *(p98)*, the Wave Organ consists of a number of underwater pipes that echo and hum with the changing tides. Listening tubes are embedded in a mini-amphitheater that has views of Pacific Heights and the Presidio. "Organ" is a little misleading: the sounds you hear are more like gurgling plumbing than organ music.

Peter Richards and
↓ George Gonzalez's
Wave Organ sculpture

EAT

Smitten Ice Cream
Ice-cream scoops are frozen to order here thanks to the huge liquid nitrogen tank rumbling overhead. Try their inventive flavors like pretzel and pumpkin chai.

📍 J2 🏠 2268 Chestnut St
🌐 smittenicecream.com

$ $ $

Jane on Fillmore
The mingled scent of freshly brewed coffee and house-baked sourdough bread wafts from the door of this café, whose healthy and hearty sandwiches and salads make it a popular lunch spot.

📍 K4 🏠 2123 Fillmore St
🌐 itsjane.com

$ $ $

Café Boho
Fresh, local seafood takes center stage here, particularly with the signature "seacuterie board": a sharing platter with tuna pastrami and octopus dip.

📍 K2 🏠 3321 Steiner St
🌐 cafebohosf.com

$ $ $

Delarosa
Expect elbow-to-elbow dining at this unpretentious pizza place, whose communal tables are routinely filled with patrons enjoying fresh pasta and perfectly chewy, Italian pizzas.

📍 K2 🏠 2175 Chestnut St
🌐 delarosasf.com

$ $ $

A SHORT WALK
PACIFIC HEIGHTS

Distance 1 mile (1.6 km) **Time** 15 minutes
Nearest bus 3, 10, 24

The blocks between Alta Plaza and Lafayette
Park are at the heart of Pacific Heights. The
streets in this upscale neighborhood are quiet
and tidy, lined with smart apartment blocks
and palatial houses. Some date from the late
19th century, while others were built after the
earthquake and fire of 1906 (p53). To the north
of the area, the streets drop steeply toward
the Marina District, affording outstanding
views of the bay. Wander through the large
Alta Plaza and Lafayette parks and past the
luxuriant gardens of the mansions in between,
then visit lively Fillmore Street, with its
numerous fashionable bars, cafés,
restaurants, and shops.

↑ Colorful Victorian houses
on Washington Street

Did You Know?

A little north of this map,
2640 Steiner St is the house
where *Mrs Doubtfire*
was filmed.

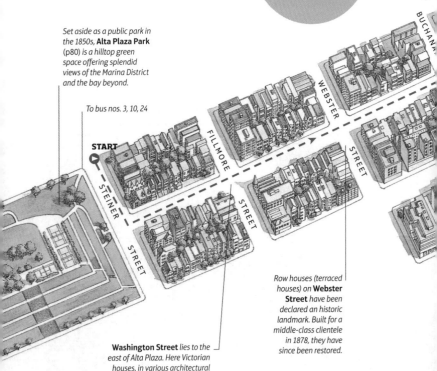

Set aside as a public park in
the 1850s, **Alta Plaza Park**
(p80) is a hilltop green
space offering splendid
views of the Marina District
and the bay beyond.

To bus nos. 3, 10, 24

START

Row houses (terraced
houses) on **Webster
Street** have been
declared an historic
landmark. Built for a
middle-class clientele
in 1878, they have
since been restored.

Washington Street lies to the
east of Alta Plaza. Here Victorian
houses, in various architectural
styles, fill an entire block.

Locator Map
For more detail see p74

PACIFIC
HEIGHTS AND
THE MARINA

Furnished in Victorian style, **Haas-Lilienthal House** *(p83) is the headquarters of the Architectural Heritage Foundation.*

The impressive limestone **Spreckels Mansion** *(p80), constructed on the lines of a Baroque palace, has been home to the family of best-selling novelist Danielle Steel since 1990.*

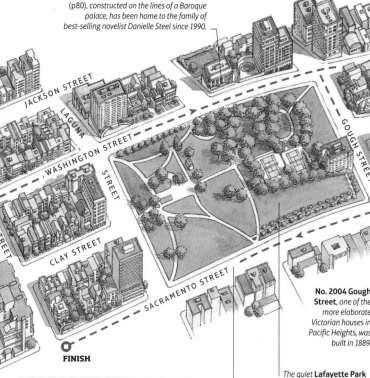

JACKSON STREET

LAGUNA

WASHINGTON STREET

STREET

CLAY STREET

STREET

SACRAMENTO STREET

GOUGH STREET

FINISH

No. 2004 Gough Street, *one of the more elaborate Victorian houses in Pacific Heights, was built in 1889.*

The quiet **Lafayette Park** *(p81) offers good views of the Victorian houses that surround it.*

No. 2151 Sacramento Street
is an ornate French-style mansion. A plaque commemorates a visit by the author Sir Arthur Conan Doyle in 1923.

↑ The hilltop Lafayette Park, a leafy green haven

A SHORT WALK
AQUATIC PARK

Distance 1.5 miles (2.5 km) **Time** 35 minutes
Nearest public transportation Powell-Hyde
cable car to Hyde Street Pier; bus 19, 28, 49 to Van
Ness Avenue-Beach Street

Side by side on San Francisco's northern waterfront, Aquatic
Park and Fort Mason offer some fascinating glimpses into the
city's past, especially its colorful history as a seaport. There
are no cars here, just walkers, cyclists, and skaters sharing
lushly overgrown paths. The route winds past historic ships
moored in the bay at Hyde Street Pier, Depression-era swim
clubs, Gold Rush cottages, and military installations dating
from Spanish colonial times to World War II. You can swim if
you don't mind the chilly bay water, fish for crabs, paddle off
a small beach, or just stop to admire the view and picnic in
one of the many grassy spots.

*The Golden Gate
Promenade climbs
upward, rounding Black
Point and giving superb
views of Alcatraz and
Angel Island.*

*At the top of the
slope, the **Youth
Hostel** is one of the
few ornate houses
open to the public.*

*Narrow steps lead down the hill
to **Fort Mason** (p76). Visit the
Mexican Museum or view the
Outdoor Exploratorium, which
illustrates the history of the shoreline
and the area's natural environment.*

Herbst
Pavilion

Mexican
Museum

Magic
Theater

Youth
Hostel

FINISH

Fort
Mason

*The grassy knolls of
Great Meadow was
where refugees from
the 1906 earthquake
camped until they
could be rehoused.*

Great
Meadow

WEBSTER
STREET

NORTH POINT STREET

BAY   STREET

LAGUNA ST

OCTAVIA ST

GOUGH ST

FRANCISCO ST

Moscone
Recreation
Center

CHESTNUT STREET

*Near the Fort Mason
General's residence is
the headquarters of
the **Golden Gate
National Recreation
Area (GGNRA)**.*

HYDE ST. PIER

←
The historic Hyde Street
Pier on San Francisco's
northern waterfront

0 meters 300
0 yards 300

N ↑

PACIFIC HEIGHTS AND THE MARINA

Locator Map
For more detail see p74

This curving concrete pier marks the western end of Aquatic Park. People fish here at all hours, mostly for crabs. The Mission-style building at the foot of the pier is an emergency pumping station.

Begin at the seaward end of **Hyde Street Pier**. Until 1938, this pier was the center of activity on the city's northern waterfront. It is now part of the Maritime Museum (p102).

Among the ships moored here is a handsome steam-powered ferry boat, the **Eureka**, built in 1890.

On the landward end of the pier, there is a **bookstore** operated by the National Park Service.

START

Hyde Street Pier

Eureka

Municipal Pier

Aquatic Park Cove

South End Club

Dolphin Club

JEFFERSON ST

Victorian Park

Bocce Ball Courts

BEACH STREET

Maritime Museum

HYDE STREET

NORTH POINT STREET

LARKIN ST

POLK ST

BAY STREET

FRANKLIN STREET

VAN NESS AVE

The two whitewashed clapboard buildings on the sandy beach house the **South End** and **Dolphin** swimming and rowing clubs.

In flower-filled **Victorian Park** street musicians perform.

The large **Casino** was built in 1939 as a public bathing club. Since 1951 it has been the West Coast home of the Maritime Museum (p102).

A topiary sign spells out "Aquatic Park." Behind this are red-and-white plastic-roofed **bocce ball courts**.

→ Skyline of San Francisco with Aquatic Park in the foreground

FISHERMAN'S WHARF AND NORTH BEACH

Fishermen from Genoa and Sicily first arrived in the Fisherman's Wharf area in the late 19th century, and founded here the San Francisco fishing industry. The district has slowly given way to tourism since the 1950s, but brightly painted boats still set out from the harbor on fishing trips early each morning.

To the south of Fisherman's Wharf lies North Beach, sometimes known as "Little Italy." This lively part of the city has an abundance of aromatic delis, bakeries, and cafes, from which you can watch the crowds. It is home to Italian and Chinese families, with a sprinkling of writers and bohemians; Jack Kerouac, among others, found inspiration here.

FISHERMAN'S WHARF AND NORTH BEACH

Must Sees
1 Alcatraz Island
2 Exploratorium

Experience More
3 PIER 39
4 USS Pampanito
5 Madame Tussauds
6 Ripley's Believe It Or Not! Museum
7 The Cannery
8 Ghirardelli Square
9 Vallejo Street Stairway
10 Maritime Museum
11 San Francisco Art Institute
12 Musée Mécanique
13 Lombard Street
14 The Beat Museum
15 Club Fugazi
16 Saints Peter and Paul Church
17 City Lights Bookstore
18 Coit Tower
19 Bocce Ball Courts
20 Filbert Steps
21 Greenwich Steps

Eat
1 Franciscan Crab Restaurant
2 Scoma's Restaurant
3 Gary Danko
4 Café de Casa

Drink
5 Player Sports Grill & Arcade
6 Gold Dust Karaoke Bar & Lounge
7 BarNua

Stay
8 Argonaut Hotel

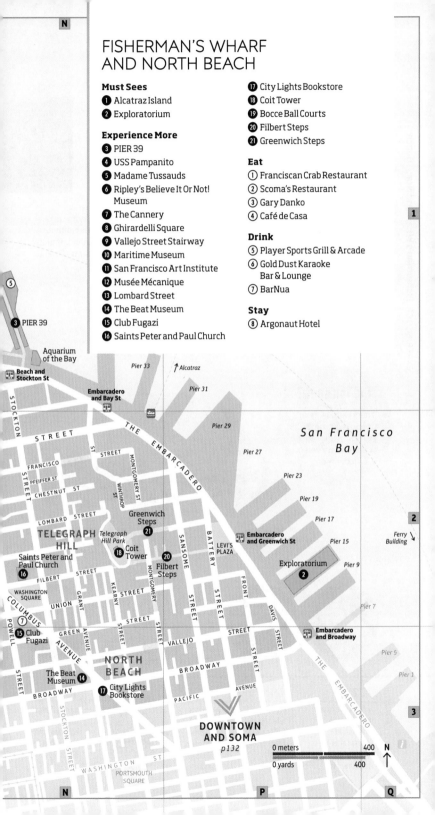

1 🗺 Ⓜ 🛍

ALCATRAZ ISLAND

📍 6 F1 🚢 Pier 33 🕐 Times vary, check website
🌐 nps.gov/alcatraz; www.alcatrazcruises.com

Even on the crowded shores of San Francisco, gazing
out at this bleak, rocky island and abandoned prison
can send a chill down anyone's spine.

Alcatraz means "pelican" in Spanish, a reference to the first
inhabitants of this rocky, steep-sided island. Lying 3 miles
(5 km) east of the Golden Gate Bridge (p64), its location is both
strategic and exposed to harsh ocean winds. In 1859, the US
military established a fort here that guarded San Francisco
Bay until 1907, when it became a military prison. From 1934
to 1963, it served as a maximum-security Federal Penitentiary.
Abandoned until 1969, the island was occupied by Indians of All
Tribes laying claim to the island as their land. The group was
expelled in 1971, and Alcatraz is now part of the Golden Gate
National Recreation Area.

The former prison ↑
and its lighthouse
standing atop
Alcatraz Island

Lighthouse

Warden's house

The officers'
apartments
stood here.

Did You Know?

There were 14 escape
attempts during the 29
years Alcatraz Federal
Penitentiary was in
operation.

Agave Trail
(open seasonally)

Military parade
ground (open
seasonally)

Timeline

1775
△ Spanish explorer
Juan Manuel de
Ayala names
Alcatraz after the
"strange birds"
that inhabit it

1848
△ Military
Governor of
Caifornia, John
Frémont, buys
Alcatraz

1850
Alcatraz is
declared a
military
reservation
by President
Fillmore

1854
▽ First Pacific Coast
lighthouse activated
on Alcatraz

1859
△ Fort Alcatraz
completed;
equipped with
100 cannon and
300 troops

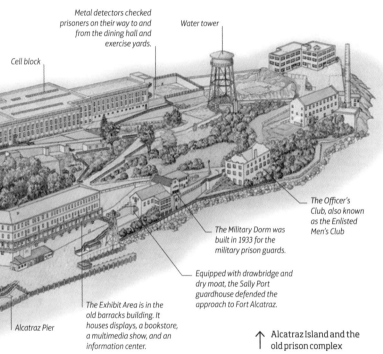

Metal detectors checked prisoners on their way to and from the dining hall and exercise yards.

Water tower

Cell block

The Officer's Club, also known as the Enlisted Men's Club

The Military Dorm was built in 1933 for the military prison guards.

Equipped with drawbridge and dry moat, the Sally Port guardhouse defended the approach to Fort Alcatraz.

The Exhibit Area is in the old barracks building. It houses displays, a bookstore, a multimedia show, and an information center.

Alcatraz Pier

↑ Alcatraz Island and the old prison complex

1909
▽ Army prisoners begin construction on the cell house

1962
▽ Frank Morris and the Anglin brothers escape

1963
Prison closed

1934
▲ Federal Bureau of Prisons turns Alcatraz into a civilian prison

1972
▲ Alcatraz becomes a national park

Inside Alcatraz

The maximum-security prison on Alcatraz, dubbed "The Rock" by the US Army, housed an average of 264 of the country's most incorrigible criminals, who were transferred here for disobedience while serving time in prisons elsewhere in the US. The strict discipline at Alcatraz was enforced by the threat of a stint in the isolation cells and by loss of privileges, including the chance at special jobs, time for recreation, use of the prison library, and visitation rights.

INSIDER TIP
Plan Ahead

Tickets for Alcatraz go on sale 90 days in advance, and sell out particularly fast in summer months. Make sure you bring a jacket or sweater, as the weather can be far wilder and colder out here than it is in the city.

↑ The corridor that separates C and B blocks, nicknamed Broadway by the prisoners

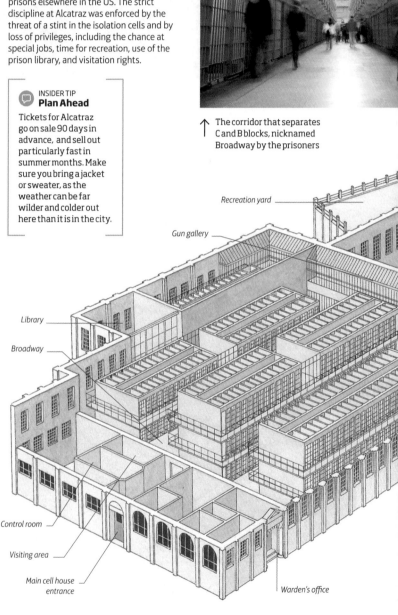

Recreation yard

Gun gallery

Library

Broadway

Control room

Visiting area

Main cell house entrance

Warden's office

↑ Cross-section of the interior of Alcatraz Federal Penitentiary

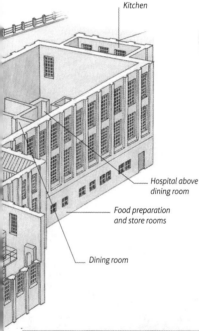

Kitchen

Hospital above dining room

Food preparation and store rooms

Dining room

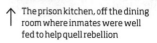

↑ The prison kitchen, off the dining room where inmates were well fed to help quell rebellion

Infamous Inmates

Al Capone

▶ The notorious Prohibition-era gangster "Scarface" Capone was actually convicted, in 1934, for income tax evasion! He spent much of his 10-year sentence on Alcatraz in a hospital isolation cell, and finally left the prison mentally unbalanced after contracting syphilis.

Robert Stroud

◀ Stroud spent all of his 17 years on The Rock in solitary confinement. Despite assertions to the contrary in the film *The Birdman of Alcatraz* (1962), Stroud was in fact prohibited from keeping birds in his prison cell.

Carnes, Thompson, and Shockley

In May 1946, a group of prisoners led by Clarence Carnes, Marion Thompson, and Sam Shockley overpowered guards and captured their guns. The prisoners failed to break out of the cell house, but three inmates and two officers were killed in the "Battle of Alcatraz." Carnes received an additional life sentence, and Shockley and Thompson were executed at San Quentin prison, for their part as ringleaders of the insurrection.

Anglin Brothers

▶ John and Clarence Anglin, along with Frank Morris, chipped through the back walls of their cells, hiding the holes with cardboard grates. They left dummy heads in their beds and made a raft to enable their escape. They were never caught. Their story was dramatized in the film *Escape from Alcatraz* (1979).

George Kelly

▶ "Machine Gun Kelly" served 17 years on The Rock for kidnapping and extortion. He was then sent to a Kansas jail, where he later died.

15595

② EXPLORATORIUM

◎ D2 ⌂ Pier 15 🚌 1, 2, 6, 10, 12, 14, 21, 31, 38, 41 🚋 E, F Ⓜ Embarcadero
🕐 10am–5pm Tue–Sun 🌐 exploratorium.edu/visit

With exhibit names like the Tinkering Studio and Tactile Dome, you'll be itching to get hands-on with all the interactive displays at the Exploratorium. Covering everything from vast topics like the science of human behavior right down to local geography, there's a topic to ignite everyone's curiosity.

Since 1969 this renowned museum and global learning center has been influencing people of all ages with its creative and interactive exhibits. The museum uses unique hands-on displays that promote playful learning, and with so many topics to explore there's something to inspire the curiosity in everyone. Learn how reflections work, how certain genes are passed on from parent to child, and examine local micro-organisms and their Bay Area habitats. Using only the sense of touch, find your way out of the Tactile Dome, a pitch-dark network of chambers and mazes. When

you need a break from all the excitement, the all-glass Fisher Bay Observatory Gallery and Terrace offers excellent views of the Bay.

There are also a variety of events to look out for on the museum's calendar, including a guided walk during the highest tide of the year (known as the "King Tide"), and Community Days when patrons can pay whatever they wish (though admission is first-come-first-served and can't be guaranteed.) After Dark Thursdays also give adults a chance to explore the exhibits in their own time (18+ only: 6–10pm Thursdays).

→ Coloured light bathing visitors to the Central Gallery, and a child blowing bubbles *(inset)*

MUSEUM GUIDE

The long building is laid out into five galleries. The Bernard and Barbro Osher Gallery 1 contains the Human Phenomena exhibit on topics such as emotions and human behavior. Gallery 2's tinkering exhibits and the Bechtel Gallery 3 on seeing and listening take up a large part of the museum, followed by Gallery 4 on living systems. Covering both the natural sciences and local history and geography are the outdoor Gallery 5, and the Fisher Bay Observatory Gallery on the upper level of the museum.

↑ The skyline of downtown San Francisco behind the Exploratoium

EXPERIENCE MORE

3

PIER 39

⦿ N1 **🚌** 4, 8, 8BX, 39, 47 **🚋** E, F **🚠** Powell-Hyde **⛴** SF Bay Ferry

Refurbished in 1978 to resemble a quaint wooden fishing village, this 1905 cargo pier now houses many tourist shops and specialty stores spread through two levels.

The pier's street performers and amusements are popular with families. You can try the two-story carousel, play games at the Riptide arcade, or brave the Turbo Ride. The Aquarium of the Bay houses 20,000 sea creatures including sharks, bat rays, and skates.

You can take a closer look at the pier's most famous residents at the Sea Lion Center; exhibits include a sea lion skeleton and interactive videos. Step outside afterward to view the sea lions at close range.

4

USS Pampanito

⦿ M1 **⌂** Pier 45 **🚌** 4, 8, 8BX, 39, 47 **🚋** E, F **🚠** Powell-Hyde **⛴** SF Bay Ferry **🕙** 9am–6pm Sun-Thu, 9am–8pm Fri & Sat (see website for seasonal variations) **🌐** maritime. org/uss-pampanito

This World War II submarine fought in, and survived, several bloody battles in the Pacific, sinking six enemy ships and severely damaging others. Tragically for the allies, two of its fatal targets were carrying British and Australian POWs. The *Pampanito* managed to rescue 73 men and carry them to safety in the US. A tour of the ship takes visitors from stern to bow to see the torpedo room, the claustrophobic kitchen, and officers' quarters. When the *Pampanito* was in service, it had a full crew of 10 officers and 70 seamen.

5

Madame Tussauds

⦿ M1 **⌂** 145 Jefferson St **🚌** 4, 8, 8BX, 30, 39, 47 **🚋** E, F **🚠** Powell-Hyde **🕙** 10am–7pm daily, (to 8pm Fri-Sun) **🌐** madame tussauds.com

Madame Tussauds San Francisco location is the brand's second in California. In addition to the expected host of historic luminaries and figures from the worlds of entertainment and sport, the complex also houses the San Francisco Dungeon (additional fee required): a thrilling journey through time exploring the darker aspects of the history of the city.

→ Ghirardelli Square shopping center, site of the original famous chocolate factory

6

Ripley's Believe It Or Not! Museum

📍M1 🏠175 Jefferson St 🚌4, 8, 8BX, 30, 39, 47 🚊E, F 🚋Powell-Hyde ⏰Sep-mid-Jun: 10am-9pm daily (to 10pm Fri & Sat); mid-Jun-Aug: 9am-11pm daily (to midnight Fri & Sat) 🌐ripleys.com/sanfrancisco

California native Robert L. Ripley was an illustrator with a penchant for collecting peculiar facts and artifacts. He earned his fame and fortune by syndicating his newspaper cartoon strip, called *Ripley's Believe It Or Not!*

1,701

The highest number of sea lions recorded on PIER 39, in November 2009.

Among the 350 oddities on display are a cable car built of 275,000 matchsticks, a two-headed calf, and an image of a man who had two pupils in each eyeball. Get lost in the Marvelous Mirror Maze and sample some candy from the factory. Some of Ripley's famous cartoon strips are on display, too.

7

The Cannery

📍M1 🏠2801 Leavenworth St 🚌4, 8, 8BX, 30, 39, 47 🚊E, F 🚋Powell-Hyde

This 1909 fruit-canning plant was refurbished in the 1960s to incorporate footbridges, sunny courtyards, and rambling passages, with restaurants and specialty shops selling clothes, collector dolls, American Indian arts and crafts, and much else.

The Cannery also used to house the Museum of the City of San Francisco, but a fire forced the premises to close. However, the collection has moved to the City Hall *(p166)*, where all the exhibits are now

← The huge crab sculpture standing in the entrance to PIER 39

on display. Among these is the massive head of the statue that capped City Hall before the 1906 earthquake *(p54)*. The glowing crown on the head is an example of early electric illumination.

8

Ghirardelli Square

📍L2 🏠900 North Point St 🚌4, 18, 19, 24, 27, 28, 30, 38, 47, 49 🚊E, F 🚋Powell-Hyde 🌐ghirardellisq.com

Once a chocolate factory and woollen mill, this is the most attractive of San Francisco's refurbished factories, a mix of old red-brick buildings and modern shops and restaurants. The shopping center retains the famous Ghirardelli trademark clock tower and the original electric roof sign. The Ghirardelli Chocolate Manufactory on the plaza beneath the tower still houses vintage chocolate-making machinery and sells the confection, although these days the chocolate bars are made in San Leandro, across the Bay.

The square's centerpiece and popular gathering point for shoppers day and evening is Andrea's Fountain, decorated with bronze sculptures of mermaids and turtles.

HIDDEN GEM
Willis Polk

The work of architect Willis Polk can be seen at several points while climbing Vallejo Street. Look out for the stylish Williams-Polk House at 1013-1019 Vallejo and the terraced stairway near Taylor Street.

9

Vallejo Street Stairway

📍 B3 🏠 Vallejo St, between Mason St and Jones St 🚌 10, 12, 41, 45 🚋 Powell-Mason

The steep climb from Little Italy to the southernmost summit of Russian Hill reveals some of the city's best views of Telegraph Hill, North Beach, and the encompassing bay. The street gives way to steps at Mason Street, which climb up through the quiet and pretty Ina Coolbirth Park. Higher still, above Taylor Street, there is a warren of lanes, with several elegant Victorian-style wooden houses *(p32)*. At the crest of the hill is one of the rare pockets of the city that was not destroyed in the earthquake and fire of 1906.

STAY

Argonaut Hotel
This grand, red-brick building has a nautically inspired interior. The most sought-after rooms have windows gazing over the San Francisco Bay.

📍 M1 🏠 495 Jefferson St 🌐 argonauthotel.com

$⑤$⑤⑤

10

Maritime Museum

📍 L2 🏠 900 Beach St 🚌 4, 8, 19, 39, 47 🚋 E, F 🚋 Powell-Hyde ⏰ Times vary, check website 🌐 maritime.org

Constructed in 1939, the Aquatic Park Bathhouse Building has housed the Maritime Museum from 1951. Visitors can still admire the renovated Streamline Moderne building with its clean lines, rather like that of an ocean liner.

Moored at nearby Hyde Street Pier is one of the world's largest collections of old ships. Among the most spectacular is the *CA Thayer*, a three-masted schooner built in 1895 and retired in 1950. The *Thayer* carried lumber along the North California coast, and was later used in Alaskan fishing.

Also at the pier are the steam tug, *Hercules* (1907), and the side-wheel ferry boat, *Eureka*, built in 1890 to ferry trains between the Hyde Street Pier and the counties north of San Francisco Bay. It carried 2,300 passengers and 120 cars, and was the largest passenger ferry of its day.

↑ The *CA Thayer*, an 1895 lumber schooner on Hyde Street Pier, part of the Maritime Museum

11

San Francisco Art Institute

📍 M2 🏠 800 Chestnut St 🚌 30, 41, 45, 91 🚋 Powell-Hyde, Powell-Mason ⏰ Diego Rivera Gallery: 9am-7pm daily; Walter and McBean Galleries: 11am-6pm Tue-Sat (to 7pm Tue) 🌐 sfai.edu

San Francisco's Art Institute dates from 1871, one of the oldest in the US, and once occupied the large wooden mansion built for Mark Hopkins' family on Nob Hill *(p126)*, which burned down in the 1906 fire. Today it is housed in a 1926 Spanish Colonial-style building, with cloisters, bell tower, and courtyard fountain. The Diego Rivera Gallery, named after the Mexican muralist and containing one of his murals, *The Making of a Fresco Showing the Building of a City*, is left of the main entrance. The Walter and McBean Galleries are the primary exhibition venues and feature changing shows from film screenings and contemporary photography to design and technology.

Musée Mécanique

📍 M1 📍 Pier 45, at the end of Taylor St 🚌 1 🚃 E, F
🕐 10am–8pm daily
🌐 museemecaniquesf.com

Kids and adults alike will love the experience of combing through and playing at this museum of penny-arcade games from the early 20th century. The privately owned collection is one of the largest of its kind in the world and consists of over 300 items, including automatons, early examples of pinball, coin-operated pianos, antique slot machines, orchestrions, laughing fortune tellers, and more. It was an insiders-only local spot for many years, and is still popular with young San Franciscans looking for a unique and fun evening out. Located close to PIER 39 and Fisherman's Wharf, Musée Mécanique can be part of a whimsical, memorable day. General admission is free, but the cost to play games ranges from a penny (true to their name!) up to a dollar.

Did You Know?

The speed limit down the twisted, one-way, route of Lombard Street is 5 mph (8 km/h).

Lombard Street

📍 M2 🚌 19, 41, 45
🚃 Powell-Hyde

Banked at a natural incline of 27°, this hill proved too steep for vehicles to climb. In the 1920s the section of Lombard Street close to the summit of Russian Hill was revamped, and the severity of its gradient lessened by the addition of eight curves.

Today it is known as "the crookedest street in the world." Cars can travel downhill only, while people take the steps or the cable car.

Cars driving down the winding ribbon of Lombard Street ↓

14

The Beat Museum

📍N3 🏠540 Broadway
🚌8, 8AX, 10, 12, 30, 39, 41, 45, 91 🕐10am–7pm daily
🌐kerouac.com

This quirky museum displays memorabilia related to the artists of the Beat Generation, associated with San Francisco in the 1950s. Photographs, books, album covers, and letters line the walls and floors of the building. The museum hosts events related to Beat culture, while the shop sells a fascinating range of books, videos, T-shirts, and posters. The property is undergoing a major renovation to help protect against earthquake damage, and may be closed for some months; please check online for the latest information before you visit.

15

Club Fugazi

📍N3 🏠678 Green St
📞421-4222 🚌8, 8BX, 30, 39, 41, 45, 91 🚋Powell-Mason 🕐Wed–Sun

Club Fugazi was originally built in 1912 as a community hall for Italians living in San Francisco in the wake of the 1906 earthquake. These days it is the home of the musical cabaret *Beach Blanket Babylon* (p14). This lively show, famous for its topical and outrageous songs, has been running now for over four decades and has become a San Francisco institution.

16

Saints Peter and Paul Church

📍N2 🏠666 Filbert St
🚌8BX, 8X, 30, 39, 41, 45, 91 🚋Powell-Mason
🕐7:30am–4pm daily (to 1pm public hols)
🌐salesiansspp.org

Known by many as the Italian Cathedral, this large church is situated at the heart of North Beach, and many Italians find it a

→
The historic City Lights Bookstore, a literary meeting place since 1953

welcome haven when they first arrive in San Francisco. The building, designed by Charles Fantoni, has an Italianesque facade, with a complex interior notable for its many columns and ornate altar. The concrete and steel structure of the church, with its elegant twin spires, was completed in 1924.

Cecil B. DeMille filmed the workers laying the foundations of Saints Peter and Paul, and used the scene to show the building of the

🔍 HIDDEN GEM
Beat Generation

Although prominent Beat figure Jack Kerouac never lived in San Francisco, his life and work are intrinsically linked to the city. An alley to the south of City Lights Bookstore was named after him in 2007, and contains plaques dedicated to the Beat Generation.

A favorite of the Beat poets and still a relevant and wonderful independent bookstore for browsing today, City Lights Bookstore is an intriguing stop.

Temple of Jerusalem in his film *The Ten Commandments*.

The church is also known as the Fishermen's Church (many Italians once earned their living by fishing), and there is a Mass to celebrate the Blessing of the Fleet every October. Masses are held in Italian, Chinese, and English.

17

City Lights Bookstore

N3 261 Columbus Ave 8, 8AX, 8BX 10am-midnight daily citylights.com

A favorite of the Beat poets and still a wonderful independent store, City Lights Bookstore and publishing press was founded in 1953 by the poet Lawrence Ferlinghetti and sociology professor Peter D. Martin. Soon after opening, Ferlinghetti and Martin were arrested for disseminating obscene literature – Allen Ginsberg's *Howl and Other Poems* (1956). However, after a lengthy, highly publicised court trial the jury ruled against the charges, and the event only worked to increase the spotlight on the Beat poets, and cement City Lights Bookstore as a cornerstone of the Beat movement.

Browsing the shelves and exploring the unique titles, it's easy to feel transported back to the 1960s. The upstairs aisles focus on poetry and offer plenty of cozy nooks to settle down into with a new title. Be sure also to check out the used books on the more expansive lower level.

←

The facade of the Beat Museum *(inset)* and a 1940's pontiac exhibited inside

EAT

Franciscan Crab Restaurant

Huge windows frame impressive views of the Golden Gate Bridge and Alcatraz at this seafood institution, whose crab-centric menu also includes fresh oysters and steamed mussels.

M1 Pier 43 1/2, Fisherman's Wharf franciscancrabrestaurant.com

$$$

Scoma's Restaurant

Jutting out onto the bay, this Italian-owned spot oozes old-school charm. Ingredients for the seafood dishes are pulled straight from local fishing boats.

M1 1965 Al Scoma Way scomas.com

$$$

Gary Danko

A refined chef-owned spot with a seasonal five-course tasting menu showcasing classic French cooking with Californian wine pairings.

M2 800 North Point St garydanko.com

$$$

Café de Casa

Great value Brazilian breakfasts, crêpes and traditional pastries are on the menu at this tiny cafe with a pretty, plant-filled patio.

M2 2701 Leavenworth St cafedecasa.com

$$$

18

Coit Tower

📍N2 🏠1 Telegraph Hill Blvd 📞249-0995 🚌8, 8BX, 8X, 30, 39, 41, 45, 91 🕐10am-6pm daily (winter: to 5pm)

Coit Tower was built in 1933 at the top of 284-ft- (87-m-) high Telegraph Hill, with funds left to the city by Lillie Hitchcock Coit, an eccentric San Franciscan pioneer and philanthropist. The 210-ft- (63-m-) reinforced concrete tower was designed as a fluted column by the architect Arthur Brown. When floodlit at night it is an eerie white and can be seen from most parts of the eastern half of the city. The view around the North Bay from the observation platform (reached by elevator) is spectacular.

> **Scenes range from the teeming streets of the city's Financial District (with a robbery in progress) to factories, dockyards, and Central Valley wheat fields.**

In the lobby of the tower are murals that are even more absorbing. These were sponsored in 1934 by a government-funded program designed to keep artists employed during the Great Depression. Twenty-five artists joined efforts to paint a vivid portrait of life in modern California. Scenes range from the teeming streets of the city's Financial District (with a robbery in progress) to factories, dockyards, and Central Valley wheat fields.

There are many fascinating details, including a real light switch cleverly incorporated into a painting and a poor family of migrants encamped by a river, plus newspaper headlines, magazine covers, and book titles. The murals are effective social commentary and yet also whimsical in spirit. There are various political themes depicting labor problems and social injustice that run through them. Many of the faces in the paintings are those of the artists and their friends, along with local figures such as Colonel William Brady, caretaker of Coit Tower. The works' political content initially caused public controversy.

19

Bocce Ball Courts

📍N2 🏠Lombard St and Mason St, Joe DiMaggio Playground 📞831-5500 🚌8BX, 8X, 30, 39, 41, 45, 91 🚋Powell-Mason 🕐6am-10pm daily

Italians have been influential in North Beach since the main wave of immigration from Italy in the late 19th and early 20th centuries. Along with their food, customs, and religion, they also brought games to their new home.

← Coit Tower and the lobby's fascinating 1930s murals *(inset)* depicting everyday Californian life

The pretty Filbert Steps with breathtaking views of the bay below

Among these was *bocce*, an Italian version of lawn bowling, played on a narrower and shorter court than the English version. In North Beach it is played most afternoons on the public court in a corner of the Joe DiMaggio Playground. There are four participants (or four teams), who roll a wooden ball at a smaller, target ball, at the opposite end of an earth court. The aim is for the balls to lightly "kiss" *(bocce)*, and the highest score goes to the player whose ball gets closest to this target.

Filbert Steps

P2 8, 8BX, 39, 82X
E, F

Telegraph Hill falls away sharply on its eastern side, and the streets here become steep steps. Descending from Telegraph Hill Boulevard, Filbert Street is a rambling, picturesque stairway, made of wood, brick, and concrete, where fuchsia, rhododendron, bougainvillea, fennel, and blackberries thrive, and offering panoramic views.

Greenwich Steps

N2 8, 8BX, 39, 82X
Powell-Mason

Descending roughly parallel to Filbert Steps, the steps of Greenwich Street have splendid views, with luxuriant foliage from adjoining gardens overflowing onto them. Going up one set of steps and down the other makes a delightful walk around the eastern side of Telegraph Hill.

DRINK

Player Sports Grill & Arcade

This lively waterside spot combines a sports-bar vibe with an arcade and a fun tiki bar serving classic beach cocktails. Families and groups of friends gather here for live music and happy hour.

N1 2 Beach St
playerssf.com

Gold Dust Karaoke Bar & Lounge

Lively crowds are drawn here by the nightly karaoke, live music and a famed menu including

Irish coffees and Napa Valley wines. The stylish, saloon-themed spot has a long, leather-fronted bar, colorful decor, and pressed-tin ceiling.

M1 165 Jefferson St
golddustsf.com

BarNua

A North Beach locals' favourite with an upscale yet unpretentious vibe, happy hour and regular live music nights, plus a decent selection of wines and craft brews on tap.

N2 561 Columbus Ave
sfbarnua.com

A SHORT WALK
FISHERMAN'S WHARF

Distance 1 mile (0.6 km)   **Time** 15 minutes   **Nearest streetcar** E, F

World-class dining, shopping, and entertainment are the focus of this vibrant neighborhood – the center of San Francisco's fishing industry. Try the city's celebrated Dungeness crab, served from November to June, at one of the many seafood restaurants or outdoor crab stands. See the fishing boats along Jefferson Street, watch fishermen at work on Fish Alley, then visit the museums and browse the many fun stores. The Wharf is also the launching point for bay cruises. Tickets for Alcatraz can be purchased from Pier 33.

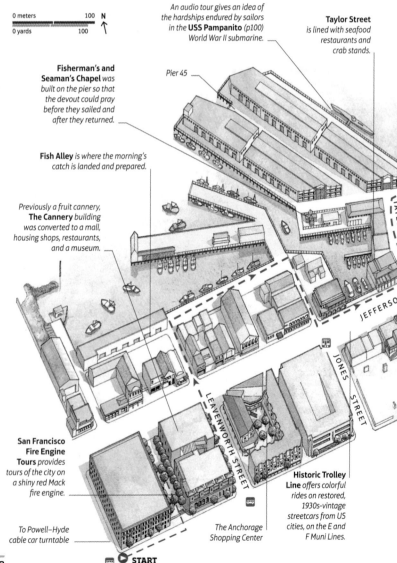

0 meters 100   N
0 yards 100

An audio tour gives an idea of the hardships endured by sailors in the **USS Pampanito** *(p100) World War II submarine.*

Taylor Street *is lined with seafood restaurants and crab stands.*

Fisherman's and Seaman's Chapel *was built on the pier so that the devout could pray before they sailed and after they returned.*

Pier 45

Fish Alley *is where the morning's catch is landed and prepared.*

Previously a fruit cannery, **The Cannery** *building was converted to a mall, housing shops, restaurants, and a museum.*

TAYLOR

JEFFERSON

JONES STREET

LEAVENWORTH STREET

San Francisco Fire Engine Tours *provides tours of the city on a shiny red Mack fire engine.*

Historic Trolley Line *offers colorful rides on restored, 1930s-vintage streetcars from US cities, on the E and F Muni Lines.*

To Powell–Hyde cable car turntable

The Anchorage Shopping Center

▶ START

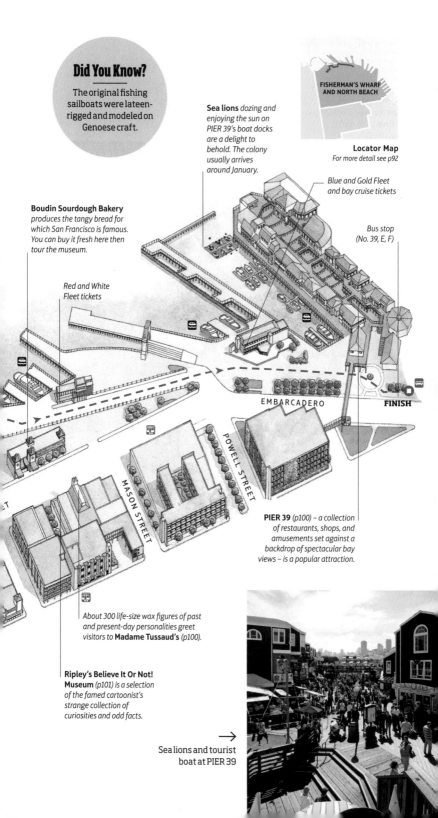

Did You Know?

The original fishing sailboats were lateen-rigged and modeled on Genoese craft.

FISHERMAN'S WHARF AND NORTH BEACH

Locator Map
For more detail see p92

Sea lions *dozing and enjoying the sun on PIER 39's boat docks are a delight to behold. The colony usually arrives around January.*

Blue and Gold Fleet and bay cruise tickets

Bus stop (No. 39, E, F)

Boudin Sourdough Bakery
produces the tangy bread for which San Francisco is famous. You can buy it fresh here then tour the museum.

Red and White Fleet tickets

EMBARCADERO

FINISH

MASON STREET

POWELL STREET

PIER 39 *(p100) – a collection of restaurants, shops, and amusements set against a backdrop of spectacular bay views – is a popular attraction.*

About 300 life-size wax figures of past and present-day personalities greet visitors to **Madame Tussaud's** *(p100).*

Ripley's Believe It Or Not! Museum *(p101) is a selection of the famed cartoonist's strange collection of curiosities and odd facts.*

→
Sea lions and tourist boat at PIER 39

A SHORT WALK
TELEGRAPH HILL

Distance 0.5 mile (0.8 km) **Nearest bus** 39
Time 15 minutes

Telegraph Hill was named for the semaphore installed on its crest in 1850 to alert merchants of the arrival of ships. Today's hill falls away abruptly on its eastern side, where it was dynamited to provide rocks for landfill and paving. There are steep paths on this side of the hill, bordered by gardens. The western side slopes more gradually into "Little Italy," the area around Washington Square. In the 1920s the hill was home to immigrants and to bohemian artists who appreciated the panoramic views. These days the quaint pastel clapboard homes are much sought after and this is one of the city's prime residential areas. Stroll through its quiet streets, finishing at the Art Deco Coit Tower, which houses interesting fresco murals in the American Social Realism style and a panoramic viewing platform at its summit.

↑ Beautiful interior of Saints Peter and Paul Church

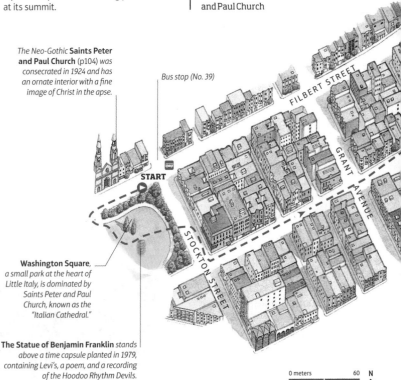

*The Neo-Gothic **Saints Peter and Paul Church** (p104) was consecrated in 1924 and has an ornate interior with a fine image of Christ in the apse.*

Bus stop (No. 39)

START

FILBERT STREET

GRANT AVENUE

STOCKTON STREET

Washington Square, *a small park at the heart of Little Italy, is dominated by Saints Peter and Paul Church, known as the "Italian Cathedral."*

The Statue of Benjamin Franklin *stands above a time capsule planted in 1979, containing Levi's, a poem, and a recording of the Hoodoo Rhythm Devils.*

0 meters   60
0 yards   60

N

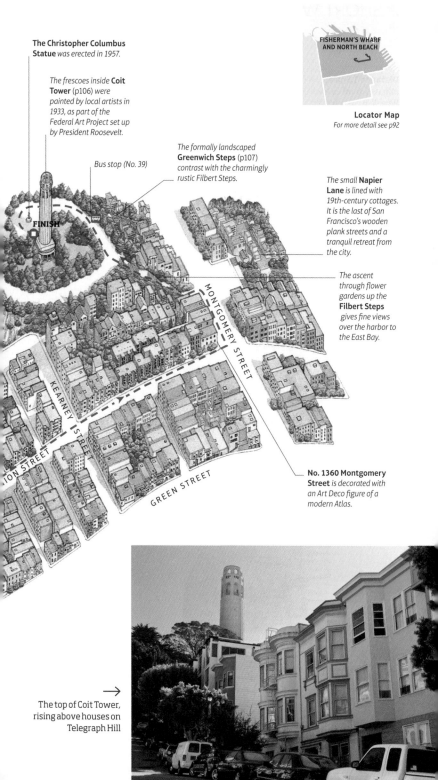

The Christopher Columbus
Statue *was erected in 1957.*

The frescoes inside **Coit
Tower** *(p106) were
painted by local artists in
1933, as part of the
Federal Art Project set up
by President Roosevelt.*

Bus stop (No. 39)

The formally landscaped
Greenwich Steps *(p107)
contrast with the charmingly
rustic Filbert Steps.*

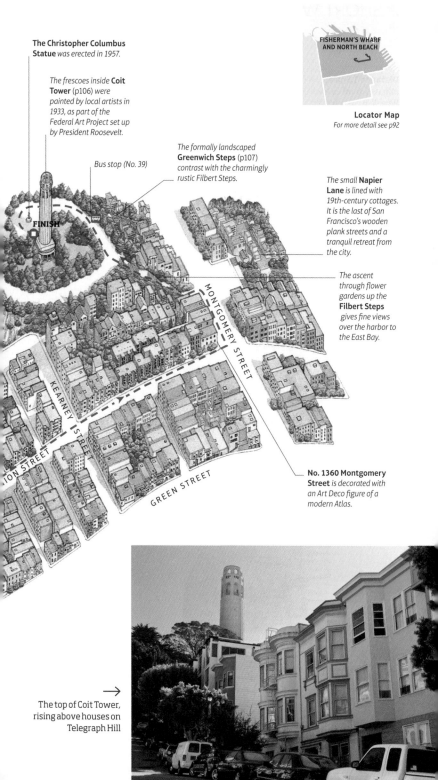

**FISHERMAN'S WHARF
AND NORTH BEACH**

Locator Map
For more detail see p92

The small **Napier
Lane** *is lined with
19th-century cottages.
It is the last of San
Francisco's wooden
plank streets and a
tranquil retreat from
the city.*

*The ascent
through flower
gardens up the*
Filbert Steps
*gives fine views
over the harbor to
the East Bay.*

FINISH

MONTGOMERY STREET

KEARNEY STREET

ION STREET

GREEN STREET

**No. 1360 Montgomery
Street** *is decorated with
an Art Deco figure of a
modern Atlas.*

→
The top of Coit Tower,
rising above houses on
Telegraph Hill

A SHORT WALK
RUSSIAN HILL

Distance 1.5 miles (2.4km) **Walking time** 35 minutes **Nearest public transportation** Powell-Hyde cable car to Hyde St & Vallejo St; bus 10 or 12 to Pacific Ave & Jones St

The rewards for scrambling up the steep stairways and leafy alleys of Russian Hill are a lovely hilltop warren of parks and rare examples of architecture that survived the 1906 earthquake. Here you will encounter few cars and fewer people as you wander among carefully preserved buildings, and enjoy the dazzling views and luxuriant hillside gardens that are the pride of the neighborhood. At the end of your walk, descend to indulge in European-style cafés and boutiques at the foot of the hill.

FISHERMAN'S WHARF AND NORTH BEACH

Locator Map
For more detail see p92

0 meters   200

0 yards   200

N ↑

*The block between Hyde and Leavenworth streets is also called "**the Paris Block**," and is lined with a number of buildings on the National Register of Historic Places.*

*Continue to **Hyde Street** where cafés and boutiques cluster between Jackson and Union streets. The charming Cocotte at No. 1521 is a great place to end the walk.*

FILBERT STREET

LEAVENWORTH STREET

ALLEN ST

UNION STREET

WARNER PL

LARKIN STREET

GREEN STREET

GREEN

VALLEJO STREET

VALLEJO STREET

HYDE STREET

BROADWAY

BROADWAY

LYNCH STREET

POLK STREET

LARKIN STREET

MORRELL ST

PACIFIC AVENUE

JACKSON STREET

FINISH

WASHINGTON STREET

CLAY STREET

← A cable car heading up the Hyde Street hill

*Proceed north on Taylor Street to **Macondray Lane**, which is accessed by a creaky stairway winding through dense vegetation. Along the two-block walkway are shingled Edwardian-inspired cottages.*

↑ A view of downtown from the secluded Ina Coolbrith Park

*At the bottom of the Vallejo Street Stairway, stroll across the street to enjoy the views from the tiny **Ina Coolbrith Park**.*

FILBERT STREET

JONES STREET

TAYLOR STREET

MASON STREET

POWELL STREET

UNION STREET

GREEN STREET

STREET

MACONDRAY LANE

RUSSIAN HILL PLACE

Ina Coolbrith Park

VALLEJO STREET

START

VALLEJO ST STAIRWAY

FLORENCE STREET

*Architect Willis Polk created the zigzagging, Beaux Arts-style **Vallejo Street Stairway** (p102). All along the extensive, three-part stairway are gardens overflowing with flowers and trees.*

GLOVER STREET

BROADWAY

BROADWAY TUNNEL

BERNARD ST

POWELL ST

*On Vallejo Street, the gems of Russian Hill are two steep-roofed, gabled houses in the Bay Area Tradition-style at **Nos. 1013–19**.*

TAYLOR STREET

JONES STREET

PACIFIC AVENUE

JACKSON STREET

LEAVENWORTH STREET

*Turn right into short Florence Street and, at the end, look across the rooftops to **Nob Hill** (p130), sprinkled with 19th-century mansions.*

*Take the stairs and walk into the short alleyway of **Russian Hill Place** to see Mission-Revival style architecture.*

→ Vallejo Street Stairway leading to a row of pastel-colored houses

Chinese-inspired architecture and street decor ion Grant Avenue

CHINATOWN AND NOB HILL

The Chinese settled in the plaza on Stockton Street in the 1850s, and today the shops and markets recall the atmosphere of a typical southern Chinese town – although the architecture, customs, and public events are distinctly American variations on a Cantonese theme.

Nob Hill is San Francisco's most celebrated hilltop. It is famous for its cable cars, plush hotels, and breathtaking views. In the late 19th century, the "Big Four," (p53) who built the first transcontinental railway, were among its richest tenants, in their large mansions on the hill. The earthquake and fire of 1906 leveled all but one of these, but the area's contemporary hotels still recall the opulence of Victorian times.

CHINATOWN AND NOB HILL

Must Sees

1. Cable Car Museum
2. Stockton Street and Grant Avenue

Experience More

3. Chinatown Gateway
4. Old St. Mary's Cathedral
5. Tin How Temple
6. Golden Gate Fortune Cookie Company
7. Grace Cathedral
8. Portsmouth Square
9. Chinese Historical Society of America
10. Pacific Heritage Museum
11. InterContinental Mark Hopkins Hotel
12. Fairmont Hotel
13. The Pacific-Union Club

Eat

1. Sam Wo
2. Good Mong Kok Bakery
3. Mister Jiu's

Shop

4. Chinatown Kite Shop

❶ 🛍

CABLE CAR MUSEUM

📍B3 🏠1201 Mason St 🚌1, 10, 12 🚋Powell-Mason, Powell-Hyde
🕙10am–6pm daily (Nov–Mar: to 5pm) 🌐cablecarmuseum.org

Get up close to the inner workings of the city's famous cable-car system. Here you're right in the middle of the action, feeling the vibrations and hearing the whirring mechanics of public transportation at work.

This is both a museum and the powerhouse of today's cable-car system *(p120)*. Anchored to the ground floor are the engines and wheels that wind the cables through the system of channels and pulleys beneath the streets. Observe them from the mezzanine, then walk downstairs to see under the street. The museum houses an early cable car and examples of the mechanisms that control the individual cars. The system is the last of its kind in the world, so after you're done getting a close-up look in the car barn don't miss a chance to hop on either the Powell-Mason or Powell-Hyde line right outside and experience a journey on one of these historic cars. (Check the website for line closures, as a few improvements are being carried out in 2019.)

→

An old cable car stoplight on display at the museum

Timeline

1869
△ Inventor Andrew Hallidie allegedly finds inspiration for the cable car system in wanting to put a stop to the use of horse-drawn trams

1873
△ Construction begins on San Francisco's first cable-car line in May, with regular service starting in September

1906
△ The San Francisco earthquake destroys most of the system's cars and lines, and electric streetcars replace most of the old cable-car lines when the city is rebuilt

1947
△ The mayor attempts to have the remaining lines closed, but a committee led by Friedel Klussmann succeeds in preserving the city's cable-car system

↑ The Cable Car Museum, also housing the city's cable-car system

REBUILDING THE CABLE CARS

San Francisco's cable-car system was introduced in 1873, and remained in use even with the advent of more modern public transportation over the years. Despite regular maintenance, the aging system began to deteriorate to the point where drastic measures had to be taken, but as a beloved and iconic feature of the city there was no chance of simply closing the lines. Instead the city initiated the Cable Car System Rehabilitation Program, an immense and thorough upgrade that involved closing the whole cable-car system from 1982-4. The work involved replacing old tracks across 69 city blocks, tidying up the cars, and carrying out important upgrades at 1201 Mason St - both on the structure of the car barn as well as the mechanisms of the powerhouse. In June 1984 the system reopened and San Franciscans celebrated its return with four days of festivites.

SAN FRANCISCO'S CABLE CARS

In their heyday, cable cars ran on 23 lines throughout the city. While San Franciscans mostly use other public transport on their commute these days, the cable cars are still a beloved and iconic feature of the city.

The cable car system was launched in 1873, with its inventor Andrew Hallidie riding in the first car. He was purportedly inspired to tackle the problem of transporting people up the city's steep slopes after seeing a horrible accident: a horse-drawn tram slipped down a hill, dragging the horses with it. His system was a great success, and by 1889 cars were running on eight lines. With the advent of the internal combustion engine, cable cars became almost obsolete, and in 1947 attempts were made to replace them with buses. However, after a public outcry – led by Friedel Klussmann's "Citizens' Committee to Save the Cable Cars" – the present three lines, using 17 miles (25 km) of track, were retained.

↑ Two of the 12 California Street cable cars passing by on the streets of San Francisco

Did You Know?

A cable-car bell-ringing contest is held in Union Square every July.

→

Cross-section illustration of a Powell Street car and cable-car tracks

Bell

POW

Grip handle

Sandbox

Emergency brake

Center plate and jaws grip the cable

Wheel brake

HOW CABLE CARS WORK

Engines in the central powerhouse wind a looped cable under the city streets, guided by a system of grooved pulleys. When the gripman in the cable car applies the grip handle, the grip reaches through a slot in the street and grabs the cable. This pulls the car along at a steady speed of 9.5 mph (15.5 km/h). To stop, the gripman releases the grip and applies the brake. Great skill is needed at corners where the cable passes over a pulley. The gripman must release the grip to allow the car to coast over the pulley.

PRESERVING HISTORY

Maintenance and renovations on the cable cars are done with attention to historical detail, because they are designated historic monuments. A cable car celebration was held in 1984 after a two-year renovation of the system. Each car was restored, and all lines were replaced with reinforced tracks. The system should now work safely for 100 years.

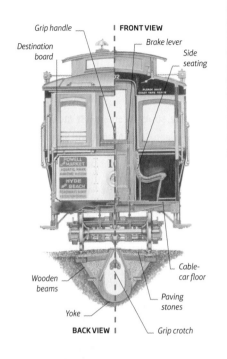

Grip handle · FRONT VIEW · Brake lever · Destination board · Side seating · Wooden beams · Yoke · Cable-car floor · Paving stones · BACK VIEW · Grip crotch

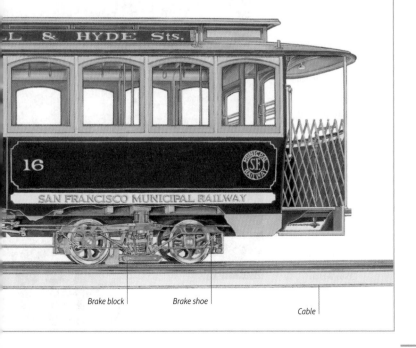

Brake block · Brake shoe · Cable

❶ 🍴 🖥 🛍

STOCKTON STREET AND GRANT AVENUE

📍C4 🚌10, 12, 30, 45 🚋California St 🌐sanfranciscochinatown.com

Tucked between Grant Avenue and Stockton Street, Chinatown exerts an irresistible pull, drawing eager visitors in with the promise of busy shops, delicious food, and colorful architecture.

Contained within a busy neighborhood, the Chinatown Alleys are situated between Grant Avenue and Stockton Street. These four narrow lanes intersect Washington Street within half a block of each other. Of these, the largest is Waverly Place, known as the "Street of Painted Balconies," for reasons that are apparent to every passerby. The alleys contain many old buildings, as well as traditional shops such as old-fashioned herbalists displaying elk antlers, sea horses, snake wine, and other exotic wares. All throughout the alleys, small restaurants, both above and below street level, serve cheap, delicious, home-cooked food.

The Story of Grant Avenue

Grant Avenue is also distinguished for being the first street of Yerba Buena, the village that preceded San Francisco. A plaque at No. 823 Grant Avenue marks the block where William A. Richardson and his wife, Maria Antonia Martinez, erected Yerba Buena's first edifice, a canvas tent, on June 25, 1835. By October, they

EAT

In Chinatown you can find family-run bakeries as well as upscale spots serving Chinese classics with Californian flair.

Sam Wo
📍U2 🏠713 Clay St
🚫Tue 🌐samwo restaurant.com

$$$

Good Mong Kok Bakery
📍T1 🏠1039 Stockton St 🌐goodmongkok.com

$$$

Mister Jiu's
📍U2 🏠28 Waverly Pl
🚫Sun & Mon
🌐misterjius.com

$$$

→
Chinese street lamps and lanterns in San Francisco's Chinatown

↑ The Ping Yuen mural, painted on Stockton Street by Darryl Mar in 1999

A CHINESE DEITY

Kuan Di is the deity most often found in shrines in Cantonese cities, and his distinctive face looks down from Taoist shrines in many Chinatown restaurants. He is typically depicted with a large sword in one hand and a book in the other – symbols of his dedication to both the martial and the literary arts. To get a good look at Kuan Di, head to the top floor above the post office on Stockton Street, where the Kong Chow Temple looks out over Chinatown and the Financial District. Although the building dates from 1977, the temple altar and statuary are possibly the oldest Chinese religious shrine in North America, and are presided over by a carved wooden statue of Kuan Di dating from the 19th century.

had replaced this with a wooden house, and the following year with a yet more permanent adobe (sun-dried brick) home, called Casa Grande. The street in which the Richardsons' house stood was named Calle de la Fundación, the "Street of the Founding." It was renamed Grant Avenue in 1885 in memory of Ulysses S. Grant, the US president and Civil War general who died that year.

→ Ingredients on sale in a Chinatown food market

EXPERIENCE MORE

❸

Chinatown Gateway

⊙ U2 ⌂ Grant Ave at Bush St 🚍 8, 30, 45

This ornate portal, opened in 1970 and designed by Chinese-American artchitect Clayton Lee, spans the entrance to Chinatown's main tourist street, Grant Avenue. Inspired by the ceremonial entrances of traditional Chinese villages, the three-arched gateway is capped with green roof tiles and a host of propitiatory animals – including two dragons and two carp chasing a large, round pearl – all of glazed ceramic. Village gateways are often commissioned by wealthy clans to enhance their status, and the names of these benefactors are inscribed on the gates. This structure was erected by a peculiarly American institution, the Chinatown Cultural Development Committee.

It is guarded by two stone lions that are suckling their cubs through their claws, in accordance with ancient lore. Once through the gate, you find yourself among some of the most elegant shops in Chinatown. Here you can buy antiques, silks, and gems, but sometimes at high prices, aimed at tourists.

❹

Old St. Mary's Cathedral

⊙ U2 ⌂ 660 California St 🚍 1, 15, 30 🚋 California St, Powell-Hyde, Powell-Mason 🖥 oldsaintmarys.org

San Francisco's first Catholic cathedral, Old St. Mary's served a largely Irish congregation from 1854 to 1891, when a new St. Mary's Church was built on Van Ness Avenue. Owing to the shortage of suitable building materials in California, the bricks for the old church were imported from the East Coast, while the granite foundation stones came from China. The clock tower bears the inscription, "Son, observe the time and fly from evil," said to have been directed at the brothels that stood across the street at the time it was built. Twice damaged by fire, the church has its original foundations and walls.

❺

Tin How Temple

⊙ U1 ⌂ Top floor, 125 Waverly Pl 📞 986-2520 🚍 1, 8, 8AX, 8BX, 30, 45 🚋 California St, Powell-Hyde, Powell-Mason ⏰ 9:30am–3:30pm daily

This unusual temple, the longest-operating Chinese temple in the United States, is dedicated to Tin How (Tien Hau), Queen of Heaven and protector of seafarers and visitors. Originally founded by the Cantonese clan association in 1852, it is situated at the top of three steep, wooden flights of stairs. The temple's narrow space is smoky with incense and burned paper offerings, and hung with hundreds of gold and red lanterns. Gifts of fruit lie on the carved altar in front of the wooden statue of Tin How. Entry is free, though a donation is expected.

❻

Golden Gate Fortune Cookie Company

⊙ U1 ⌂ 56 Ross Alley 📞 781-3956 🚍 1, 8, 8AX, 8BX, 30, 45 🚋 California St, Powell-Hyde, Powell-Mason ⏰ 8am–6pm daily

The Golden Gate Fortune Cookie Company has been in business since 1962. The cookie-making machine nearly fills the tiny bakery, where dough is poured onto griddles and baked on a conveyor belt. An attendant inserts the "fortunes" (slips of paper bearing mostly positive predictions) before the cookies are folded.

Ironically, despite its association with Chinese culture, the fortune cookie is unknown in China. It was actually invented in 1909 in

↑ Chinatown Gateway, at the entrance to Chinatown's main street, Grant Avenue

San Francisco's Japanese Tea Garden *(p198)*, by then chief gardener, Makota Hagiwara.

↑ The labyrinth inside Grace Cathedral and its imposing exterior *(inset)*

Grace Cathedral

📍 S2 🏛 1100 California St 🚌 1, 27 🚋 California St 🕐 8am–6pm daily (to 7pm Sun) 🌐 gracecathedral.org

Grace Cathedral is the mother church of the Episcopal Diocese of California and the third-largest Episcopal cathedral in the US. Designed by Lewis P. Hobart, it stands on the site of the two Charles and William H. Crocker mansions. Although building started in September 1928, the cathedral was not completed until 1964, and the interior vaulting remains unfinished to this day. Notre Dame in Paris was one of the inspirations for the building, which incorporates a number of traditional elements such as a rose window, which was made in Chartres in 1964.

The interior is replete with marble and stained glass. Its leaded-glass windows were designed by Charles Connick, inspired by the blue glass of Chartres. The rose window, made with 1-inch- (2.5-cm-) thick faceted glass, is illuminated from inside at night. Other windows, by Henry Willet and Gabriel Loire, include depictions of modern heroes such as Albert Einstein. Objects in the cathedral include a 13th-century Catalonian crucifix and a 16th-century silk and gold Brussels tapestry. The doors of the main entrance are cast from molds of Ghiberti's "Gates of Paradise," made for the Baptistry in Florence, Italy.

> The temple's narrow space is smoky with incense and burned paper offerings, and hung with hundreds of gold and red lanterns.

❽ Portsmouth Square

📍 U1 🚌 1, 8, 8AX, 8BX, 30, 45

San Francisco's original town square was laid out in 1839. Also known as the Portsmouth Plaza, it was once the social center for the small village of Yerba Buena. On July 9, 1846, less than a month after rebels declared California's independence from Mexico, a party of marines rowed ashore. They raised the American flag above the square, seizing the port as part of the United States. For a while the square was the hub of an increasingly dynamic city, but in the 1860s the business district shifted southeast and the plaza gradually declined in civic importance.

Portsmouth Square today is very much the social center of Chinatown. In the morning, people practice *t'ai chi*, and others gather to play checkers and cards throughout the day.

Chinese Historical Society of America

📍 T2 🏠 965 Clay St ☎ 391-1188 🚋 Powell-Mason 🚌 1, 8, 8X, 8BX, 30, 45 🕐 11am-4pm Wed-Sun 🌐 chsa.org

Founded in 1963, this is the oldest organization in the country dedicated to the interpretation, promotion, and preservation of the history and contributions of Chinese people in America. One of the exhibits is a multimedia display chronicling the complex history of the Chinese in America, replicas of Angel Island barracks and interrogation room, and paintings by

↑ An exhibition at the Chinese Historical Society of America

Chinese American artists such as Jake Lee and Stella Wong.

The Chinese contribution to California's development was extensive. Chinese workers helped build the western half of the first transcontinental railroad and constructed dikes throughout the Sacramento River delta. The society sponsors oral history projects, an "In Search of Roots" program, and a monthly speakers' forum.

🔟 Pacific Heritage Museum

📍 U2 🏠 608 Commercial St ☎ 399-1124 🚌 1, 8, 8AX, 8BX, 30X, 41 🕐 10am-4pm Tue-Sat

As elegant as the frequently changing collections of Asian arts displayed within, this is actually a synthesis of two distinct buildings. The US Sub-Treasury was built here in 1875–7 by William Appleton Potter, on the site of San Francisco's original mint.

→ Top of the Mark rooftop bar, a perfect place to sip a cocktail and watch the sun set

You can look into the old coin vaults through a cutaway section on the ground floor, or descend in the elevator for closer inspection. In 1984, architects Skidmore, Owings, and Merrill designed the 17-story headquarters of the Bank of Canton (now East West Bank) above the existing building, incorporating the original street-level facade and basement.

🔢 InterContinental Mark Hopkins Hotel

📍 T2 🏠 999 California St 🚋 1 🚋 California St, Powell-Mason, Powell-Hyde 🌐 intercontinental markhopkins.com

At the behest of his wife Mary, Mark Hopkins, one of the founders of the Central Pacific Railroad, arranged for a fantastic wooden mansion, surpassing every other for ostentatious ornamentation, to be built on Nob Hill. When Mrs. Hopkins died, the house became home to the fledgling San Francisco Art Institute. It

burned in the fire after the earthquake of 1906, and only the granite retaining walls remain. The present 25-story tower, capped by a flag visible from all over the city, was built in 1925 by architects Weeks and Day. Top of the Mark, the glass-walled cocktail bar on the 19th floor, is one of San Francisco's most celebrated drinking establishments, enjoying spectacular panoramic views of the city. World War II servicemen customarily drank a farewell toast to the city here before leaving for overseas.

THE NOBS OF NOB HILL

"Nob" was one of the kinder names reserved for the unscrupulous entrepreneurs who amassed huge fortunes during the development of the American West. Many of the "nobs" who lived on Nob Hill acquired other nicknames that hint at the wild stories behind their vast wealth. "Bonanza King" James Flood formed a partnership with three Irish immigrants and, in 1872, the four men bought controlling interests in some dwindling Comstock mines, sinking new shafts and striking a "bonanza" – a rich pocket of high-grade silver ore. Flood returned to San Francisco as a millionaire and bought a parcel of land on the summit of Nob Hill.

Fairmont Hotel

♀ T2 ♠ 950 Mason St
🚋 1 🚋 California St, Powell-Mason, Powell-Hyde
🌐 fairmont.com/san-francisco

Built by Tessie Fair Oelrichs (1871–1926), an American socialite and wife of steamship magnate Heinrich Oelrichs, this Beaux Arts building was completed on the eve of the 1906 major

earthquake, and stood for two days before it was burned down. Rebuilt by architect Julia Morgan within the original white terracotta façade, it opened for business one year later. After World War II it was the scene of meetings that led to the founding of the United Nations. For some stunning views, ride the elevator to the city's highest observation point, the Fairmont Crown; or, enjoy a cocktail at the hotel's famed Tonga Room and Hurricane Bar, which serves Polynesian fusion cuisine and is well known for its extravagant tropical decor.

The Pacific-Union Club

♀ T2 ♠ 1000 California St
📞 775-1234 🚋 1
🚋 California St, Powell-Mason, Powell-Hyde
🚫 To the public

In 1885, Augustus Laver built this townhouse for one of the Nobs of Nob Hill – the "Bonanza King" James Flood. Its brown sandstone facade survived the 1906 fire, though the other mansions, built of wood, were destroyed. The gutted building was bought by the Pacific-Union Club, an exclusive gentlemen's club.

A SHORT WALK
CHINATOWN

Distance 1 mile (0.6 km) **Time** 15 minutes
Nearest bus 8, 30, 45, 91

Grant Avenue is the tourist Chinatown of dragon lampposts, upturned rooflines and stores packed to the rafters with everything from kites to cooking utensils. Locals shop on Stockton Street, where the freshest produce and fish spill over in boxes onto crowded sidewalks. In the alleys in between, look for traditional temples, shops, and family-run restaurants.

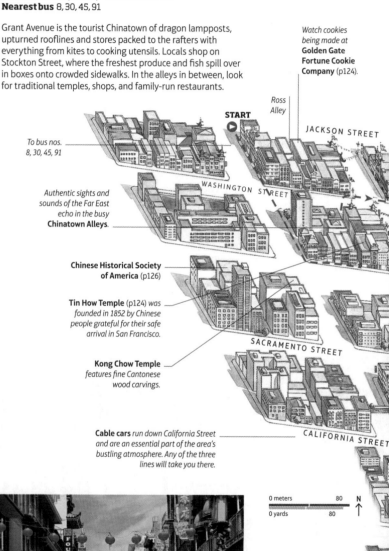

Watch cookies being made at **Golden Gate Fortune Cookie Company** *(p124).*

Ross Alley

START

JACKSON STREET

To bus nos. 8, 30, 45, 91

Authentic sights and sounds of the Far East echo in the busy **Chinatown Alleys**.

WASHINGTON STREET

Chinese Historical Society of America (p126)

Tin How Temple (p124) *was founded in 1852 by Chinese people grateful for their safe arrival in San Francisco.*

Kong Chow Temple *features fine Cantonese wood carvings.*

SACRAMENTO STREET

Cable cars *run down California Street and are an essential part of the area's bustling atmosphere. Any of the three lines will take you there.*

CALIFORNIA STREET

| 0 meters | 80 |
| 0 yards | 80 |

N ↑

BUSH

← Grant Avenue, Chinatown's main commercial thoroughfare

← The elegant interior of Old St. Mary's Cathedral

Locator Map
For more detail see p116

Laid out in 1839, **Portsmouth Square** *(p125) was the social center for the village of Yerba Buena, the original settlement that later became San Francisco. Today people gather here to play cards and mahjong.*

Did You Know?

San Francisco's Chinatown is the oldest one in North America.

The Chinese Cultural Center *contains an art gallery and a small crafts shop. It sponsors a lively series of lectures and seminars.*

Housed in an elegant building, the small **Pacific Heritage Museum** *(p126) has fine exhibitions of Asian art.*

In the mid-19th century, **Grant Avenue** *(p122) was the main thoroughfare of Yerba Buena. It is now the busy commercial center of Chinatown.*

The clock tower of **Old St. Mary's Cathedral** *(p124), built while the city was still in its infancy, bears an arresting inscription.*

St. Mary's Square *is a quiet haven in which to take a rest.*

To bus nos. 8, 30, 45, 91

Also known as the "Dragons' Gate," **Chinatown Gateway** *(p124) marks Chinatown's southern entrance.*

KEARNY STREET

CLAY STREET

AVENUE

STOCKTON STREET

PINE STREET

FINISH

STREET

A SHORT WALK
NOB HILL

Distance 0.5 mile (0.8 km) **Time** 15 minutes
Nearest bus 1, 27

Nob Hill is the highest summit of the city center, rising 338 ft (103 m) above the bay, and affording splendid views of the city. Its steep slopes were treacherous for carriages and kept prominent citizens away until the opening of the California Street cable car line in 1878. After that, the wealthy "nobs" soon built new homes on the peak of the hill. Though many of the grandiose mansions were burned down in the great fire of 1906 (p53), Nob Hill still attracts the affluent to its many splendid hotels. A stroll through this well-heeled neighborhood will lead you past some of the most expensive real estate in the US.

The Pacific-Union Club (p127), *now an exclusive men's club, was once the mansion of Comstock millionaire James Flood.*

Huntington Park *is on the site of Collis P. Huntington's mansion.*

Grace Cathedral (p125) *is a replica of Notre Dame in Paris.*

SACRAMENTO STREET

TAYLOR STREET

START

JONES STREET

The Nob Hill Masonic Auditorium *honors Freemasons who died in American wars.*

Huntington Hotel *with its Big Four Bar and Restaurant exudes the opulent urbane atmosphere of the Victorian era on Nob Hill.*

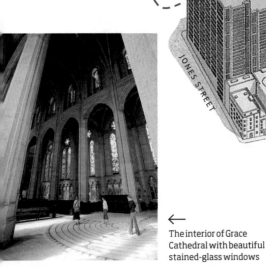

← The interior of Grace Cathedral with beautiful stained-glass windows

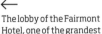

The lobby of the Fairmont Hotel, one of the grandest hotels on Nob Hill

Locator Map
For more detail see p116

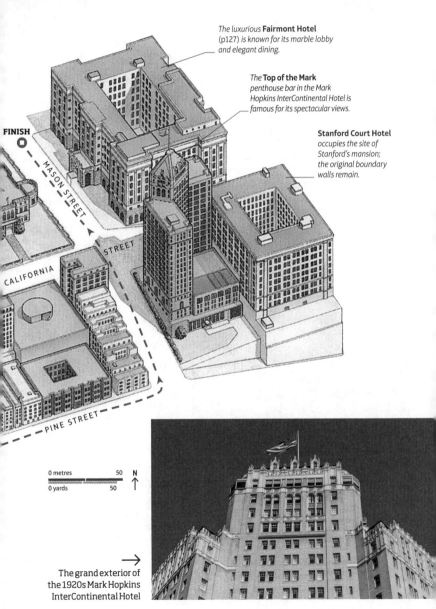

The luxurious **Fairmont Hotel**
(p127) is known for its marble lobby and elegant dining.

The **Top of the Mark**
penthouse bar in the Mark Hopkins InterContinental Hotel is famous for its spectacular views.

Stanford Court Hotel
occupies the site of Stanford's mansion; the original boundary walls remain.

FINISH

MASON STREET

STREET

CALIFORNIA

PINE STREET

| 0 metres | 50 |
| 0 yards | 50 |

N ↑

The grand exterior of the 1920s Mark Hopkins InterContinental Hotel

Facade of SFMOMA on 3rd Street

DOWNTOWN AND SOMA

Montgomery Street, now in the heart of downtown San Francisco, was once a street of small shops, where miners came to weigh their gold dust. It roughly marks the old shoreline of the shallow Yerba Buena Cove, which was filled in during the Gold Rush years *(p52)* to create more land. Today, old-style banking halls from the early 20th century stand in the shadow of glass and steel skyscrapers, and crowds of office workers throng the streets.

Bordering this high-profile hub is SOMA – "South of Market" – which has had a dramatic, and often tragic, history. The original residential district here was almost completely destroyed during the 1906 earthquake, and the gay community based here several decades later was threatened when City Hall tried to close down and redevelop much of the area during the 1970s and 80s. Now, however, the area has found a firm place as a contemporary and bustling district of galleries, fine dining, and office towers.

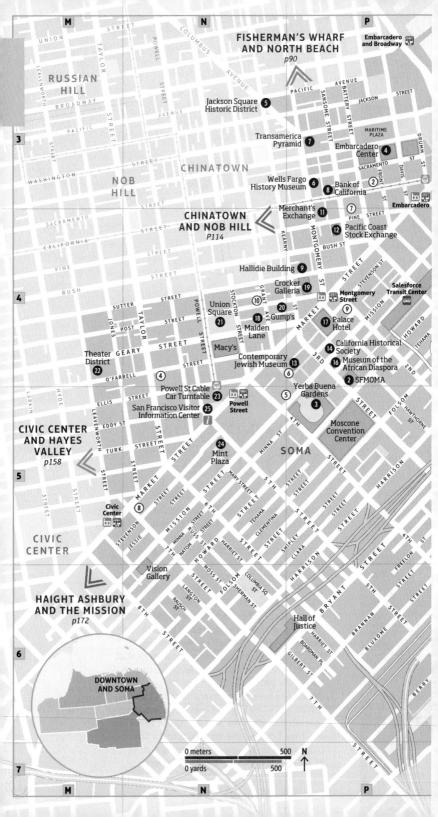

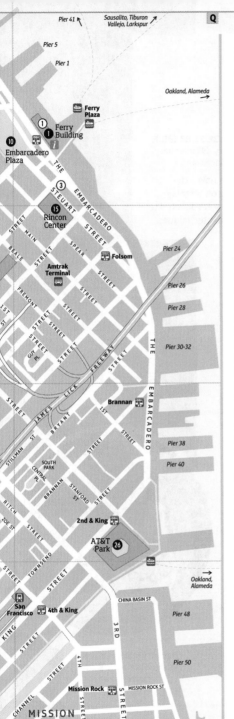

DOWNTOWN AND SOMA

Must Sees
1. Ferry Building
2. SFMOMA
3. Yerba Buena Gardens

Experience More
4. Embarcadero Center
5. Jackson Square Historic District
6. Wells Fargo History Museum
7. Transamerica Pyramid
8. Bank of California
9. Hallidie Building
10. Embarcadero Plaza
11. Merchants' Exchange
12. Pacific Coast Stock Exchange
13. Contemporary Jewish Museum
14. California Historical Society
15. Rincon Center
16. Museum of the African Diaspora
17. Palace Hotel
18. Maiden Lane
19. Crocker Galleria
20. Gump's
21. Union Square
22. Theater District
23. Powell Street Cable Car Turntable
24. Mint Plaza
25. San Francisco Visitor Information Center
26. AT&T Park

Eat
1. Donut Farm, El Porteño, The Slanted Door, MarketBar
2. Tadich Grill
3. Boulevard

Drink
4. Cityscape Bar & Lounge
5. The View Lounge
6. Press Club

Stay
7. Loews Regency San Francisco
8. YOTEL San Francisco

Shop
9. Alexander Book Company
10. Hats on Post

1 🚫 🍴 🖥 🛍

FERRY BUILDING

📍E3 🚇Embarcadero at Market St 🚌2, 6, 21, 31, 82 🚊E, F, J, K, L, M, N 🚋California St ⛴ SF Bay Ferry 🕐Times vary, check website 🌐ferrybuildingmarketplace.com

This historic entry point into the city is now a chic marketplace and food hall. Everything on offer is made with flair and care by local producers devoted to sustainability and traditional production techniques.

Once an important point of entry into the city, the Ferry Bulding is now a marketplace. It houses many gourmet shops, several restaurants and eateries, and hosts a farmers' market on Tuesdays and Saturdays. There's a distinctly northern California feel to the Ferry Building Marketplace in the way it celebrates popular modern principles like using regional produce, traditional farming, and local and artisan producers.

The Old Ferry Terminal

Constructed between 1896 and 1903, the Ferry Building survived the great fire of 1906 through the intercession of fireboats pumping water from the bay. The clock tower is 235 ft (71 m) high, and was inspired by the Moorish bell tower of Seville Cathedral. In the early 1930s more than 50 million passengers a year passed through the building. With the opening of the Bay Bridge in 1936, the Ferry Building ceased to be the city's main point of entry, but even today ferries still cross the bay to Larkspur and Sausalito in Marin County and Alameda and Oakland in the East Bay.

The Ferry Building at night and the farmers' market (inset) ↑

← The Ferry Building's clock tower, an iconic feature of the lcoal skyline

→ Inside the open and inviting Ferry Building Marketplace

Did You Know?

At the farmers' market, local celebrity chefs shop for local, farm-to-table ingredients.

EAT

Donut Farm
Vegan-friendly menu with delightful donuts and great breakfast options.

 Sat only Ⓦ vegan donut.farm

$$$$$$

El Porteño
Argentinian empanadas passed down from an old family recipe.

Ⓦ elportenosf.com

$$$$$$

The Slanted Door
A highly acclaimed Vietnamese restaurant overlooking the Bay.

Ⓦ slanteddoor.com

$$$$$$

MarketBar
This brasserie uses ingredients from the venue's Farmers' Market in its seasonal seafood.

Ⓦ marketbar.com

$$$$$$

2 🛠 Ⓜ 🍴 🖥 🛍

SFMOMA

📍 C1 🏠 151 3rd St 🚌 5, 9, 12, 14, 30, 38, 45 🚊 J, K, L, M, N, T
🕙 10am–5pm Thu–Tue (to 9pm Thu) 🌐 sfmoma.org

Standing proudly on the northeast side of the Yerba Buena Gardens art and entertainment complex, the exterior of the San Francisco Museum of Modern Art (SFMOMA) is as artistically innovative as the works displayed within it.

This museum forms the nucleus of San Francisco's reputation as a leading center of modern art. Opening in 1935 at the Veterans Building (p167), it moved into its current quarters in 1995, and in spring 2016 reopened after a major three-year $365 million expansion that doubled its capacity. Designed by the international architecture firm Snøhetta, the 235,000 sq ft (21,832 sq m) expansion is seamlessly integrated with Swiss architect Mario Botta's 1995 modernist building. The museum offers a dynamic schedule of special exhibitions and permanent collection presentations.

Museum Highlights

SFMOMA is both an outstanding repository of modern and contemporary art and a powerhouse of inspiration and encouragement to the local art scene. With more than 30,000 works of art in the museum's permanent collection, you'll see works ranging from traditional paintings to media arts, architecture, and design. The museum's main strengths lie in US and Latin American modernism, Fauvism, Surrealism, Abstract Expressionism, Minimalism and post-Minimalism, Pop art, postwar German art, and the art of California. The 2016 expansion brought a notable addition: the 15,000-sq-ft (1,393-sq-m) Pritzker Center for Photography, the largest space dedicated to this artform in any art museum in the country.

↑ The Howard Street entrance and visitors at a media arts exhibit (inset)

Gallery Guide

Level One
Here you'll find the excellent museum store, the Michelin-starred restaurant In Situ, a theater, and large abstract works by Julie Mehretu

Level Two
The permanent collection, Education Center, and library are housed on the second floor, interspersed with some temporary exhibits

↑ The vibrant *Figures with Sunset* (1978) by Roy Lichtenstein

Level Three

⊿ The fabulous Center for Photography sits on the third floor along with the Sculpture Terrace, Graphic Design Gallery, and the 30-ft-(9-m-) high Living Wall

Level Four

⊿ The Agnes Martin and Kelly Elsworth Galleries, event space, and many temporary exhibits

Level Five

⊿ The fifth floor houses a variety of museum highlights including the Oculus Bridge, Andy Warhol gallery, and Sculpture Garden

Level Six

⊿ The Anselm Kiefer and Gerhard Richter Galleries

Level Seven

Sculpture Terrace and temporary exhibits

LOWER FLOORS

California Arts

On the second floor there are galleries dedicated to works by California artists. These painters and sculptors have drawn their inspiration from local materials and scenes to create an influential body of art that is unique to the West Coast. Collage and assemblage artists exhibited on rotation from the museum's collection make use of everyday materials such as felt-tip pens, junkyard scraps and old paintings, producing art with a distinctive West Coast flavor.

Photography

Drawing on its enormous permanent collection of over 17,800 photographs, the museum presents wonderful exhibitions of the photographic arts in the Pritzker

A display in the Pritzker Center for Photography ↓

Center for Photography, located on the third-floor.

The collection of Modernist American masters includes Berenice Abbott, Walker Evans, Edward Steichen, and Alfred Stieglitz, with special attention paid to California photographers. It has the finest collection of Japanese photography outside of Japan, as well as extensive collections from Latin America and Europe, including German avant-garde photographers of the 1920s, and European Surrealists of the 1930s.

Did You Know?

SFMOMA's collection began with paintings donated by Albert M. Bender, a dedicated patron of the arts.

Paintings and Sculpture

Included in the museum's permanent holdings are over 8,000 paintings, sculptures, and works on paper. American Abstract Expressionism is well represented at the museum by Philip Guston, Franz Kline, and Jackson Pollock, whose first ever museum exhibition took place here at SFMOMA.

Other prominent North and Latin American artists whose works are displayed in the museum collections include Frida Kahlo, Diego Rivera, and Georgia O'Keeffe. Another exhibition area permanently shows works by Jasper Johns, Robert Rauschenberg, and Andy Warhol, among others. There is a good collection of the European Modernists, including notable paintings by Pablo Picasso from various periods. A large collection of works by Paul Klee are accommodated in an individual gallery, with works by the famous French painter of the Fauvist school, Henri Matisse, nearby on the second floor.

> An actively changing schedule of contemporary art exhibits supplements the museum's historical collection and does much to encourage today's art scene.

↑ Alexander Calder sculptures; *Frieda and Diego Rivera* (1931), by Frida Kahlo *(inset)*

UPPER FLOORS

Architecture and Design

SFMOMA's Department of Architecture and Design was founded in 1983. Its function is to procure and maintain a collection of historical and contemporary architectural drawings, models, and design objects, and to examine and illuminate their influences on modern art. Its current holding of over 6,000 items focuses on architecture, furniture, product design, and graphic design, and is widely considered one of the most significant in the United States. The new sixth-floor galleries offer rotating exhibitions.

Among items included in the permanent collection are models, drawings, prints, and prototypes by well-known and emerging designers. These include the famous architect Bernard Maybeck,

who was responsible for some of the most beautiful buildings in the Bay Area, including the Palace of Fine Arts *(p68)*. Other noted San Francisco Bay Area architects represented are Timothy Pflueger, William Wurster, and Willis Polk, known for his design of the glass and steel Hallidie Building *(p146)*, as well as the California design team of Charles and Ray Eames. The permanent collection also includes works by Frank Lloyd Wright, Frank Gehry, and Fumihiko Maki.

Media Arts

Established in 1988, the Department of Media Arts collects, conserves, documents, and exhibits art of the moving image, including works in video, film, projected image, electronic arts, and time-based media. The seventh-floor galleries deploy state-of-the-art equipment to present photographic, multi-image and multimedia works, film, video, and selected programs of interactive media artwork.

The museum's growing permanent collection includes pieces by artists such as Nam June Paik, Don Graham, Peter Campus, Joan Jonas, Lynn Hershman Leeson, Bill Viola, Doug Hall, and Mary Lucier.

Contemporary Art and Special Exhibitions

The fourth floor features special exhibition galleries. An actively changing schedule of contemporary art exhibits supplements the museum's historical collection and does much to encourage today's art scene. The museum also has regular film screenings and public talks in the theater.

 INSIDER TIP
In Situ

SFMOMA's Michelin-starred restaurant brings together a collection of dishes from around the world. Walk-ins are welcome, but it's best to book in advance *(insitu.sfmoma.org/reservation)*.

---

3 🍴 🖥

YERBA BUENA GARDENS

📍 C5 🚇 Mission, 3rd, Folsom, 4th & Howard streets 🚌 9, 14, 30, 45, 76 🚊 J, K, L, M, N, T 🕐 6am–11pm daily 🌐 yerbabuenagardens.com

Teeming with art installations, green spaces, and museums spread out across several modern buildings, the Yerba Buena Gardens feel like a mini artists' community. With so much to explore, it's the perfect location for both art lovers and urban adventurers.

The construction of the Moscone Center, San Francisco's largest venue for conventions, was just the first in a series of ambitious development plans for Yerba Buena Gardens. Housing, hotels, museums, galleries, gardens, and restaurants have all followed, and now the area is a vibrant hub of activity. Check the Yerba Buena Gardens website for information about hours and admission prices for the individual buildings on site.

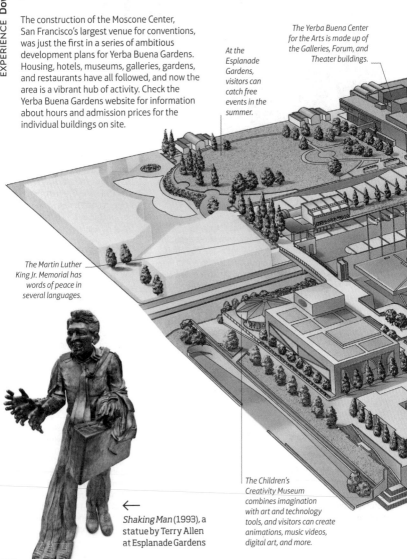

The Yerba Buena Center for the Arts is made up of the Galleries, Forum, and Theater buildings.

At the Esplanade Gardens, visitors can catch free events in the summer.

The Martin Luther King Jr. Memorial has words of peace in several languages.

← Shaking Man (1993), a statue by Terry Allen at Esplanade Gardens

The Children's Creativity Museum combines imagination with art and technology tools, and visitors can create animations, music videos, digital art, and more.

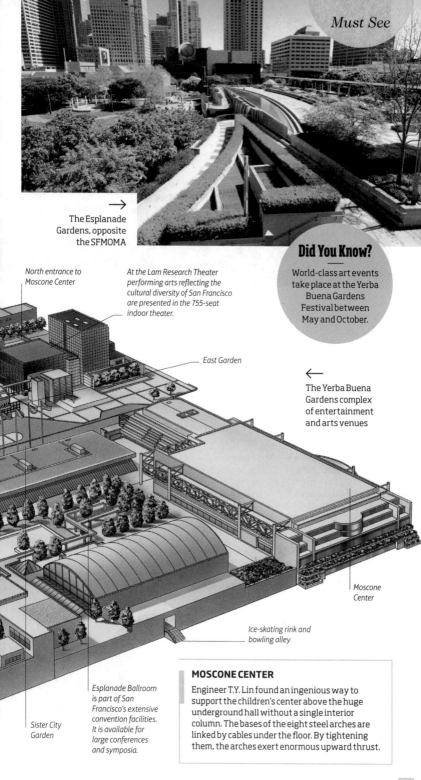

→
The Esplanade Gardens, opposite the SFMOMA

North entrance to Moscone Center

At the Lam Research Theater performing arts reflecting the cultural diversity of San Francisco are presented in the 755-seat indoor theater.

East Garden

Did You Know?

World-class art events take place at the Yerba Buena Gardens Festival between May and October.

←
The Yerba Buena Gardens complex of entertainment and arts venues

Moscone Center

Ice-skating rink and bowling alley

Esplanade Ballroom is part of San Francisco's extensive convention facilities. It is available for large conferences and symposia.

Sister City Garden

MOSCONE CENTER

Engineer T.Y. Lin found an ingenious way to support the children's center above the huge underground hall without a single interior column. The bases of the eight steel arches are linked by cables under the floor. By tightening them, the arches exert enormous upward thrust.

EXPERIENCE MORE

④
Embarcadero Center

📍P3 🚌 Many buses 🚆 E, F, J, K, L, M, N, T 🚋 California St

The Embarcadero Center was completed in 1981 after a decade of construction, the largest redevelopment project in the city's history. The complex of hotels and office and retail space reaches from Embarcadero Plaza (p147) to Battery Street. Four separate high-rise towers reach upward 35 to 40 stories above the landscaped plazas and elevated walkways.

Embarcadero Center's most spectacular interior is the lobby of the Hyatt Regency Hotel. Its 17-story atrium contains an immense sculptured globe, made up of 1,440 interlacing aluminium tubes, by Charles O. Perry, entitled *Eclipse* (1973). Glass elevators glide up and down one wall, carrying visitors to and from their rooms. Also housed in the center is an array of shops and a movie theater screening independent and foreign movies.

⑤
Jackson Square Historic District

📍N3 🚌 8AX, 8BX, 10, 12, 41, 82X 🌐 jackson squaresf.com

Renovated in the early 1950s, this low-rise neighborhood contains many historic ornate brick, cast-iron, and granite facades dating from the Gold Rush era. From 1850 to 1910, it was notorious for its squalor and the crudeness of its inhabitants, and was known as the Barbary Coast. The Hippodrome at No. 555 Pacific Street used to be a theater; the bawdy relief sculptures in the recessed front recall the risqué shows that were performed there. Today the buildings of the Jackson Square Historic District are used as showrooms, law offices, top-notch restaurants, design and fashion boutiques, art galleries, and antique shops; the most attractive buildings can be seen on Jackson Street, Gold Street, Hotaling Place, and Montgomery Street.

⑥ 🛍
Wells Fargo History Museum

📍P3 🏠 420 Montgomery St 🚌 1, 3, 8, 8AX, 8BX, 10, 12, 30X, 41 🚋 California St 🚇 Montgomery 🕒 9am–5pm Mon-Fri 🌐 wellsfargo history.com/museums/san-francisco

Founded in 1852, Wells Fargo & Co. became the greatest banking and transportation company in the West and was influential in the development of the American frontier. The company moved people and

↑ A mail coach on display in the Wells Fargo History Museum

← Charles O. Perry's dramatic sculpture, *Eclipse,* in the Hyatt Regency Hotel's lobby

Francis Brocklehurst, an immigrant, and view exhibits that include Pony Express mail, a working telegraph, weaponry, and gold nuggets.

 7

Transamerica Pyramid

P3 ⌂ **600 Montgomery St** ▣ **1, 8AX, 8BX, 10, 12, 41** ⊘ **To the public** ⓦ **pyramidcenter.com**

Capped with a pointed spire on top of its 48 stories, the pyramid reaches 853 ft (256 m) above sea level. It is the most recognized building in the city and was the tallest until it was overtaken by the Salesforce Tower, which was completed in 2018.

Although San Franciscans disliked it when it opened in 1972, they have since accepted it as part of their

Did You Know?

SOMA's new Salesforce Tower is 1,070 ft (326 m) tall.

city's skyline. Designed by William Pereira & Associates, the pyramid houses 1,500 office workers on a historically rich site. The Montgomery Block was built here in 1853. In the basement was the Exchange Saloon, frequented by Mark Twain. In the 1860s artists and writers took up residence in the Montgomery Block. The Pony Express terminus, marked by a plaque, was at Merchant Street opposite the pyramid. The building has been closed to the public since September 11, 2001, though there is a visitors' center in the lobby.

goods from the East to the West Coast, and between California mining camps and towns. It also transported gold from the West Coast to the East and delivered mail. Wells Fargo put mail boxes in convenient locations and messengers sorted the letters en route. Wells Fargo played a major role in the mail service venture, Pony Express.

The stagecoaches, like the one on display in the museum, are famous for the legends of heroic drivers and the bandits who robbed them. The best-known bandit was Black Bart, who left poems at the scene of his crimes. He stalked the roads from Calaveras County to the Oregon border between 1875 and 1883, holding up stagecoaches. In one hold-up he mistakenly left a hand-kerchief with a distinctive laundry mark, revealing him to be a mining engineer named Charles Boles.

Visitors to the museum can experience how it felt to sit for days in a jostling stagecoach, listen to the recordings of

→ The Transamerica Pyramid, one of San Francisco's most recognizable sights

8
Bank of California

📍P3 🏛️400 California St
📞765-0400 🚌1, 30X, 41
🚃California St

William Ralston and Darius Mills founded this bank in 1864. Ralston, known as "the man who built San Francisco," invested profitably in Comstock mines, and used the bank and his personal fortune to finance many civic projects in San Francisco. These included the city's water company, a theater, and the Palace Hotel (p148). However, when economic depression struck in the 1870s, Ralston's empire also collapsed. The present

---

💬 INSIDER TIP
Naming the Plaza

In 2017 city officials voted to change the name of the Justin Herman Plaza. Embarcadero Plaza, its current title, is only temporary until a new name can be decided upon.

---

colonnaded building was completed in 1908. In the basement there is a pleasant arcade of shops, restaurants, and art exhibits.

9
Hallidie Building

📍P4 🏛️130 Sutter St
🚌3, 8, 30, 45 🚃K, L, M, N
🚃California St 🚇Montgomery 🚈Embarcadero
🔒To the public

A unique and important architectural achievement, the Hallidie Building was the first building in the United States to use the glass-curtain style, in which glass panes are suspended in a steel-mullion grid. When constructed in 1918 by Willis Polk, the seven-floor building was breathtakingly modern. It juxtaposes minimalist elements like the glass curtain with classic Gothic architectural details such as embellished cornices, balconies, fire escapes, and

→

The Vaillancourt Fountain in the Embarcadero Plaza

thin zinc panels adorned with birds and flowers. A major restoration of the facade was completed in 2013.

10
Embarcadero Plaza

📍P3 🚌Many buses 🚃E, F, J, K, L, M, N 🚃California St

Formerly known as the Justin Herman Plaza, this open square is popular with lunchtime crowds from the

← The grand colonnaded facade of the Pacific Coast Stock Exchange building

EAT

Tadich Grill

Operating since 1849, this old-school favorite pulls in the after-work crowds for famously large portions of seafood.

📍 P3 🏠 240 California St
🕐 Sun
🌐 tadichgrillsf.com

$$$

Boulevard

Indulgent ingredients from Pacific swordfish to Burgundy truffles are used to create refined, regionally focused dishes. The waterfront setting and low lighting make this a favorite date spot.

📍 Q3 🏠 1 Mission St
🌐 boulevardrestaurant.com

$$$

nearby Embarcadero Center and other offices. The plaza is mostly known for its avant-garde Vaillancourt Fountain, made in 1971 by Canadian artist Armand Vaillancourt. The fountain is modeled from huge concrete blocks, and some find it ugly, especially when it runs dry in times of drought. However, you can climb on and through it, and its pools and columns of falling water make it an intriguing public work of art when functioning as intended.

 Merchants' Exchange

📍 P4 🏠 465 California St
🚌 1, 3, 8, 30X, 41
🚋 California St 🕐 9am–5pm Mon–Fri; Sat & Sun by appointment only
🌐 mxbuilding.com

The exchange, designed by Willis Polk in 1903, survived the great fire of 1906 with little damage. Inside, fine seascapes by the Irish painter William Coulter line the walls. These depict epic maritime scenes from the age of steam and sail. The building was the focal point of San Francisco's commodities exchange in the early 20th century, when lookouts in the tower relayed

Did You Know?

California architect Julia Morgan helped to redesign parts of the Merchants' Exchange.

news of ships arriving from abroad. The building is now an office and events space.

 Pacific Coast Stock Exchange

📍 P4 🏠 301 Pine St 🚌 3, 8, 30X, 41 🚫 To the public

This was once America's largest stock exchange outside New York. Founded in 1882, it occupied these buildings, which were remodeled by Miller and Pflueger in 1930 from the existing US Treasury. The monumental granite statues that flank the Pine Street entrance to the building were made by the renowned San Francisco sculptor, painter, and muralist Ralph Stackpole, also in 1930. No longer a stock exchange, the building is now a fitness club.

18

A lucky number in Jewish culture – which is why 18 steps lead up to the Contemporary Jewish Museum.

13

Contemporary Jewish Museum

📍P4 🏠736 Mission St 🚌8, 14, 30, 45, 81X 🚋J, K, L, M, N, T 🕐11am-8pm Thu, 11am-5pm Fri-Tue 🚫Major Jewish holidays 🌐thecjm.org

This museum partners with national and international cultural institutions to present a variety of art, photography, and installations celebrating and exploring Judaism.

The museum is housed in an early 20th-century Pacific Gas & Electric (PG&E) Power Substation, adapted and redesigned by world-renowned architect Daniel Libeskind and unveiled in 2005. The space features more than 10,000 sq ft (930 sq m) of exhibition space and an impressive education center.

14

California Historical Society

📍P4 🏠678 Mission St 🚌8, 14, 30, 45, 81X 🚋J, K, L, M, N, T 🚇Montgomery 🕐Times vary, check website 🌐california historicalsociety.org

The society promotes understanding of the history of California, and houses research libraries and a bookstore. The galleries are particularly interesting and thorough, and include a photographic collection, 900 paintings and watercolors by American artists, a decorative arts exhibit, and a unique collection of costumes.

15

Rincon Center

📍Q4 🏠121 Spear St 🚌14

This shopping center, with its soaring atrium, was added on to the old Rincon Annex Post Office Building in 1989. The Rincon Annex is known for 27 painted panels titled *The History of California*, executed in Social Realist style by Russian-born Anton Refregier between 1940 and 1948.

16

Museum of the African Diaspora

📍P4 🏠685 Mission St 🚌8, 14, 30, 45, 81X 🚋J, K, L, M, N, T 🕐11am-6pm Wed-Sat, noon-5pm Sun 🚫Major hols 🌐moadsf.org

A contemporary art museum, MoAD celebrates black culture. Three to four innovative exhibitions are held at any one time, in addition to multiple public events every week. The museum has emerged as an important destination within the Yerba Buena Center for the Arts campus.

17

Palace Hotel

📍P4 🏠2 New Montgomery St 🚌8, 12, 14, 30, 45, 81X 🚋J, K, L, M, N, T 🌐sfpalace.com

The original Palace Hotel was opened by William Ralston, one of San Francisco's best-known financiers, in 1875.

→

The Contemporary Jewish Museum, redesigned by D. Libeskind

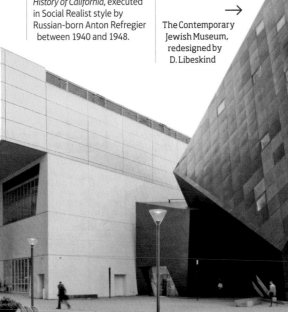

It was the most luxurious of San Francisco's early hotels and was regularly frequented by the rich and famous. Among its patrons were Sarah Bernhardt, Oscar Wilde, and Rudyard Kipling. The celebrated tenor Enrico Caruso was a guest at the time of the earthquake of 1906, when the hotel caught fire. It was rebuilt by the architect George Kelham, and reopened in 1909. It is best known for the Garden Court, its fabulous glass-ceilinged, colonnaded restaurant, and its Pied Piper bar. The bar is decorated with a beautiful mural by Maxfield Parrish, which was commissioned by the hotel on its reopening in 1909. The hotel's palm-filled Garden Court also provides a memorable brunch or high tea experience.

> **Among the Palace Hotel's patrons were Sarah Bernhardt, Oscar Wilde, and Rudyard Kipling.**

↑ The magnificent Garden Court restaurant at the Palace Hotel, dating from 1909

STAY

Loews Regency San Francisco

The reliably luxurious chain occupies the top floors of a high-rise and takes full advantage of its lofty perch with a stylish, open-air lounge on the roof. Some of the plush rooms have great views of Alcatraz.

📍P4 🏠222 Sansome St
🌐loewshotels.com

⑤⑤⑤

YOTEL San Francisco

Compact, high-tech rooms with rainfall showers, a rooftop terrace, and numerous social spaces inspired by first-class airline lounges are housed in one of the few buildings to survive the terrible 1906 earthquake.

📍N5 🏠1095 Market St
🌐yotel.com

⑤⑤⑤

Pedestrianized Maiden Lane, a pretty, tranquil haven away from the city bustle

20

Gump's

📍N4 🏠135 Post St 🚌3, 5, 6, 8, 9, 21, 30, 38, 45 🚊J, K, L, M, N, T 🚋Powell-Mason, Powell-Hyde ⏰11am-6pm Mon-Sat 🌐gumps.com

Founded in 1861 by German immigrants, this homegrown San Francisco department store is a local institution.

18

Maiden Lane

📍N4 🏠Between Stockton St and Kearny St 🚌3, 30, 38R 🚋Powell-Mason 🚋Powell

In the heady days of the Gold Rush, this prim-sounding street played host to San Francisco's most popular red light district. Today, its name is associated with its high-end boutiques, opera-singing buskers, and art galleries. A traffic-free mall located just off Union Square, lined with shops and open-air cafés, the street offers a respite from the hustle and bustle just a block away. One notable building, the V. C. Morris Gift

Did You Know?

The street underwent several name changes before the city landed on Maiden Lane in 1922.

Shop, is a designated San Francisco landmark, since it's the only Frank Lloyd Wright-designed structure in the city. Film buffs will get a kick out of touring one of the city spots where Alfred Hitchcock shot a scene for his movie *The Birds*.

19

Crocker Galleria

📍P4 🏠Between Post, Kearny, Sutter, and Montgomery Sts 🚌3, 5, 6, 8, 21, 30, 38, 45 🚊J, K, L, M, N, T 🚋Montgomery ⏰Sun 🌐thecrockergalleria.com

The Crocker Galleria was built in 1982, by the architects Skidmore, Owings & Merrill. Inspired by the Galleria Vittorio Emanuele in Milan, this building features a central plaza underneath a vaulting sky-light glass roof.

A rooftop garden, farmers' market, food court, and dozens of shops, from gourmet patisseries to one-off homeware and fashion boutiques, are housed here on three floors.

DRINK

Cityscape Bar & Lounge

Craft cocktails and a vast selection of wines are served up with views of the Golden Gate Bridge at this chic rooftop bar.

📍N4 🏠333 O'Farrell St 🌐cityscapesf.com

The View Lounge

Those in the know head to this rooftop before sunset to grab a cocktail and a seat for one of the city's best views over skyscrapers toward the San Francisco Bay.

📍P5 🏠780 Mission St 🌐sfviewlounge.com

Press Club

This underground bar is the place to be for happy hour, offering generous discounts on local craft brews and wines by the glass.

📍P4 🏠20 Yerba Buena Lane 🌐pressclubsf.com

Many local couples register their wedding present list with the store. Gump's has the largest collection of fine china and crystal in the US.

The store is also celebrated for its Oriental treasures, furniture, and the rare works in the art department. The Asian art is particularly fine, especially the remarkable jade collection, which enjoys a worldwide reputation. In 1949 Gump's imported the great bronze Buddha and presented it to the Japanese Tea Garden (p198). Gump's has an exclusive, refined atmosphere and is frequented by the rich and famous. It is also renowned for its colorful and extravagant window displays.

1861–5. The rallies galvanized popular support in San Francisco for the Northern cause, and this was instrumental in bringing California into the war on the side of the Union. The square is at the heart of the city's shopping district; large department stores can be found here, including Macy's and Sak's Fifth Avenue, as well as major flagship stores. The square is bordered on the west side by the famous Westin St Francis Hotel, and at the center there is a statue of *Victory* atop a 90-ft (27-m) column. This monument commemorates Admiral Dewey's victory at Manila Bay during the Spanish-American War of 1898.

 HIDDEN GEM
Frank Lloyd Wright

Architect Frank Lloyd Wright experimented with the use of ramps in the small V. C. Morris Gift Shop at 140 Maiden Lane. It is considered one of his most influential works.

the title of San Francisco's theater district. The two biggest venues are on Geary Boulevard, two blocks west of the square. These are the Curran Theater – which was built in 1922 and sports a grand carved ceiling and glass chandelier – and the Geary Theater, built in 1909 and now the home of the American Conservatory Theater (ACT). Drama has flourished in San Francisco since the days of the Gold Rush, and great actors and opera stars have been attracted to the city. Isadora Duncan, the innovative 1920s dancer, was born nearby on Taylor Street.

21

Union Square

N4 2, 3, 5, 6, 8, 9, 21, 30
J, K, L, M, N, T Powell-Mason, Powell-Hyde

Union Square was named for the big, pro-Union rallies held there during the Civil War of

22

Theater District

M4 2, 3, 27, 38, 45
J, K, L, M, N, T Powell-Mason, Powell-Hyde

Several theaters are located near Union Square, all within a six-block area, giving the area

↑ Union Square surrounded by high-end stores such as Saks and Tiffany & Co

SHOP

Alexander Book Company

A labyrinthine, independent bookstore with stacks of new and used tomes spread over three floors. Comfy chairs dotted between shelves give you a chance to sit down and flip through the books.

P4 **50 2nd St** **Sun** **alexander book.com**

Hats on Post

Tucked inside the Victorian-era Shreve Building, this charming shop stocks head-turning headgear for special occasions and everyday wear. The vintage-look cloche hats and fascinators are handcrafted by West Coast milliners.

N4 **210 Post St** **Sun & Mon** **hatsonpost.com**

Powell Street Cable Car Turntable

N5 **Hallidie Plaza, Powell St at Market St** **Many buses** **J, K, L, M, N, T** **Powell-Mason, Powell-Hyde**

The Powell-Hyde and the Powell-Mason cable-car lines are the most spectacular routes in San Francisco. They start and end their journeys to Nob Hill, Chinatown, and Fisherman's Wharf at the corner of Powell Street and Market Street. Unlike the double-ended cable cars on the California Street line, the Powell Street cable cars were built to move in one direction only – hence the need for a turntable at every terminus.

After the car's passengers have disembarked, it is pushed onto the turntable and rotated manually by the conductor and gripman (the person who operates the "grip," which by grasping or releasing the cable, starts or stops the car). Prospective customers for the return journey wait amid an ever-moving procession of street musicians, shoppers, tourists, and office workers.

Did You Know?

Both the Powell-Mason and Powell-Hyde lines end near Fisherman's Warf, but in different areas.

A cable car at the Powell Street cable car turntable ↓

→ AT&T Park, the home of the San Francisco Giants and a statue of Hall of Famer, Willie Mays *(inset)*

24

Mint Plaza

N5 8AX, 9R, 14, 27, 45, 88X J, K, L, M, N, T Powell mintplazasf.org

With plenty of outdoor chairs scattered about, this public plaza offers a comfortable space to rest your feet or to grab a bite after sightseeing near Union Square. Tucked away off Market Street, the square is framed by trees, flower beds, and historic buildings. The plaza is a popular conduit for San Franciscans walking to work during rush hour and makes for excellent people-watching. During the summer months, you will frequently find live music being played. The original Blue Bottle café, renowned for its quality coffee, is located just off the plaza, and sandwich shops and lunch spots abound. You'll also find popular restaurants and wine bars for happy hour.

25

San Francisco Visitor Information Center

N5 900 Market St Many buses J, K, L, M, N, T Powell-Mason, Powell-Hyde 9am-5pm Mon-Fri, 9am-3pm Sat & Sun) Nov-Apr: Sun sftravel.com

Enquire here for information on tours of the city and surrounding areas, festivals, special events, restaurants, accommodations, and sightseeing. Maps and a wide range of brochures are available in English and other languages, while a multilingual staff is on hand to answer questions. You can make enquiries by phone, or use their 24-hour information recording.

For baseball fans, no trip to the Bay Area would be complete without catching a game at AT&T Park.

26

AT&T Park

Q5 24 Willie Mays Plaza 10, 30, 45, 47, 81, 82, 83 E, N, T mlb.com/giants/ballpark

AT&T Park is the home of the World Series-winning San Francisco Giants. For baseball fans, no trip to the Bay Area would be complete without catching a game here. The stadium is located right on the water in the southwest quadrant of the city; spectators at afternoon games are treated to spectacular views and plenty of sunshine. Like everything in San Francisco, the food options are top-notch for stadium cuisine, with many local chefs collaborating on independent food stands.

Outside of baseball season, visitors can come to enjoy other events at the park, from Cirque du Soleil productions to food festivals.

A SHORT WALK
FINANCIAL DISTRICT

Distance 0.5 mile (0.6 km) **Time** 15 minutes
Nearest bus 1, 8AX, 8BX, 10, 12, 41

San Francisco's economic engine is fueled largely by the Financial District, one of the chief commercial centers in the US. It reaches from the imposing modern towers and plazas of the Embarcadero Center to staid Montgomery Street, sometimes known as the "Wall Street of the West." All the principal banks, brokers, exchanges, and law offices are situated within this compact area. The Jackson Square Historical District, north of Washington Street, was once the heart of the business community.

Embarcadero Center (p144) *houses both commercial outlets and offices. A shopping arcade occupies the first three tiers of the towers.*

Jackson Square Historical District (p144) *recalls the Gold Rush era more than any other.*

Hotaling Place, *a narrow alley leading to the Jackson Square Historical District, has several good antiques shops.*

The Golden Era Building, *built during the Gold Rush, was the home of the paper Golden Era for which Mark Twain wrote.*

Once the tallest skyscraper in the city, the **Transamerica Pyramid** (p145) *has now been eclipsed by the Salesforce Tower.*

The Wells Fargo History Museum (p144) *has displays on transportation and banking. An original stagecoach, evoking the wilder days of the old West, is one of the many exhibits.*

The grand banking hall in the **Bank of California** *is guarded by fierce stone lions carved by sculptor Arthur Putnam.*

The former world headquarters of Bank of America at **555 California** *was the city's tallest skyscraper until 1972.*

Epic paintings line the walls of **Merchant's Exchange** (p147).

START

WASHINGTON STREET

BATTERY STREET

CLAY STREET

SANSOME STREET

MONTGOMERY STREET

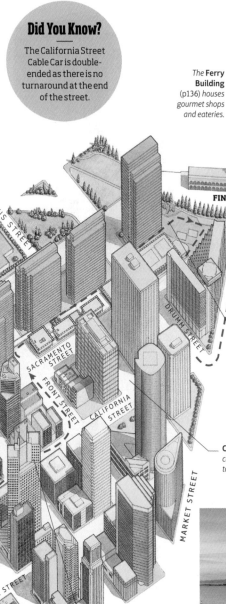

Did You Know?

The California Street Cable Car is double-ended as there is no turnaround at the end of the street.

The **Ferry Building** (p136) *houses gourmet shops and eateries.*

Locator Map
For more detail see p134

DOWNTOWN AND SOMA

FINISH

The Gandhi Monument *(1988) was designed by K.B. Patel and sculpted by Z. Pounov and S. Lowe. It bears an inscription of Gandhi's words.*

Embarcadero Plaza (p146) *is filled with lunchtime crowds on sunny days.*

| 0 meters | 100 | N |
| 0 yards | 100 | |

California Street, *busy with clanging cable cars, sweeps to the top of Nob Hill.*

First Interstate Center, *home of the Mandarin Oriental Hotel*

The **Pacific Coast Stock Exchange** (p147) *was once the focal point of the city's trade.*

↑ The iconic Ferry Building at sunset, a San Francisco landmark

A LONG WALK
AROUND SOMA

Distance 2.25 miles (3.5 km) **Time** 45 minutes **Terrain** Flat streets, busy with pedestrians and traffic **Nearest BART station** Powell Street

Once a grubby warehouse district, SOMA (a contraction of "South of Market") is a model of urban revitalization. This was once the "wrong side" of the Market Street cable-car tracks when Gold Rush-era immigrants worked in the factories here in the 19th century. Today, a four-block square area surrounding the Moscone Convention Center (*p143*) is packed with major art galleries and history museums, high-rise hotels, and shops, and on this walk you will encounter vestiges of the city's lively past among its dazzling 21st-century architecture.

↑ San Francisco's impressive Old Mint, completed in 1874

Turn left on Howard Street, then take a right on 5th Street. At the corner of Mission Street, you will see the magnificent facade of the "Granite Lady," the Greek Revival-style **Old Mint**, *erected in 1869–74 to make coins from California gold and Nevada silver. Its last coins were produced in 1937.*

← Daniel Libeskind's extension to the Contemporary Jewish Museum, unveiled in 2005

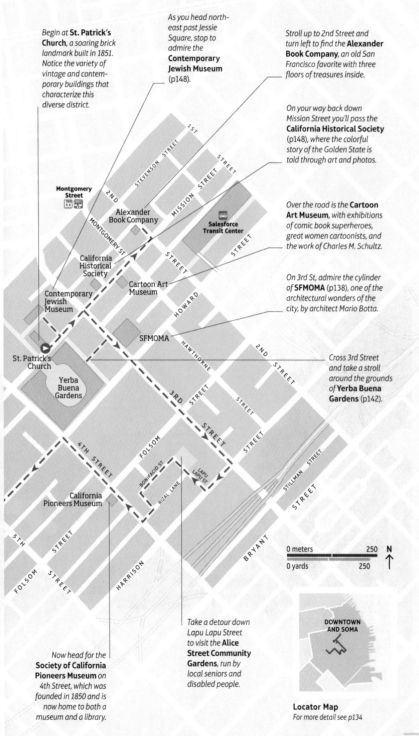

Begin at **St. Patrick's Church**, a soaring brick landmark built in 1851. Notice the variety of vintage and contemporary buildings that characterize this diverse district.

As you head northeast past Jessie Square, stop to admire the **Contemporary Jewish Museum** (p148).

Stroll up to 2nd Street and turn left to find the **Alexander Book Company**, an old San Francisco favorite with three floors of treasures inside.

On your way back down Mission Street you'll pass the **California Historical Society** (p148), where the colorful story of the Golden State is told through art and photos.

Over the road is the **Cartoon Art Museum**, with exhibitions of comic book superheroes, great women cartoonists, and the work of Charles M. Schultz.

On 3rd St, admire the cylinder of **SFMOMA** (p138), one of the architectural wonders of the city, by architect Mario Botta.

Cross 3rd Street and take a stroll around the grounds of **Yerba Buena Gardens** (p142).

Take a detour down Lapu Lapu Street to visit the **Alice Street Community Gardens**, run by local seniors and disabled people.

Now head for the **Society of California Pioneers Museum** on 4th Street, which was founded in 1850 and is now home to both a museum and a library.

Montgomery Street

1ST STREET
STEVENSON STREET
2ND
MISSION STREET
MONTGOMERY ST
Alexander Book Company
Salesforce Transit Center
STREET
California Historical Society
Cartoon Art Museum
HOWARD STREET
Contemporary Jewish Museum
SFMOMA
HAWTHORNE STREET
2ND STREET
St. Patrick's Church
Yerba Buena Gardens
3RD STREET
FOLSOM STREET
STREET
STILLMAN STREET
4TH STREET
BONIFACIO ST
RIZAL LANE
LAPU LAPU ST
California Pioneers Museum
5TH STREET
FOLSOM STREET
HARRISON
BRYANT STREET

0 meters 250
0 yards 250
N ↑

DOWNTOWN AND SOMA

Locator Map
For more detail see p134

CIVIC CENTER AND HAYES VALLEY

The administrative center of San Francisco has as its focal point the Civic Center Plaza, which features some of the best architecture in the city. Its grand government buildings and palatial performing arts complex are the source of great local pride. The former City Hall was destroyed in the earthquake of 1906, creating an opportunity to build a civic center more in keeping with San Francisco's fast-emerging role as a major port.

Adjoining this historic government district, Hayes Valley has a much more humble history, originally being used as farmland during the mid-19th century. The area was long considered a dangerous neighborhood, but with gentrification Hayes Valley has become an upscale district full of charming houses, boutiques, and restaurants.

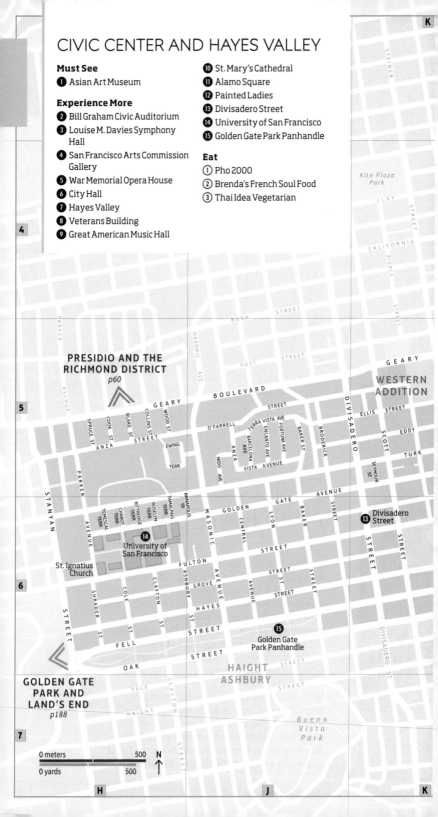

CIVIC CENTER AND HAYES VALLEY

Must See
1 Asian Art Museum

Experience More
2 Bill Graham Civic Auditorium
3 Louise M. Davies Symphony Hall
4 San Francisco Arts Commission Gallery
5 War Memorial Opera House
6 City Hall
7 Hayes Valley
8 Veterans Building
9 Great American Music Hall
10 St. Mary's Cathedral
11 Alamo Square
12 Painted Ladies
13 Divisadero Street
14 University of San Francisco
15 Golden Gate Park Panhandle

Eat
1 Pho 2000
2 Brenda's French Soul Food
3 Thai Idea Vegetarian

❶ ⊘ ⊛ ⊡ ⊞

ASIAN ART MUSEUM

📍F5 🏛200 Larkin St 🚌5, 7X, 9, 19, 21, 31, 47, 49 🚋F, J, K, L, M, N, T
🚇Bart Civic Center 🕐10am-5pm Tue-Sun 🌐asianart.org

Heading up the grand staircase of the Asian Art Museum is like setting out on a historical and cultural tour of the world's largest continent. The 2,000 works on display celebrate both tradition and history as well as the contemporary cultures of many Asian nations.

The Asian Art Museum is located on Civic Center Plaza in a building that was the crown jewel of the Beaux Arts movement in San Francisco. The former Main Library, built in 1917, underwent major renovation in 2001 to create the largest museum outside Asia devoted exclusively to Asian art. The museum's holdings include more than 18,000 art objects spanning 6,000 years of history and representing cultures and countries throughout Asia. There are also venues for performances and festivals, a library, a hands-on discovery center, and classrooms. Work is underway on a new special exhibitions pavillion and art terrace, due to open in early 2020, so some of the third floor may be closed in spring 2019.

↑ Facade of the Asian Art Museum, a Beaux Arts building dating back to 1917

GALLERY GUIDE

Temporary exhibits are housed on the first floor. The second floor is dedicated to Japanese, Korean, and Chinese art from 960 CE to the present day. The third floor covers countries and cultures from the Philippines in the southeast to Turkey in the west.

↑ Children painting copies of artworks from the museum's collection

Highlights

1000 BC
The museum's pair of sculptures of Shiva and Parvati are from the inner sanctuary of a Hindu temple in Cambodia.

c 1500
◀ This complex Buddha sculpture from China's Ming Dynasty is made of many small pieces that were fitted together before firing.

1870
▲ This watercolour portrait of Maharaja Mahinder Singh of Patiala was copied from a photograph, which was a common practice.

2014
▲ Covered in motifs from Taiwnese culture and folklore, Hung Yi's *Dragon Fortune* is a photogenic sculpture outside the museum.

A visitor admiring some
of the museum's more
modern artworks ↑

EXPERIENCE MORE

EAT

Pho 2000
Tucked unassumingly in the area known as "Little Saigon," this Vietnamese eatery is a favorite with locals.

📍M5 🏠637 Larkin St
🕐Tue 🌐pho2000sf.com

$ $ $

Brenda's French Soul Food
New Orleans classics made with regionally sourced ingredients.

📍M5 🏠653 Polk St
🌐frenchsoulfood.com

$ $ $

Thai Idea Vegetarian
A bright and breezy café with a meat-free menu of Thai specialities. Vegan options are also on offer.

📍M5 🏠710 Polk St
🌐thaiideaveggiesf.com

$ $ $

② Bill Graham Civic Auditorium

📍M6 🏠99 Grove St 🚌5, 7X, 9, 19, 21, 31, 47, 49 🚋J, K, L, M, N, T 🚇Civic Center
🌐billgrahamcivic auditorium.com

This venue was designed in Beaux Arts style *(p36)* by architect John Galen Howard to form a major part of the Panama-Pacific International Exposition. Orignally named the San Francisco Civic Auditorium, the venue opened in 1915 and was inaugurated by the French composer and pianist Camille Saint-Saëns. The building was completed along with City Hall, in the course of the massive architectural renaissance that followed the natural disasters of 1906. It was built, together with the adjoining Brooks Exhibit Hall, beneath the Civic Center Plaza.

The Civic Auditorium now serves as the city's main conference center, and has the capacity to seat 7,000 people. In 1992 its name was changed in honor of Bill Graham, the local rock music impresario who was a pivotal figure in both the development and promotion of the city's trademark psychedelic sound.

---

③

Louise M. Davies Symphony Hall

📍M6 🏠201 Van Ness Ave 🚌7X, 19, 21, 47, 49 🚋J, K, L, M, N, T 🚇Civic Center
🌐sfsymphony.org

Loved and loathed in equal measure by the citizens of San Francisco, this curving, glass-fronted concert hall was constructed in 1980 – the creation of architects Skidmore, Owings & Merrill. The ultra-modern hall is named for the prominent philanthropist who donated $5 million of the $35 million construction cost. It is home to the San Francisco Symphony Orchestra and

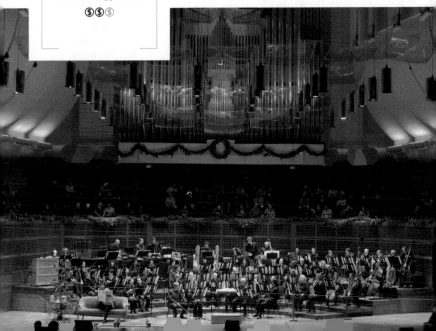

also welcomes many visiting orchestras and artists.

The acoustics of the building were disappointing when it first opened, but measures were taken to improve them. After many years of negotiations a new sound system was installed. The interior was also redesigned, and the walls were resculptured to better reflect sound.

4

San Francisco Arts Commission Gallery

M5 401 Van Ness Ave
5, 7X, 19, 21, 47, 49 J, K, L, M, N, T 11am–6pm Tue–Sat sfartscommission.org/gallery

Located in the Veterans Building (p167), this dynamic gallery shows paintings, sculptures, and multimedia works made by local artists. Their website also lists public artworks that can be found throughout the city, including some photography exhibitions at City Hall.

←

An orchestral performance at the Louise M. Davies Symphony Hall

5

War Memorial Opera House

M5 301 Van Ness Ave
5, 7X, 9, 19, 21, 47, 49 J, K, L, M, N, T Civic Center sfwmpac.org

Opened in 1932, the War Memorial Opera House, designed by Arthur Brown, was dedicated to the memory of World War I soldiers. It was

↑ The War Memorial Opera House, with its impressive colonnaded facade

a key venue during the 1945 conference which led to the creation of the United Nations Charter, and in 1951 it was used for the signing of the peace treaty between the US and Japan. It is now home to the San Francisco Opera and San Francisco Ballet.

THE SOUNDS OF 1960S SAN FRANCISCO

During the Flower Power years of the late 1960s, and most notably during the 1967 Summer of Love, young people from all over the US flocked to San Francisco. They came not just to "turn on, tune in, and drop out," but also to listen to music. Janis Joplin, Jimi Hendrix, and the Grateful Dead all emerged out of a seminal music scene. The Avalon Ballroom, now the Regency II theater on Van Ness Avenue, was the first and most significant rock venue, pioneering the use of colorful psychedelic posters.

6

City Hall

M5 **400 Van Ness Ave** **5, 7X, 9, 19, 21, 47, 49** **J, K, L, M, N, T** **8am–8pm Mon–Fri** **sfciviccenter.org/visit**

City Hall, completed in 1915, just in time for the start of the Panama-Pacific International Exposition, was designed by Arthur Brown when he was at the height of his career. The original building was completely destroyed in the 1906 earthquake. Its grand Baroque golden dome was modeled on St. Peter's Church in Rome and is higher than the US Capitol in Washington, DC. The upper levels of the dome are open to the public.

The restored building is at the heart of the Civic Center complex and is a magnificent example of the Beaux Arts style *(p36)*. Allegorical figures evoking the city's Gold Rush past can be seen in the pediment above the main Polk Street entrance, which leads into the marble-floored Rotunda. Guided tours of City Hall are available on weekdays; see the website for details on booking.

7

Hayes Valley

L6 **6, 7, 21, 22**

Just west of City Hall, Hayes Valley became one of San Francisco's trendier leisure districts after US 101 highway was badly damaged in the Loma Prieta earthquake of 1989. The road was then torn down, having previously cut Hayes Valley off from the wealthy power brokers and theater-goers of the Civic Center. A few of the local cafés and restaurants, such as Hayes Street Grill, had already begun to mix in with the Hayes Street secondhand furniture and thrift shops. This was followed by an influx of expensive art galleries, interior design shops, top-notch restaurants, trendy nightspots, craft coffee roasters, and clothing boutiques – all of which has transformed the area into one of San Francisco's coolest neighborhoods.

Brandon Flowers performing with The Killers at the Great American Music Hall

8 Veterans Building

📍 M5 🏛 401 Van Ness Ave
🚌 5, 7X, 9, 19, 21, 47, 49 🚊 J, K, L, M, N, T 🌐 sfwmpac.org

Like its almost identical twin – the War Memorial Opera House *(p165)* – this building was designed by Arthur Brown and built in 1932 to honor World War I soldiers. It was rededicated in 2015 after the opening of a 3,000 sq ft (280 sq m) art gallery. In addition to displays of historic weapons, there are showcases of military memorabilia. The building is also home to the Herbst Theater, a 928-seat classical music concert hall. The theater was the site of the signing of the United Nations Charter during the San Francisco Conference of 1945.

9 Great American Music Hall

📍 M5 🏛 859 O'Farrell St
📞 885-0750 🚌 19, 31, 38, 47, 49

Built in 1907 as a place for bawdy comedy shows, the Great American Music Hall is now an excellent performance space, with a rich interior containing tall marble columns and elaborate balconies, adorned with ornate gilt plasterwork. The venue is intimate and stylish, and the views are good from almost every table. Famous artists such as Carmen McCrae, B. B. King, Duke Ellington, Van Morrison, and Tom Paxton have played every kind of music here, from blues to rock 'n' roll.

---

10 St. Mary's Cathedral

📍 L5 🏛 1111 Gough St 🚌 2, 3, 31, 38 🕐 7am–5pm Mon– Fri & Sun, 8am–5pm Sat 🌐 stmarycathedralsf.org

Situated at the top of Cathedral Hill, the ultra-modern St. Mary's is the city's principal Roman Catholic church and one of its most prominent landmarks. Designed by architect Pietro Belluschi and engineer Pier Luigi Nervi, the church was completed in 1971. The four-part arching paraboloid roof stands out like a white-sailed ship on the horizon. The 200-ft- (60-m-) high concrete structure, which supports a cross-shaped stained-glass ceiling, seems to hover effortlessly over the nave. A sunburst canopy made of aluminum rods sparkles above the plain stone altar.

←

San Francisco's City Hall, built in Beaux Arts style and topped with a splendid dome

Did You Know?

"Painted Ladies" refers to any Victorian and Edwardian houses repainted in three or more colors.

Alamo Square

Q K6 🚌 5, 21, 22, 24

San Francisco's most photographed row of colorful Victorian houses, the so-called "Seven Sisters" or "Painted Ladies," lines the eastern side of this sloping green square, which is located some 225 ft (68 m) above the Civic Center, giving grand views of City Hall backed by the Financial District skyscrapers. Alamo Square was laid out at the same time as the pair of Pacific Heights squares, but it was developed later and much more quickly, with speculators building large numbers of very nearly identical houses.

So many grand old Victorian houses line the streets around Alamo Square that the area has been declared a historic district.

Painted Ladies

Q K6 **🏠** 710–720 Steiner St & Hayes St 🚌 5, 21, 22, 24

These grand Victorian homes from the Queen Anne era, set against the backdrop of the downtown city skyscrapers, are a wonderful visual treat, and one of the most photogenic spots in the city. Also called "Postcard Row" and mistakenly known as the "Full House house" *(p57)*, the seven Painted Ladies are found on the east side of grassy Alamo Square.

Designed by Matthew Kavanaugh, with the last house completed in 1896, the houses are still private residences and tourists should be mindful not to trespass when coming by to admire the architecture and snap that perfect photo.

Divisadero Street

Q K6 🚌 5, 21, 24, 31

A San Francisco hotspot that delights locals and visitors alike, Divisadero Street has seen tremendous change in recent decades. Once a rather dull, middle-class street lined with cheap stores, Divisadero is now chock-full of hip lunch spots, restaurants, independent boutiques, bakeries, and more. The street has a fresh, creative vibe, with plenty of art and music, a weekly farmers' market and lots of community events.

The strip is the perfect place to spend the better part of a day. Start with brunch and window-shop your way down the street, enjoying the unique shops and people-watching. Or stop at Bi-Rite, the famous upscale grocer, to grab homemade ice cream or picnic lunch and head a couple blocks over to Alamo Square to take in the jaw-dropping views.

> Divisadero is now chock-full of hip lunch spots, restaurants, independent boutiques, bakeries, and more.

The leafy campus of the University of San Francisco, on the site of a former cemetery

University of San Francisco

**⌖ H6 ⌂ 2130 Fulton St
🚌 5, 21, 33, 43 🌐 usfca.edu**

Established back in 1855 as St. Ignatius College, the University of San Francisco (USF) is still a Jesuit-run institution, though classes are now coeducational and non-denominational. The landmark of the campus is the striking St. Ignatius Church, which serves as the chapel for the university and as a parish church. It was completed in 1914 and built in exuberant Italian Baroque style, with liberal use of columns and pilasters. Its buff-colored twin towers are visible from all over the western half of San Francisco, especially when lit up at night. The church is regularly used for student graduation and convocation ceremonies. The university campus and residential neighborhood that surrounds it occupy land that historically formed San Francisco's main cemetery district, on and around Lone Mountain.

Golden Gate Park Panhandle

⌖ J6 🚌 5, 6, 7, 7X, 21, 24, 33, 43 🚃 N

This stretch of parkland, one block wide and eight blocks long, forms the narrow "Panhandle" to the giant rectangular pan that is Golden Gate Park (p144). It was the first part of the park to be reclaimed from the sand dunes that rolled across west San Francisco, and its stately eucalyptus trees are among the oldest and largest in the city. The Panhandle's winding carriage roads and bridle paths were first laid out in the 1870s, and the upper classes came here to walk and ride. They built large mansions on the outskirts of the park; many can still be seen today. In 1906 the Panhandle was a refuge for families made homeless by the earthquake. Today the old roads and paths are used regularly by joggers and cyclists.

The Panhandle is still remembered for its "Flower Power" heyday of the 1960s (p165), when bands gave impromptu concerts here.

The eye-catching "Painted Ladies" Victorian houses, facing onto Alamo Square

VICTORIAN HOUSES IN SAN FRANCISCO

Despite earthquakes, fires, and the inroads of modern life, thousands of ornate, late 19th-century houses still line the streets of San Francisco. In fact, in many neighborhoods they are by far the most common type of housing. Victorian houses are broadly similar, in that they all have wooden frames, elaborately decorated with mass-produced ornament. Most were constructed on narrow plots to a similar floor plan, but they differ in the features of the facade. Four main styles prevail in the city, although in practice many houses, especially those built in the 1880s and 1890s, combine aspects of two or more styles.

Balustrades on the porch betray the origins of the style in the Deep South.

Wide porches can be reached by a central staircase.

Tall cornices, often with decorative brackets, conceal a pitched roof.

A gabled roof with decorated vergeboards is the clearest mark of Gothic Revival.

The pitched roof over the main facade often runs lengthwise, allowing the use of dormer windows.

Timeline

Gothic Revival (1850–80)

These houses are the easiest to identify, since they always have pointed arches over the windows, and sometimes over the doors. Other features are pitched gabled roofs, decorated vergeboards, and porches that run the width of the building. The smaller, simpler houses of this type are usually painted white, rather than the vibrant colors often associated with later styles.

Italianate (1850–85)

The Italianate style was more popular here than elsewhere in the US, perhaps because the compact form was suited to San Francisco's high building density. The most distinctive feature of the Italianate style is the tall cornice, usually with a decorative bracket, which adds a palatial air to even modest homes. Elaborate decoration around doors and windows is another typical feature.

↑ Neo-Classical doorways on an Italianate house

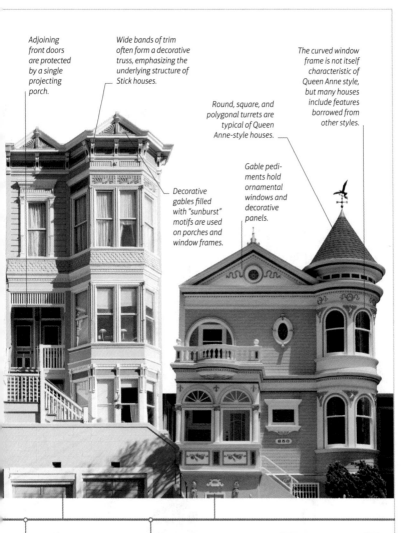

Adjoining front doors are protected by a single projecting porch.

Wide bands of trim often form a decorative truss, emphasizing the underlying structure of Stick houses.

Round, square, and polygonal turrets are typical of Queen Anne-style houses.

The curved window frame is not itself characteristic of Queen Anne style, but many houses include features borrowed from other styles.

Decorative gables filled with "sunburst" motifs are used on porches and window frames.

Gable pediments hold ornamental windows and decorative panels.

Stick
(1860–90)

This style is perhaps the most prevalent among Victorian houses in the city. Sometimes also called "Stick-Eastlake" after London furniture designer Charles Eastlake, the style was intended to be architecturally "honest." Vertical lines are emphasized, both in the wood-frame structure and in ornamentation. Bay windows, false gabled cornices and square corners are key identifiers.

Queen Anne
(1875–1905)

The name "Queen Anne" does not refer to a historical period; it was coined by the English architect Richard Shaw. Queen Anne houses freely combine elements from many decorative traditions, but are marked by their turrets and towers and large, often decorative, panels on wall surfaces. Most houses also display intricate spindle-work on balustrades, porches, and roof trusses.

WHERE TO FIND THEM

Haas-Lilienthal House *(p83)*

Octagon House *(p83)*

Pacific Heights *(p86)*

Painted Ladies *(p168)*

(Richard) Spreckels Mansion *(p180)*

Clarke's Folly *(p182)*

HAIGHT ASHBURY AND THE MISSION

To the north of Twin Peaks – two windswept hills rising 900 ft (274 m) above the city – lies Haight Ashbury. With its rows of beautiful late Victorian houses, it is mostly inhabited by the wealthy middle classes, although this is where thousands of hippies lived in the 1960s. The Castro District, to the east, is the center of San Francisco's gay community. Well-known for its wild hedonism in the 1970s, the area is quieter these days, although its cafés and shops are still lively.

The Mission District, farther east still, was originally settled by Spanish monks and is home to many Hispanics.

HAIGHT ASHBURY AND THE MISSION

Must Sees

1. Castro Street
2. Haight Ashbury

Experience More

3. (Richard) Spreckels Mansion
4. Buena Vista Park
5. Lower Haight Neighborhood
6. Randall Museum
7. Vulcan Street Steps
8. GLBT History Museum
9. Clarke's Folly
10. Dolores Street
11. Mision Dolores
12. Dolores Park
13. Sutro Tower
14. Twin Peaks
15. Mission Cultural Center for Latino Arts
16. Noe Valley
17. Carnaval Mural

Eat

1. Loló

Shop

2. Loved to Death
3. Paxton Gate
4. Cole Valley Antiques
5. 826 Valencia Pirate Supply Store

1 🍴 🖥 🛍

CASTRO STREET

📍 D2 🚌 24, 33, 35, 37 🚋 F, K, L, M, T

The hilly neighborhood around Castro Street between Twin Peaks and the Mission District is the heart of San Francisco's high-profile LGBT+ community. It's a lively district of entertainment venues and nightlife with a side of beautiful architecture and proud history.

Focused on the intersection of Castro Street and 18th Street, the self-proclaimed "Gayest Four Corners of the World" emerged as an LGBT+ nexus during the 1970s. Gay people of the Flower Power generation moved into this predominantly working-class district and began restoring Victorian houses and setting up businesses. They also opened gay bars including Mary Ellen Cunha and Peggy Forster's Twin Peaks Tavern (*www. twinpeakstavern.com*) on the corner of Castro Street and 17th Street. Unlike earlier bars, where gay people had to hide in dark corners out of public view, the Twin Peaks Tavern had large windows that made it the first gay bar where passersby could see inside. Though the many shops and restaurants attract all kinds of people, the Castro's openly queer identity has made it a place of pilgrimage for people in the LGBT+ community. It symbolizes for this minority group a freedom not generally found in cities elsewhere.

> **The Castro's openly queer identity has made it a place of pilgrimage for LGBT+ people.**

A rainbow-colored street crossing and the famous Twin Peaks Tavern (*inset*) ↑

THE CASTRO THEATER

Completed in 1922, this brightly lit neon marquee is a Castro Street landmark. It is the most sumptuous and best preserved of San Francisco's neighborhood film palaces, with a lavish interior inspired by *Arabian Nights* and a glorious Wurlitzer organ that rises from the floor between screenings. The venue hosts the San Francisco International LGBT Film Festival, held each June.

Rainbow Honor Walk

Bronze plaques on the Castro Street sidewalk commemorate important figures in the international LGBT+ community. Whilst the honorees come from various backgrounds, they all shared in the battle for equality and are held up as inspirational figures in this walk of fame. Names range from famous artists like Freddie Mercury to local heroes like Major League Baseball's Glenn Burke, who is credited with inventing the high five.

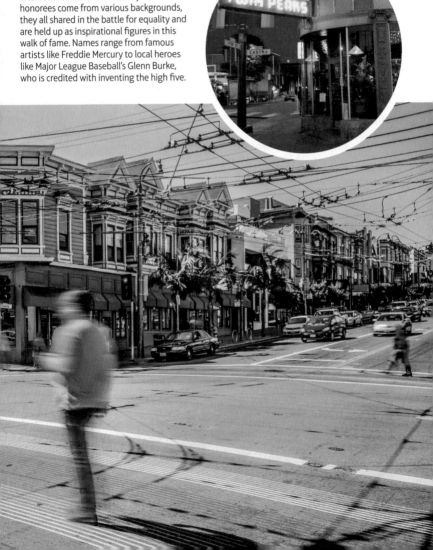

2 🍽 ☕ 🛍

HAIGHT ASHBURY

📍C1 🚌5, 6, 7, 24, 31, 33, 37, 43 🚃N

The birthplace of hippy counterculture in the 1960, the Haight retains its anti-establishment atmosphere, and an aura of the past can still be found in its congenial cafés and vintage clothing shops.

Taking its name from the junction of two main streets – named after the San Francisco pioneers Henry Haight and Munroe Ashbury – this district contains independent bookstores, large Victorian houses, cafés, and hip clothing boutiques. The neighborhood's origins date back to the 1890s, when the area was rapidly built up following the reclamation of Golden Gate Park (p199) and the opening of a large amusement park called The Chutes. The district became a middle-class suburb – hence the dozens of elaborate Queen Anne-style houses (p170) lining its streets.

The Hippie Haight

After the streetcar tunnel under Buena Vista Park was completed in 1928, the middle classes began their exodus to the suburbs in the Sunset. After World War II the area reached its lowest ebb, and the big Victorian houses were divided into apartments offering low rents. While North Beach became the place for the beatniks in the 1950s, many creatives and free-thinkers began to venture to Haight Ashbury, as it was the cheaper place to live. By the 1960s the Haight had become host to a bohemian community that was a hotbed of

> **While North Beach became the place for the beatniks in the 1950s, many creatives and free-thinkers began to venture to Haight Ashbury, as it was the cheaper place to live.**

← Street-side seating at Cafe Cole in the Haight

← Italianate-style Victorian houses in Haight Ashbury

anarchy. A component of this "hippie scene" was rock music, but the area stayed low-key until 1967. Then the media-fueled "Summer of Love" brought some 75,000 young people in search of free love, music, and drugs, and the area became the focus of a worldwide youth culture.

← Vintage second-hand clothing at the Decades of Fashion store

FAMOUS FACES OF HAIGHT ASHBURY

Famous residents of Haight Ashbury include American singer Janis Joplin, who moved to her second-floor apartment at 635 Ashbury Street with her lover Peggy Caserta in 1967. Band members of The Grateful Dead lived at 710 Ashbury Street from 1965–68 but left after the scene became too intense. Graham Nash, the singer-songwriter, also lived in "The Haight" in the 60s and 70s, in a house opposite Buena Vista Park.

EXPERIENCE MORE

3

(Richard) Spreckels Mansion

Q J7 **A** 737 Buena Vista West **⊞** 6, 7, 24, 33, 37, 43 **⟳** To the public

This house should not be confused with the larger and grander Spreckels Mansion on Washington Street (p80). It was, however, also built by the millionaire "Sugar King" Claus Spreckels, for his nephew Richard. The elaborate Queen Anne-style house (p36), built in 1897, is a typical late-Victorian Haight Ashbury home. It was once a recording studio, and later a guesthouse, but is now in private hands. Guests have included the acerbic journalist and ghost-story writer Ambrose Bierce, and Jack London, who wrote *White Fang* here in 1906.

The mansion is situated on a hill near Buena Vista Park. Rows of Victorian houses, many of them well preserved and some palatial, are nearby. One of these, a block away at 1450 Masonic Street, is an onion-domed house, one of

Did You Know?

Claus Spreckels immigrated from Germany to the US in 1846 with just one coin in his pocket.

the most unusual of the many eccentric mansions built in the Haight since the 1890s.

4

Buena Vista Park

Q J7 **⊞** 6, 7, 24, 33, 37, 43

Buena Vista Park rises steeply, 569 ft (18 m) above the geographical center of San Francisco. First landscaped in 1894, it is a pocket of land left to nature. A network of paths winds up from Haight Street to the crest, where densely planted trees frame views of the Bay Area. Many of the trails are overgrown and eroded, but there is a paved route up to the summit from Buena Vista Avenue. It is best to avoid the park at night.

5

Lower Haight Neighborhood

Q K6 **⊞** 6, 7, 22 **⊞** K, L, M, N, T

Halfway between City Hall and Haight Ashbury, and marking the southern border of the Fillmore District, the Lower Haight neighborhood is an area in transition. New markers of gentrification line the streets, such as hip art galleries, salons, eclectic boutiques, and shops, including Rooky Ricardo's

> **Guests have included the acerbic journalist and ghost-story writer Ambrose Bierce, and Jack London, who wrote *White Fang* here in 1906.**

→ Splendid views of the city from Corona Heights, home of the Randall Museum

Sunlight filtering through trees in Buena Vista Park

this unusual museum for children. The Randall Museum, a museum of natural history, science, and the arts, has a menagerie of over 100 animals, including a raccoon, owls, snakes, tortoises, and various sea creatures. There are exhibitions on the Native American tradition of basket-making, as well as earth-quakes and ocean life. The emphasis of the museum is on participation. It also offers hands-on experiences with woodworking, ceramics, creative play, theater, model railroads, and much more.

Corona Heights was gouged out by brick-making oper-ations in the 19th century. It was never planted with trees, so its bare red-rock peak offers a panoramic view over the city and East Bay, inclu-ding the winding streets of Twin Peaks.

Records – which sells rare and unusual records. These sit alongside inexpensive cafés, bars, and restaurants serving a bohemian clientele that were already in business in the area. The combination has created one of the most lively districts in San Francisco.

As in nearby Alamo Square (*p168*), the Lower Haight neighbrhood is full of dozens of beautiful, old houses built from the 1850s to the early 1900s, in the beautiful and elaborate styles that are so famous in San Francisco (*p36*).

Highlights of the area's architecture include the Nightingale House at 201 Buchanan Street, which was built in the 1880s.

6
Randall Museum

Q K7 **A** 199 Museum Way
🚌 24, 37 **🕙** 10am-5pm Tue-Sat **W** randallmuseum.org

Clinging to the side of Corona Heights Park, a dusty and undeveloped rocky peak, is

---

7

Vulcan Street Steps

Q J8 **A** Vulcan St **🚌** 37

Apart from a tiny figure of Spock standing on the mailbox of one of the houses, there is no connection between the popular *Star Trek* series and this block of almost rural houses climbing up steeply between Ord Street and Levant Street.

Like the Filbert Steps on Telegraph Hill (*p107*), however, Vulcan Streets Steps does feel light years away from the busy streets of the Castro District below. The small vegetable and flower gardens of the houses spill out and soften the edges of the steps, and a canopy of pines muffles the city sounds. There are grand views of the Mission District and beyond for those who take on the climb.

Did You Know?

The GLBT Historical Society hosts regular events including readings, discussions, and screenings.

8
GLBT History Museum

9 K8 **4** 4127 18th St **24, 33, 35, 37** F, K, L, M, S, T **11am-6pm Wed-Mon, noon-5pm Sun** Tue in fall and winter months glbthistory.org

This is the first full-scale, stand-alone museum devoted to the evolution of the liberation of the gay, lesbian, bisexual, and transgender community in the United States. Though fairly small, the museum packs a punch, celebrating the city's vast queer past through dynamic

and surprising exhibitions and programming. Discover treasures from the archives of the GLBT Historical Society that reflect the fascinating stories of this vibrant community.

9
Clarke's Folly

9 K8 **4** 250 Douglass St **33, 35, 37** To the public

This resplendent white manor house was surrounded by extensive grounds originally. It was built in 1892 by Alfred Clarke, known as Nobby, who worked in the San Francisco Police Department at the time of the Committee of Vigilance. The house is said to have cost $100,000, a huge sum in the 1890s. It was used as a hospital for a while. It is now divided into private apartments, and its turrets and other features make it a wonderfully evocative example of Victorian-era domestic architecture.

EAT

Loló
A family-owned spot with stylish decor and a menu that's equally bold. This is Mexico via the Mission District, with an array of tasty small plates.

L/M8 **4** 974 Valencia St lolosf.com

$$$

10
Dolores Street

9 E2 **22, 33, 48** J

Lined by lovingly maintained late Victorian houses *(p36)* and divided by an island of palm trees, Dolores Street is one of the city's most attractive public spaces. The boulevard forms the western border of the Mission District. It starts at Market Street, where a statue in honor of Spanish-American War soldiers is overwhelmed by the hulking US Mint.

The Mission High School, with the characteristic white walls and red-tile roof of Mission-style architecture, is on Dolores Street, as is the historic Mission Dolores.

11
Mission Dolores

9 L7 **4** 16th St and Dolores St **22** J **9am-4pm daily** missiondolores.org

Preserved intact since it was completed in 1791, Mission Dolores is the oldest building in the city and constitutes

← The fascinating GLBT History Museum, the first of its kind in the US

 Dolores Park, popular with sunbathers, tennis players and dog walkers by day

the embodiment of San Francisco's religious Spanish colonial roots. The mission was founded by a Franciscan friar, Father Junipero Serra, and formally known as the Mission of San Francisco de Asís. The name Dolores reflects its proximity to Laguna de los Dolores (Lake of Our Lady of Sorrows). The adobe building's 4-ft- (1.2-m-) thick walls have survived without serious decay. Paintings by American Indians adorn the ceiling.

There is a fine Baroque altar and reredos, as well as a display of historical artifacts in the small museum. Most services are held in the basilica, which was built next to the original mission in 1918. The white-walled cemetery contains graves of prominent San Franciscans from the Gold Rush days. A statue honoring the graves of 5,000 Indians,

most of whom died in the great measles epidemics of 1806 and 1826, was stolen and then returned in 1993. It stands on a pedestal reading, "In Prayerful Memory of our Faithful Indians."

___

12

Dolores Park

◉ L8 ⬛ 22, 33 🚋 J

Originally the site of the city's main Jewish cemetery, Dolores Park was transformed in 1905

into one of the Mission District's few large open spaces. Bounded by Dolores, Church, 18th, and 20th streets, it is situated high on a hill with a good view of the city center.

Dolores Park is popular during the day with visitors, and dog walkers, but after dark can draw drug dealers. Above the park to the south and west, the streets rise so steeply that many turn into pedestrian-only stairways. Here are some of the city's finest Victorian houses, especially on Liberty Street.

> **The adobe building's 4-ft- (1.2-m-) thick walls have survived without serious decay. Paintings by American Indians adorn the ceiling.**

LEVI STRAUSS & CO.

In 1853 Levi Strauss left New York to set up a branch of his family's cloth firm in San Francisco. In the 1860s he pioneered the use of durable blue canvas to make workpants for miners. In the 1870s his company began to use metal rivets to increase the strength of stress points in the garments, and demand increased. Levi's blue denim jeans are now produced and worn all over the world, and the company is still owned by Levi Strauss's descendants.

SHOP

The quirky characters of both Haight Ahbury and the Mission extend to the locally owned stores scattered along their streets. Prepare for maze-like shops filled with vintage antiques, new age curios, eccentric home design ideas, and even a few pirate treasures.

Loved to Death
📍H7 🏠1685 Haight St
🕐Tue 🅦lovedto
death.com

Paxton Gate
📍L8 🏠824 Valencia St
🅦paxtongate.com

Cole Valley Antiques
📍H7 🏠854 Stanyan St
🅦colevalley
antiques.com

826 Valencia Pirate Supply Store
📍L8 🏠826 Valencia St
🅦shop.826
valencia.org

Sutro Tower

📍G8 🚌36, 37 🕐To the public

Marking the skyline like an invading robot, Sutro Tower is 970 ft (290 m) high. It was named after local landowner and philanthropist Adolph Sutro, and it carries antennae for the signals of most of the city's TV and radio stations. Built in 1973, it is still much used, despite the rise of cable networks. The tower is visible from all over the Bay Area, and sometimes seems to float above the summer fogs that roll in from the sea. On the north side of the tower there are dense eucalyptus groves, first planted in the 1880s by Adolph Sutro. They drop down to the medical center campus of the University of California San Francisco (UCSF), one of the most highly rated teaching hospitals in the United States.

Twin Peaks

📍J9 🚌36, 37

These two hills were first known in Spanish as El Pecho de la Chola, "the Bosom of the Indian Girl." At the top there is an area of parkland with steep and grassy slopes, from which you can enjoy incomparable views of the city.

Twin Peaks Boulevard circles both hills near their summits, and there is a parking and viewing point from which to look out over the city. Visitors who are prepared to climb up the steep footpath to the very top can leave the crowds behind and enjoy a 360° view. The residential districts on the lower slopes have streets that wind around

↑ Fabulous view of downtown from the Twin Peaks

the contours of the slopes, rather than following the formal grid that is more common in San Francisco.

15

Mission Cultural Center for Latino Arts

📍 M9 🏠 2868 Mission St
🚌 12, 14, 27, 36, 49 🚉 J
🚇 24th St. Mission ⏰ 10am–5pm Tue-Sat 🌐 mission culturalcenter.org

This dynamic arts center displays and promotes Latino culture. It offers classes and workshops including Argentine tango, Brazilian samba, and guitar, and stages theatrical events and temporary exhibitions in its gallery. One of the highlights of its calendar is the parade held in November to celebrate the Day of the Dead (p50).

16

Noe Valley

📍 K/L 10 🚌 24, 35, 48 🚉 J

Noe Valley is known as "Noewhere Valley" by its residents, who are intent on keeping it off the tourist map. It is a comfortable neighbor-hood mainly inhabited by

← The Sutro Tower, a TV and radio mast and a prominent landmark on the city skyline

 GREAT VIEW
Noe Valley Views

The neighborhood's eastern boundaries provide excellent vistas. There's a 30 per cent gradient on 24th Street between Grand View Avenue and Fountain Street, but the effort is rewarding.

young families. Named after its original land-grant owner, José Noe, the last *alcalde* (mayor) of Mexican Yerba Buena, the area was first developed in the 1880s following the completion of a cable-car line over the steep Castro Street hill. Like many other areas of San Francisco, this once working-class district underwent wholesale gentrification in the 1970s, resulting in today's engaging mix of boutiques, bars, and restaurants. The Noe Valley Ministry, at 1021 Sanchez Street, is a late 1880s Presbyterian church in the "Stick Style" (p36), with an emphasis on vertical lines.

 17

Carnaval Mural

📍 M9 🏠 24th St and South Van Ness Ave 🚌 12, 27, 48, 67 🚉 J 🚇 24th St. Mission

One of the many brightly painted murals to be seen in the Mission District, the *Carnaval Mural* is painted above the House of Brakes and measures an impressive 24-ft- (7-m-) high and 75-ft- (23-m-) wide. It celebrates the diverse people who come together for the Carnaval festival. This event, held annually in late spring, is the high spot of the year.

Guided tours of other murals, some with political themes, are given by civic organizations. There is also an outdoor gallery with murals in Balmy Alley, near Treat and Harrison streets. Many of these murals are protests against government injustice.

Did You Know?

The *Carnaval Mural* was created in 1983 by muralist Daniel Galvez with the help of local artists.

↑ The *Carnaval Mural*, created in 1983 by Daniel Galvez and a group of local artists

A SHORT WALK
HAIGHT ASHBURY

Distance 1 mile (0.6 km) **Time** 15 minutes
Nearest bus 7, 33

Stretching from the hilly Buena Vista Park to the flat expanses of Golden Gate Park, Haight Ashbury (p178) was a place to escape to from the city center in the 1880s. It developed into a residential area, but between the 1930s and 1960s it changed dramatically to become the center of the "Flower Power" world. It is now one of the liveliest and most bohemian places in San Francisco, with an eclectic mix of people, excellent book and record stores, and good cafés. This route takes you past some of the area's main highlights.

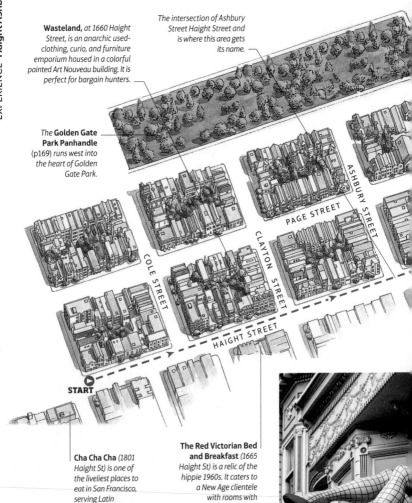

Wasteland, at 1660 Haight Street, is an anarchic used-clothing, curio, and furniture emporium housed in a colorful painted Art Nouveau building. It is perfect for bargain hunters.

The intersection of Ashbury Street and Haight Street is where this area gets its name.

The **Golden Gate Park Panhandle** (p169) runs west into the heart of Golden Gate Park.

ASHBURY STREET

PAGE STREET

CLAYTON STREET

COLE STREET

HAIGHT STREET

START

Cha Cha Cha (1801 Haight St) is one of the liveliest places to eat in San Francisco, serving Latin American food in a variety of small dishes.

The **Red Victorian Bed and Breakfast** (1665 Haight St) is a relic of the hippie 1960s. It caters to a New Age clientele with rooms with transcendental themes.

Downtown San Francisco skyline seen from Buena Vista Park

Locator Map
For more detail see p174

HAIGHT ASHBURY AND THE MISSION

OAK STREET

LYON STREET

CENTRAL STREET

MASONIC STREET

BUENA VISTA WEST

0 meters   100   N
0 yards   100

Through its mass of twisting trees, the dramatic **Buena Vista Park** *(p180) offers magnificent views over the city.*

No. 1220 Masonic Avenue *is one of many ornate Victorian mansions built on a steep hill to the south of Haight Street.*

The grand home at No. 737 Buena Vista Avenue is **(Richard) Spreckels Mansion** *(p180), built in 1897.*

FINISH

← Legs sticking out of the window of the Piedmont Boutique on Haight Street

187

GOLDEN GATE PARK AND LAND'S END

Lying to the south of the Richmond District *(p60)* is the spectacular Golden Gate Park, a masterpiece of landscape gardening, created in the 1890s out of a sandy wasteland. Little grows here by chance, and trees have been planted where they will best deflect the prevailing winds. All shrubs and bushes are carefully chosen to ensure there is color in every season. More parklands lie to the north and west of the Richmond District, linked by the Coastal Trail. This is where rugged Land's End, the scene of so many shipwrecks, meets the sea.

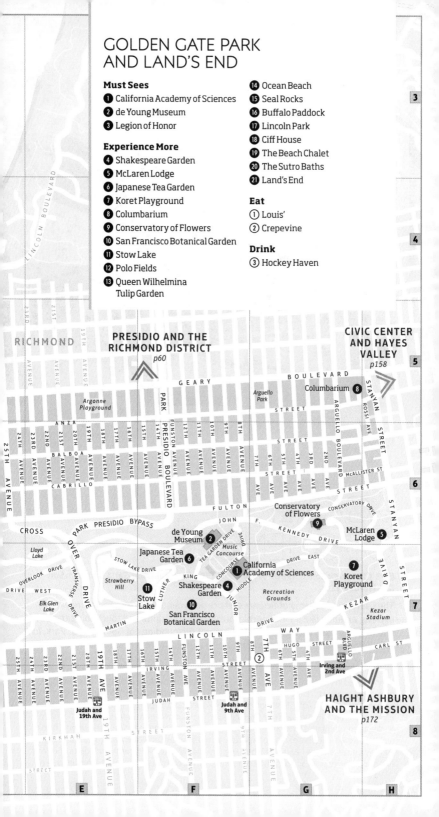

GOLDEN GATE PARK AND LAND'S END

Must Sees

1. California Academy of Sciences
2. de Young Museum
3. Legion of Honor

Experience More

4. Shakespeare Garden
5. McLaren Lodge
6. Japanese Tea Garden
7. Koret Playground
8. Columbarium
9. Conservatory of Flowers
10. San Francisco Botanical Garden
11. Stow Lake
12. Polo Fields
13. Queen Wilhelmina Tulip Garden
14. Ocean Beach
15. Seal Rocks
16. Buffalo Paddock
17. Lincoln Park
18. Ciff House
19. The Beach Chalet
20. The Sutro Baths
21. Land's End

Eat

1. Louis'
2. Crepevine

Drink

3. Hockey Haven

Did You Know?

The museum's website has live video cams for exhibits such as the penguin colony and coral reef.

① ⊘ Ⓜ Ⓨ ▱ ⑪

CALIFORNIA ACADEMY OF SCIENCES

📍F2 🏛55 Music Concourse Dr 🚌5, 44 🚇N 🕐9:30am–5pm Mon–Sat, 11am–5pm Sun
🌐calacademy.org

The California Academy of Sciences lets curious minds get close to nature with exciting exhibits like an indoor rainforest, vast aquarium, and touchable tidepool. The building itself blends in with the natural surroundings of Golden Gate Park, in an environmentally friendly structure with a beautiful roof of local plantlife.

The California Academy of Sciences has been located in Golden Gate Park since 1916, settling into a new building in late 2008. It houses the Steinhart Aquarium, Morrison Planetarium, and the Kimball Natural History Museum, and combines innovative green architecture with flexible exhibition spaces. A lovely piazza is at the heart of the building. Filled with native plant species, the 2.5-acre (1-ha) living roof, which can be seen from the rooftop deck, is designed to make the museum blend in with the surrounding parkland. Explore the fascinating exhibits at your own pace or flit between the many workshops and talks held throuhout the day. Ther museum's calendar is also full of lectures, weekly late-night events for adults of 21 and over, and sleepovers for children aged 5–17.

Visitors in the Osher Rainforest exhibit, a four-story indoor rainforest

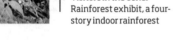

MUSEUM GUIDE

Steinhart Aquarium displays are spread throughout the museum, but most of the tanks are on the lower level beneath the Piazza. The main floor is the gateway to all the other key exhibits, including the Kimball Natural History Museum, Morrison Planetarium and Osher Rainforest, with some exhibits extending up several floors. An auditorium above the cafe hosts traveling exhibits as well as special performances and programs. The third floor houses the geology collection and Naturalist Center, and on the roof there is an observation deck.

Morrison Planetarium

Visitors leave planet Earth behind as stunning films send them flying through space and time.

Living Roof

▽ An observation deck offers views of the park and allows visitors to see the green roof up close.

Discovery Tidepool

Located on the main floor, this exhibit allows visitors to touch sea creatures from local rock pools.

T. Rex

▷ Part of the Kimball Natural History Museum, the skeleton of a *Tyrannosaurus Rex* sits at the museum entrance. This gigantic predator was the most powerful carnivore ever to walk the earth.

Steinhart Aquarium

◁ The amazing aquarium exhibit on the lower floor includes the world's largest indoor reef.

Tusher African Hall

▷ Preserved animals from Africa are displayed here in lifelike dioramas. This area is also home to a colony of endangered African penguins *(right)*.

② ⬦ Ⓜ ⬚ 🏛

DE YOUNG MUSEUM

📍F2 🏠50 Hagiwara Tea Garden Dr 🚌5, 44 🚈N 🕐9:30am–5:15pm Tue–Sun 🌐deyoung.famsf.org

A bastion of American, Oceanian, and African art, the immense, copper-clad de Young Museum looms as a cultural and architectural landmark above a canopy of plane trees in the Golden Gate Park.

Founded in 1895, this stunning gallery suffered such bad damage in the Loma Prieta earthquake (1989) that the structure couldn't be saved. However, an exciting new facility opened in 2005 and has become as much a city landmark as its predecessor.

The museum contains a broad range of American art from the 17th century to contemporary works. With pieces by Native Americans, early immigrants, and African slaves, the collection offers a look at the diversity of American experiences and cultures. Alongside displays of American origin are exhibits from the Department of Africa, Oceania, and the Americas, which owes its collection mainly to donations. These have developed into a broad and fascinating selection of exhibits from cultures around the world, and one of the most impressive textile and costume collections in the US.

↑ Visitors admiring sculptures in the beautiful museum gardens

→ The Piazzoni Mural Room and sculpture of Diana *(inset)* from 1889

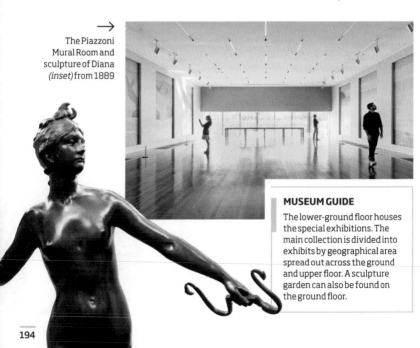

MUSEUM GUIDE

The lower-ground floor houses the special exhibitions. The main collection is divided into exhibits by geographical area spread out across the ground and upper floor. A sculpture garden can also be found on the ground floor.

14,000

The number of items in the museum's textile collection, from rugs to costumes.

The tower and observation deck on the north end of the De Young museum →

③ 🖉 🅜 🖵 🏛

LEGION OF HONOR

📍B5 🏛Lincoln Park, 100 34th Ave (at Clement St) 🚌1, 18, 38 🕐9:30am–5:15pm Tue–Sun 🌐legionofhonor.famsf.org

Set in the gorgeous natural landscape of Land's End and housed in a replica of the Palais de la Légion d'Honneur in Paris, this museum features medieval to 20th-century European art, and is famous for hosting fanastic temporary exhibits.

Alma de Bretteville Spreckels (heiress to the Spreckels sugar fortune) commissioned this museum in the 1920s to promote French art in California, and to commemorate the state's casualties in World War I. It contains mostly European art from the last eight centuries, with paintings by famous figures including Monet, Rubens, and Rembrandt, as well as over 70 sculptures by Rodin. The gallery also houses collections on photography and ancient art covering 6,000 years of world history and cultures. The Achenbach Foundation, a famous collection of around 90,000 graphic works, is displayed in rotating exhibits.

GALLERY GUIDE

The museum's permanent collection is displayed in 19 galleries on the first floor. Beginning at the left of the entrance, works are arranged chronologically from the medieval period to the 20th century.

Gallery Highlights

c 1880

▽ This Oval leaf molded plate was designed by the famous Wedgwood Factory.

c 1904

▽ The bronze cast of Rodin's *The Thinker* was made by Rodin's assistant, Henri Lebossé.

1642

△The Raising of Lazarus, one of several hundred Rembrandt works in the Achenbach Foundation collection.

1889

△ Konstantin Makovsky's *The Russian Bride's Attire* depicts a Russian woman preparing for her wedding day.

↑ A gallery of European sculptures; the museum facade (*inset*), inspired by a historic palace in Paris

1924

▽ The Skinner pipe organ was built by the Ernest M. Skinner Organ Company, and is used in organ concerts here throughout the year.

c 1914

△ This version of *Water Lilies* is just one of around 250 paintings Monet created of the water lilies in his garden.

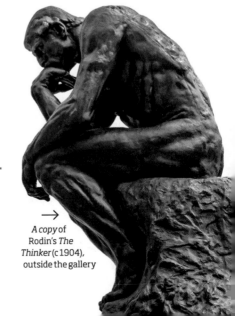

→ A copy of Rodin's *The Thinker* (c 1904), outside the gallery

EXPERIENCE MORE

4

Shakespeare Garden

F7 Music Concourse, Golden Gate Park
6, 7, 43, 44

Gardeners here have tried to cultivate all the plants mentioned in William Shakespeare's works. The relevant quotations are written on plaques set in a wall at the back of the garden.

5

McLaren Lodge

H6 Near junction of Stanyan St and Fell St on the park's east side 831-2700 8am-5pm Mon-Fri 7X, 21, 33

This sandstone villa, designed by Edward Swain, was built in 1896. As superintendent of the park, John McLaren lived here with his family until his death in 1943. His portrait hangs on the wall, and every December the cypress tree outside is lit with colored lights in his memory.

6

Japanese Tea Garden

F7 Music Concourse, Golden Gate Park 44
9am-6pm daily (Nov-Feb: to 4:45pm) japanese teagardensf.com

This garden was established by the art dealer George Turner Marsh for the California Midwinter Fair of 1894. Paths

←

Looking onto the picturesque Japanese Tea Garden from the Tea House

200

The number of different flower and plant species in the Shakespeare Garden.

wind through the carefully manicured Japanese trees, shrubs, and flowers. The steeply arched Moon Bridge forms a dramatic circular reflection in the pond below. The largest bronze Buddha to be found outside Asia, cast in Japan in 1790, is seated at the top of the garden stairs.

 Koret Playground

G7 **Kezar Drive, near First Ave** **231-0077**
5, 71 **N** **Times vary, call ahead**

A great place for young visitors who need to let off some steam, this is the oldest public children's playground in the United States. In 1978 it was redesigned with sandboxes, swings, slides, and a fortress, and recent additions include a wave-inspired climbing wall. On the Herschell-Spillman merry-go-round, housed in a Greek-

↑ Stunning cherry trees blossoming in the Shakespeare Garden

inspired structure that dates from 1892, children ride on brightly painted beasts (additional fee required).

THE CREATION OF GOLDEN GATE PARK

As San Francisco prospered in the 1860s, its citizens demanded the same amenities as other great cities. Prominent among these was a large city park, so city planners turned to a surveyor and engineer named William Hammond Hall. Hall started work at the east end, laying out meandering roads and trying to create a seemingly natural landscape. The developing park soon proved popular: families came to picnic and young dandies raced their carriages.

Despite the popularity of the park, it was nearly prevented from reaching maturity by budget cuts and public corruption, with city officials siphoning off funds. Hall was falsely accused of corruption and resigned in protest. The park fell into a period of decline, but after a decade of decay, Hall was asked to resume the task of managing it, which he agreed to do with the help of John McLaren, who shared his passion and vision for the park.

8

Columbarium

◉ G5 ◈ 1 Loraine Court
☎ 771-0717 🚌 33, 38
🕐 8am-5pm Mon-Fri,
10am-3pm Sat & Sun

The San Francisco Columbarium is the sole survivor of the old Lone Mountain Cemetery, which once covered sizable tracts of the Richmond District. Most of the remains were disinterred and moved to Colma in 1914. This Neo-Classical rotunda houses the remains of 6,000 people in elaborate decorated urns. Unused for several decades, it was rescued and restored by the Neptune Society in 1979. The ornate, bright interior under the dome has lovely stained-glass windows. The narrow passages encircling the dome are remarkable for their acoustics.

9

Conservatory of Flowers

◉ G6 ◈ John F. Kennedy Drive, Golden Gate Park
🚌 5, 21, 33, 44 🚋 N
🕐 10am-4pm Tue-Sun
🌐 conservatoryof flowers.org

This beautiful, ornate Victorian-style glasshouse is full of flowers and plants from around the world, especially from tropical zones. There are five distinct galleries, each focusing on a different

┌─────────────────────────────┐
│ 📷 PICTURE PERFECT
│ **Light Shows**
│
│ The Conservatory of Flowers is illuminated with light projections every night from dusk to midnight. The installation can be viewed from JFK Drive and in Conservatory Valley - no admission is necessary.
└─────────────────────────────┘

ecosystem. The original building, opened in 1879, was largely destroyed by a storm in 1995. A campaign for its repair was launched, and it reopened in 2003.

10

San Francisco Botanical Garden

◉ F7 ◈ 9th Ave at Lincoln Way, Golden Gate Park
🚌 5, 7, 44 🚋 N 🕐 Mar-Sep: 7:30am-6pm daily (Oct: to 5pm; Nov-Jan: to 4pm)
🌐 sfbotanicalgarden.org

On display at the Botanical Garden are 8,500 species of plants, trees, and shrubs from around the world. There are Mexican, African, South American, and Australian gardens, and one devoted to native California plants.

Well worth a visit is the enchanting Moon-Viewing Garden. It exhibits East Asian plants in a setting that, unlike that of the Japanese Tea Garden (p198), is naturalistic rather than formal. Both

> **Well worth a visit is the enchanting Moon-Viewing Garden. It exhibits East Asian plants in a setting that is naturalistic rather than formal.**

medicinal and culinary plants are grown in the Garden of Fragrance, which is designed for the visually impaired. Here the emphasis is on the senses of taste, touch, and smell, and the plants are identified in Braille. Another area is planted with indigenous California redwood trees, with a small stream winding through. This recreates the flora and atmosphere of a northern Californian coastal forest. There is also a New World Cloud Forest, with flora from the mountains of Central America. Surprisingly, all these gardens thrive in the coastal fog. The garden has a shop, selling seeds and books, and also houses the Helen Crocker

Russell Library of Horticulture, open to the public. The shop is the starting point for free guided tours on weekdays at 1:30pm, and from 10:30am to 1:30pm on weekends.

Stow Lake

📍F7 🏠50 Stow Lake Drive, Golden Gate Park 🚌28, 29, 44 ⏰Daily 🌐goldengatepark.com/stow-lake.html

This artificial lake, created in 1895, encircles Strawberry Hill such that the summit of the hill now forms an island, linked to the mainland by two stone-clad bridges.

Stow Lake's pretty circular stream is ideal for rowing laps on a boat rented from the boathouse, though leisurely drifting feels more appropriate in this tranquil setting.

The Chinese moon-watching pavilion on the island's shore was a gift from San Francisco's sister city Taipei, in Taiwan. The red and green pavilion was shipped to

↑ Boating on Stow Lake, one of the park's main attractions

San Francisco in 6,000 pieces, then assembled on the island.

The millionaire Collis P. Huntington donated the money to create the reservoir and the waterfall that cascades into Stow Lake and is one of the park's most attractive features.

EAT

Louis'
Owned and run by the same family since 1937, Louis' doesn't accept reservations but it's worth trying your luck as a walk-in for stellar views of the wild coastline as you dine on classic American fare.

📍A5 🏠902 Point Lobos Ave 🌐louissf.com

Crepevine
With an exhaustive menu of sweet and savoury crêpes and other breakfast and lunch options, this is a great place to fill up before setting out to explore Golden Gate Park.

📍G7 🏠624 Irving St 🌐crepevine.com

← Tropical plants fill the magnificent Conservatory of Flowers

Did You Know?

A velodrome was built around the Polo Fields in 1906 and is still used by cyclists to this day.

 12

Polo Fields

📍C7 🚩John F. Kennedy Drive, Golden Gate Park 🚌5, 29

You are far more likely to see joggers and soccer teams than polo ponies using the Polo Fields stadium in the more open western half of Golden Gate Park. Horses, on which to explore the park's equestrian trails and the Bercut Equitation Field, are available by the hour at the adjacent riding stables. For anglers, there are several fly-casting pools nearby.

To the east of the stadium, in the green expanse of Old Speedway Meadows, many celebrations were held during the late 1960s, including some notable rock concerts. The Grateful Dead and Jefferson Airplane, among others, played here. Here, in the spring of 1967, thousands attended a huge "Be-in," one of many events that led to the "Summer of Love."

 13

Queen Wilhelmina Tulip Garden

📍B7 🚌5, 18, 31, 31AX

The Dutch windmill was built near the northwest corner of Golden Gate Park in 1903. Its original purpose was to pump water from an underground source to irrigate the park, but it is no longer in use. Its companion, the Murphy Wind-mill, was erected in the park's southwest corner in 1905. The garden was named after the Dutch Queen Wilhelmina, and tulip bulbs are donated each year by the Dutch Bulb Growers' Association; early spring is the best time of year to see the colorful display of tulips in full bloom.

 14

Ocean Beach

📍A7 🚌5, 7X, 18, 31, 31AX, 48 🚃L, N

Most of San Francisco's western boundary is defined by this broad sweep of sandy beach. Though sublime when viewed from Cliff House or Sutro Heights, the sea here is dangerous for swimming because of its icy waters and a strong undertow. Surfers in wet suits are a common sight,

←

The Queen Wilhelmina Tulip Garden with its windmill and glorious flower beds

but there is often a stiff wind, or fog. On rare hot days, it is also a popular spot for sunbathers and picnickers; and locals come for barbecue and to watch the sun go down.

↑ Seal Rocks, a haven for sea lions *(inset)* and sea birds jut off Ocean Beach

Seal Rocks

⑮ A6 🚌 18, 38

Seal Rocks is a collection of small rocky islands (not accessible to visitors) in the Lands End area, popular with basking sea lions and sea birds. They are best viewed from Ocean Beach (at low tide), Cliff House, or Sutro Heights Park. Bring binoculars to watch them in their natural setting. At night, the barking of the sea lions is somehow both reassuring and eerie, especially when it is foggy. On a clear day you can see the Farallon Islands, which lie 32 miles (51 km) off the coast. This group of islands and sea stacks are also inhabited by sea lions and contain a rookery that has been protected by the state since 1907.

Buffalo Paddock

⑯ C7 🏛 John F. Kennedy Drive, Golden Gate Park 🚌 5, 29

The shaggy buffalo that graze in this paddock are the largest North American land animals. With its short horns and humped back, the buffalo (or "American bison") is the symbol of the American plains. This paddock was opened in 1892. In 1902 William Cody, alias "Buffalo Bill," traded one of his bulls for one from the Golden Gate Park herd. Both parties thought that they had rid themselves of an aggressive beast, but Cody's newly purchased bull jumped a high fence once back at his encampment and escaped. Apparently, it took a total of 80 men to recapture it.

⓱ Lincoln Park

🚩 B4 🚌 1, 1AX, 18, 38

This splendid park, located above the Golden Gate Park, is the setting for the Legion of Honor *(p196)*. The land was originally allocated to Golden Gate Cemetery, where graves were segregated according to the nationality of their occupants. When these graves were cleared in the first decade of the 20th century, the park was established and landscaped by John McLaren, who served as superintendent of the Golden Gate Park for many years *(p198)*.

The park now boasts an 18-hole golf course and scenic walks. City views from the hilltop course are, as you might expect, superb.

⓲ Cliff House

🚩 A6 🏠 1090 Point Lobos 🚌 38AX 🕐 Daily 🌐 cliffhouse.com

Cliff House is a wonderful place to come for a meal and enjoy dramatic views of the ocean. Built in 1909, the present building, which was renovated in 2004, is the third on this site. Its predecessor, an elaborate eight-story Gothic structure that burned down in 1907, was built by the flamboyant entrepreneur Adolph Sutro. His estate on the hill overlooking Cliff House is now Sutro Heights Park. There are several restaurants on the upper levels, live jazz on Friday nights, and three observation decks with panoramic views. A camera obscura is located on the lower level and uses a series of mirrors and lenses to produce a 360° panorama of the ocean and rocks around.

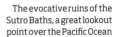

The evocative ruins of the Sutro Baths, a great lookout point over the Pacific Ocean

⓳ The Beach Chalet

🚩 A7 🏠 1000 Great Hwy 🚌 5, 5R, 31, 31AX, 38 🕐 Times vary, check website 🌐 beachchalet.com

Where the Golden Gate Park meets the ocean, you'll find this charming historic building. Noteworthy architect Willis Polk designed the chalet in 1925, while other artisans have added their touches over the years, creating a distinctly "only-in-San Francisco" establishment. Elaborate murals by famed artist Lucien Labaudt were commissioned by the Works Progress Administration in 1936 and depict famous places and people in San Francisco. Intricate wood carvings by Michael von Meyer show seaside imagery such as mermaids, octopuses, and old ships, underscoring the sweeping views of the Pacific Ocean right outside the Beach Chalet windows. You can browse historic artifacts housed on the first floor, view a three-dimensional model of Golden Gate Park, sample

📷 PICTURE PERFECT
A Labyrinth

Inspired by other historic labyrinths and the awe-inspiring coastal landscape, artist Eduardo Aguilera created his own rock labyrinth at Land's End. It can be found down an offshoot of the Land's End Trail.

← Cliff House, perched on rugged rocks above the Pacific Ocean

seasonal beers from the brewery, and enjoy live entertainment and good food in the restaurant.

20

The Sutro Baths

 A5 🏠 **1004 Point Lobos** 🚌 **38, 38AX, 38R** 🕐 **Sunrise-sunset daily**

Today, all that remains of the Sutro Baths are atmospheric ruins in a wild and rocky setting. Developed in 1890 by Adolph Sutro, an entrepreneur and former city mayor, the baths housed the largest indoor pools in the country. The incoming tide would fill and refresh the water of the pools every five days. The pools were a popular destination for visitors and locals in the first half of the twentieth century, but they

> **Set within the craggy cliffside near the famed Cliff House and close to the wide expanse of the ocean, these brooding ruins afford striking views.**

eventually fell out of favor. In the 1960s, a myst-erious fire laid waste to the once iconic buildings. Set within the craggy cliffside near the famed Cliff House and close to the wide expanse of the ocean, these brooding ruins afford striking views.

21

Land's End

 B4 🚌 **1, 1AX, 18, 38**

A rugged seascape of rock, cliff, and matted cypress woods, Land's End is the wildest part of San Francisco.

It is reached on foot along the Coastal Trail, which can be accessed by stairs from the Legion of Honor, or from a parking area at Point Lobos. The Coastal Trail ends in a spectacular viewing point overlooking the Golden Gate Bridge (p64). It is inadvisable to leave the trail, as there is a risk of being stranded by incoming tides; call the National Park Service for tide information (415 561 4700). Mile Rocks Lighthouse can be seen offshore from here, or at least what is left of it. The tower was removed in 1966 and the top converted into a helicopter pad.

↑ The Coastal Trail at Land's End, offering city and ocean views

A SHORT WALK
GOLDEN GATE PARK

Distance 0.5 mile (0.6 km) **Time** 10 minutes
Nearest bus 5, 44

Golden Gate Park is one of the largest urban parks in the world. It stretches from the Pacific Ocean to the center of San Francisco, forming an oasis of greenery and calm in which to escape from the bustle of city life. Within the park an amazing number of activities are possible, both sporting and cultural. The landscaped area around the

Music Concourse, with its fountains, plane trees, and benches, is the most popular and developed section. Here you can enjoy free Sunday concerts at the Spreckels Temple of Music. Two museums stand on either side of the Concourse, and the Japanese and Shakespeare gardens are in walking distance.

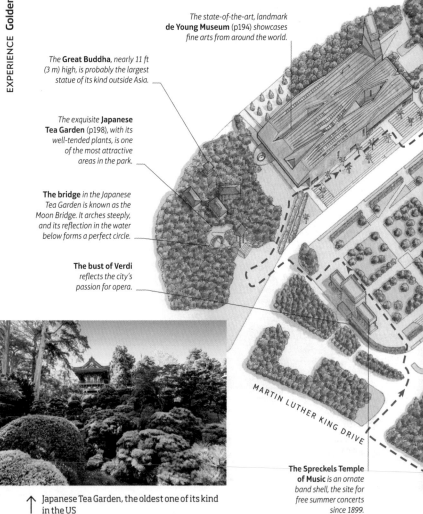

The state-of-the-art, landmark **de Young Museum** (p194) *showcases fine arts from around the world.*

The **Great Buddha**, *nearly 11 ft (3 m) high, is probably the largest statue of its kind outside Asia.*

The exquisite **Japanese Tea Garden** (p198), *with its well-tended plants, is one of the most attractive areas in the park.*

The bridge *in the Japanese Tea Garden is known as the Moon Bridge. It arches steeply, and its reflection in the water below forms a perfect circle.*

The bust of Verdi *reflects the city's passion for opera.*

MARTIN LUTHER KING DRIVE

The Spreckels Temple of Music *is an ornate band shell, the site for free summer concerts since 1899.*

↑ Japanese Tea Garden, the oldest one of its kind in the US

← The Spreckels Temple of Music band shell

GOLDEN GATE PARK AND LAND'S END

Locator Map
For more detail see p190

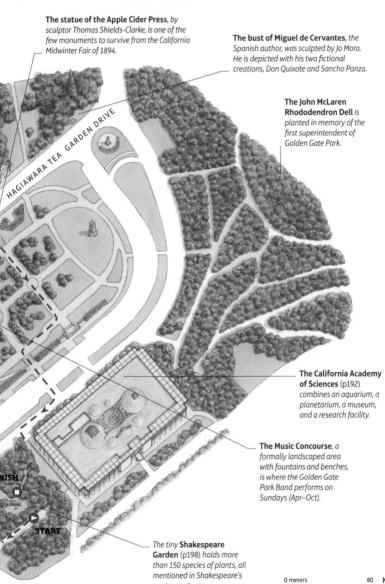

The statue of the Apple Cider Press, *by sculptor Thomas Shields-Clarke, is one of the few monuments to survive from the California Midwinter Fair of 1894.*

The bust of Miguel de Cervantes, *the Spanish author, was sculpted by Jo Mora. He is depicted with his two fictional creations, Don Quixote and Sancho Panza.*

The John McLaren Rhododendron Dell *is planted in memory of the first superintendent of Golden Gate Park.*

HAGIAWARA TEA GARDEN DRIVE

The California Academy of Sciences (p192) *combines an aquarium, a planetarium, a museum, and a research facility.*

The Music Concourse, *a formally landscaped area with fountains and benches, is where the Golden Gate Park Band performs on Sundays (Apr–Oct).*

The tiny **Shakespeare Garden** (p198) *holds more than 150 species of plants, all mentioned in Shakespeare's poetry or plays.*

FINISH

START

0 meters   80
0 yards   80

N ↑

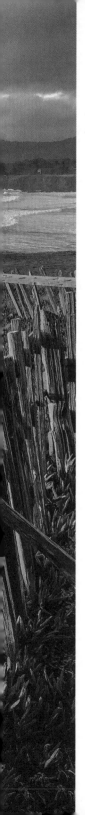

Sunset over the Sonoma County coast

THE BAY AREA

San Francisco is the smallest in size of the seven counties that encircle the San Francisco Bay. To the north of Golden Gate Bridge, Marin County has a wild, windswept coastline, forests of redwoods, and Mount Tamalpais, which offers magnificent views across the Bay Area. In the East Bay, popular destinations are Oakland's Museum of California and the famous university, Gourmet Ghetto, and the botanical gardens of Berkeley. The Peninsula area stretching to the south of San Francisco is full of interesting urban areas that hug the beautiful coastline, while the Napa Valley and Sonoma counties to the north are famous for the manicured beauty of their vineyards, and their famous wines and upscale resorts.

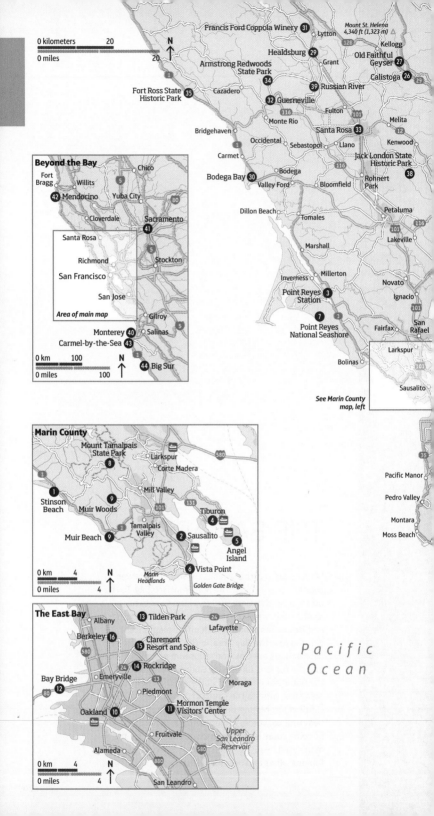

0 kilometers   20

0 miles   20

N

Francis Ford Coppola Winery **31** Lytton   Mount St. Helena
4,340 ft (1,323 m)

Kellogg

Healdsburg **29**   Old Faithful
Geyser **27**

Armstrong Redwoods
State Park   Grant   Calistoga **26**

34   **39** Russian River

Fort Ross State   Cazadero
Historic Park **35**   **32** Guerneville

Fulton

Monte Rio   101   Melita

Bridgehaven   Santa Rosa **33**

Occidental   Sebastopol   Kenwood

Carmet   Llano   Jack London State
Historic Park

Bodega Bay **30**   Bodega   **38**

Valley Ford   Bloomfield   Rohnert
Park

Dillon Beach   Tomales

Petaluma

Marshall   Lakeville

Inverness   Millerton   Novato

Point Reyes **3**   Ignacio
Station

Point Reyes **7**   Fairfax   San
National Seashore   Rafael

Larkspur

Bolinas   Sausalito

*See Marin County
map, left*

Beyond the Bay

Fort   Chico
Bragg   Willits   5

42 Mendocino   Yuba City   80

Cloverdale   Sacramento
41

Santa Rosa   5   Stockton

Richmond

San Francisco   5

San Jose   Gilroy

Area of main map   Salinas   5

Monterey **40**

Carmel-by-the-Sea **43**   1

0 km   100   N   **44** Big Sur

0 miles   100

Marin County

Mount Tamalpais   580
State Park   Larkspur

8   Corte Madera

Mill Valley

1   **9**   101   131

Stinson   Muir Woods   Tiburon
Beach   **4**

Tamalpais   **2** Sausalito   **5**
Valley

Muir Beach **9**   Angel
Island

Marin   **6** Vista Point
Headlands

0 km   4   N   *Golden Gate Bridge*

0 miles   4

Pacific Manor

Pedro Valley

35

Montara

Moss Beach

The East Bay

13 Tilden Park   24

Albany   Lafayette

Berkeley **16**

15 Claremont
Resort and Spa

24 **14** Rockridge

Bay Bridge   Emeryville   Moraga

12   **13**

Piedmont

Oakland **10**   **11** Mormon Temple
Visitors' Center

Fruitvale   *Upper
San Leandro
Reservoir*

Alameda   880

0 km   4   N   580

0 miles   4   San Leandro

*Pacific
Ocean*

THE BAY AREA

Marin County
1. Stinson Beach
2. Sausalito
3. Point Reyes Station
4. Tiburon
5. Angel Island
6. Vista Point
7. Point Reyes National Seashore
8. Mount Tamalpais State Park
9. Muir Woods and Beach

The East Bay
10. Oakland
11. Mormon Temple Visitors' Center
12. Bay Bridge
13. Tilden Park
14. Rockridge
15. Claremont Resort and Spa
16. Berkeley

The Peninsula
17. **Must See:** Santa Cruz Beach Boardwalk
18. **Must See:** Half Moon Bay
19. San Jose
20. Stanford University
21. Año Nuevo
22. Pescadero
23. Filoli

Napa Valley
24. **Must See:** Napa Valley Wine Country
25. St. Helena
26. Calistoga
27. Old Faithful Geyser
28. Napa

Sonoma County
29. **Must See:** Healdsburg
30. Bodega Bay
31. Francis Ford Coppola Winery
32. Guerneville
33. Santa Rosa
34. Armstrong Redwoods State Park
35. Fort Ross State Historic Park
36. Gloria Ferrer Champagne Caves
37. Sonoma
38. Jack London State Historic Park
39. Russian River

Beyond the Bay
40. **Must See:** Monterey
41. Sacramento
42. Mendocino
43. Carmel-by-the-Sea
44. Big Sur

GETTING TO KNOW
THE BAY AREA

The Bay Area has no official boundaries, but is roughly made up of the nine counties that border the San Francisco Bay. San Francisco itself is only a small part of this region, so take a coach or hire a car and head out to explore the beautiful, varied, and historic region of northern California.

MARIN COUNTY

PAGE 216

A wild, windswept coastline, redwood forests, and seaside villages are all just a few minutes north from the Golden Gate Bridge. Accessible by ferry, Sausalito and Tiburon are charming bayside hamlets loaded with boutique shops, galleries, and scenic cafés and restaurants. Hugging the Pacific, a wide bay, and a wildlife-rich estuary, Point Reyes National Seashore is for hikers, bikers, and wilderness lovers.

Best for
Hiking and nature

Home to
Vista Point and Mount Tamalpais State Park

Experience
A ferry ride to Angel Island for an afternoon of hiking

THE EAST BAY

PAGE 222

The cities in the East Bay have enough highlights of their own to lure people across the Bay from San Francisco. Just 20 minutes by car over the Bay Bridge you'll find museums, galleries, waterfront walks, and historic sights abound in Oakland, while Berkeley boasts a verdant university campus and the "Gourmet Ghetto" of California cuisine.

Best for
City life and museums

Home to
Oakland and Berekely

Experience
Exploring trendy shopping districts like Fourth Street in Berkeley

THE PENINSULA

PAGE 230

South of San Francisco are coastal sights from the lively Santa Cruz Beach Boardwalk to the natural beauty of Half Moon Bay. Some of this area is also known as Silicon Valley, home of Apple, Google, and a plethora of tech-centric companies. Families will love the interactive Tech Museum of Innovation and the spooky Winchester Mystery House in San Jose, while others can enjoy some time in quiet, picturesque towns like Pescadero.

Best for
Families, beaches and cool towns

Home to
Santa Cruz Beach Boardwalk and Half Moon Bay

Experience
A day at California's oldest amusement park by the ocean in Santa Cruz

$\rightarrow$

PAGE 238

NAPA VALLEY

Hundreds of world-famous wineries have celebrity status in this region, making it the perfect place for a luxury break. But the pelasures of Napa Valley aren't restricted to wine connoisseurs. Hot-air balloons float over the hills and vineyards, while passengers on the Napa Valley Wine Train enjoy a fine dining experience as they ride the rails through beautiful rolling hills.

Best for
Wine tasting and upscale resorts

Home to
Napa Valley Wine Country

Experience
The ultimate indulgence in food and drink at the French Laundry

PAGE 242

SONOMA COUNTY

From early California history in the small town of Sonoma, to exquisite drinking and dining in verdant wine valleys, Sonoma County is another must-see stop on any good tour of the Bay Area. Along winding country roads, hundreds of premium wineries welcome visitors, offering tastes of the grape, plus music festivals and cuisine-focused events. For families and nature lovers, there's a gorgeous, rugged coastline and beautiful national parks.

Best for
Wine and national parks

Home to
Healdsburg

Experience
Taking the family for a day of sun and outdoor fun at the Russian River

PAGE 248

BEYOND THE BAY

Head out for a day trip from San Francisco and you'll find all kinds of adventures to remind you of the irresistible pull of the Pacific coast that has drawn settlers and inspired writers and artists for centuries. Explore Sacramento and Mendocino to the north, and the lovely town of Monterey in the south – but make sure you take time out to drive down Highway 1 and enjoy the breathtaking coastline of Big Sur.

Best for
History, beaches and old towns

Home to
Monterey

Experience
Visiting the historic Old Town in Sacramento, the capital of California

Hanging out on the waterfront and enjoying the views at Sausalito ↑

MARIN COUNTY

1

Stinson Beach

🚗 US 101 N to Highway 1 🕐 7am–one hour after sunset daily 🌐 nps.gov/goga/stbe.htm

Since the early days of the 20th century this has been a popular vacation spot; the first visitors came on ferries from San Francisco and were met by horse-drawn carriages. Stinson remains the preferred swimming beach for the whole area, with shallow water making it very safe for children, and an expansive stretch of soft white sand, where surfers mingle with swimmers and sunbathers. The village nearby (also named Stinson Beach) has a few cafés and restaurants, and some good bookstores.

2

Sausalito

🚗 US 101 N, first exit after Golden Gate Bridge, to Bridgeway 🚌 From Ferry Building

In this attractive small town that was once a fishing community, Victorian bungalows cling to steep hills rising from the bay. Parallel to the waterfront, Bridgeway serves as a promenade for the weekend crowds that come to patronize the popular waterfront restaurants, gift shops, food markets, art studios, and boutiques and to enjoy the views.

The **US Army Corps of Engineers Bay Model Visitor Center** is well worth a look to see a working hydraulic scale model, which simulates the movement of the tides and currents of San Francisco Bay.

US Army Corps of Engineers Bay Model Visitor Center

🏛 2100 Bridgeway 🕐 Times vary, check website 🌐 spn.usace.army.mil

3

Point Reyes Station

ℹ 1 Bear Valley Rd; www.pointreyes.org

A delightful hamlet (population 350) built along the now defunct railroad at the southern end of Tomales Bay, this is the Marin Coast's main commercial and social hub. Its

---

> **Stinson remains the preferred beach for the whole area, with shallow water making it very safe for children, and an expansive stretch of soft white sand.**

→

Elephant seals basking on the beach at Point Reyes National Seashore

coastal area on hiking or horse-riding trips.

---

④

Tiburon

🚗 US 101 N, Tiburon Blvd exit 🚌 Golden Gate Transit bus 8 ⛴ From Ferry Building or Pier 43

The waterfront of this chic town is fringed with lovely parks, and the main street is lined with shops and restaurants housed in "arks." These are houseboats dating from the turn of the 20th century that were pulled ashore when the lagoon was filled in, and refurbished. They now stand in what is called "Ark Row."

---

red-brick, vaguely Italianate architecture reflects its founding by northern Italian settlers. Many original buildings still stand on Main Street, including the Old Creamery, Livery Stable, and original rail depot (today the post office). This charming hamlet is a great place to stay while exploring the beautiful Point Reyes National Seashore (p218) and surrounding

⑤

Angel Island

⛴ From Pier 41 and Tiburon 🌐 angelisland.org

Angel Island is reached by ferry from Tiburon and San Francisco. Boats dock at Ayala Cove. Hiking trails loop the wooded island, rising to 776 ft (237 m) above sea level, and past an old military garrison that once housed immigrants from Asia. During World War II, prisoners of war were held here. No motor vehicles are allowed, so it's a great place for walking or cycling.

EAT

Curled around the edge of Richardson Bay, Sausalito has plenty of options for dining with a waterfront view.

The Spinnaker
🏠 100 Spinnaker Dr
🌐 spinnaker
sasausalito.us

$$$

The Trident
🏠 558 Bridgeway
🌐 thetrident.net

$$$

Barrel House Tavern
🏠 660 Bridgeway
🌐 barrelhousetavern.
com

$$$

Fish.
🏠 350 Harbor Drive
🌐 331fish.com

$$$

 The Golden Gate Bridge shrouded in fog, seen from Vista Point

6

Vista Point

🚗 US 101 N, then take Conzelman Rd 🚌 Golden Gate Transit bus 30, 70 🌐 goldengatebridge.org

This famous viewpoint, immediately northeast of the Golden Gate Bridge (p64) offers an iconic vista of San Francisco and the Bay from atop Fort Baker. If you are coming by car, be aware that the parking lot often fills up quickly in summer, especially on weekends, so get there early or take public transport.

More spectacular vistas can be enjoyed from the Marin Headlands, on the northwest side of the bridge. A path from Fort Baker leads under the bridge then via Conzelman Road (accessible off southbound US 101) up to the first viewpoint at Battery Spencer, a World War II gun emplacement. The road snakes uphill to two other viewpoints. The most spectacular view awaits at the top, at Hawk Hill.

The **Bay Area Discovery Museum** close to Fort Baker is a wonderful, hands-on children's museum that is worth a visit once you're done admiring the scenery. With a focus on STEM subjects, it allows children to test their creative problem-solving skills with its interactive exhibits.

Bay Area Discovery Museum

⊘ ⊖ 🏠 557 McReynolds Rd ⏰ 9am–4pm Tue–Fri, 10am–5pm Sat, 9am–5pm Sun 🌐 bayareadiscovery museum.org

Point Reyes National Seashore

🚗 US Hwy 1 to Olema; then follow signs for Point Reyes National Seashore 🚌 Golden Gate Transit buses 70 & 101 to San Rafael Center, then West Marin Stage 68

Point Reyes peninsula is wild and windswept, and a haven for wildlife, including a herd of tule elk. There are cattle and dairy ranches, and three small towns: Olema, Point Reyes Station (p216), and Inverness. The peninsula is due west of the San Andreas Fault, which caused the devastating 1906 earthquake. A displaced fence on the Earthquake Trail near Bear Valley Visitor Center shows how the Fault caused the peninsula to move a full 20 ft (6 m) north of the mainland.

Point Reyes Lighthouse, built in 1870 and located at the peninsula's tip, may be the windiest and foggiest place on the Pacific Coast. The lighthouse is now automated;

← Visitors taking the 307 steps to reach The Point Reyes Lighthouse

 Walking amid the giant redwoods in Muir Woods National Monument

the original Fresnel lens is only for show. It's reached via a 307-step staircase from the clifftop **Lighthouse Visitor Center** – a great place to spot migrating whales.

Lighthouse Visitor Center

🏛 27000 Sir Francis Drake Blvd 🕐 10am–4:30pm Fri–Mon 🌐 nps.gov/pore/planyourvisit/lighthouse.htm

8

Mount Tamalpais State Park

🏛 3801 Panoramic Hwy 🕐 7am–sunset 🌐 parks.ca.gov

Mount Tamalpais State Park is a wilderness nature preserve with trails that wind through redwoods and alongside creeks. There are picnic areas, campsites, and meadows for kite flying. Mount Tamalpais, at 2,571 ft (784 m), is one of the highest peaks in the Bay Area; the rough tracks gave rise to the invention of the mountain bike. Near the summit is the **Mountain Theater**, a natural amphitheater where musicals and plays are performed.

Mountain Theater

⌖ 🏛 East Ridgecrest 🎭 Performances: May–Jun: 2pm Sun 🌐 mountain play.org

9

Muir Woods and Beach

🏛 US 101 N, then Hwy 1 to Muir Beach turnoff 🌐 gomuirwoods.com

Nestling at the foot of Mount Tamalpais is Muir Woods National Monument, one of the few remaining stands of first-growth coast redwoods. These giant trees (the oldest is at least 1,000 years old) once covered the coastal area of California. The woods were named in honor of John Muir, a 19th-century naturalist who was one of the first to persuade Americans of the need for conservation.

Redwood Creek bubbles out of Muir Woods and makes its way down to the sea at Muir Beach, a wide expanse of sand popular with beachcombers and picnickers. The road to the beach passes the Pelican Inn. This 16th-century style inn is extremely proud of its English menu, and its welcoming hospitality.

The beach is likely to be crowded on weekends, but if you are prepared to walk a mile or so farther you will probably find that you have the place to yourself.

A LONG WALK

THE MARIN HEADLANDS

Distance 2 miles (3 km) **Time** 45 minutes **Terrain** Hilly; some paved roads; the Coastal Trail is a woodland track **Nearest transportation** Bus 76X to Bunker Rd & Field Rd

At its northern end, the Golden Gate Bridge is anchored in the rolling green hills of the Marin Headlands. This is an unspoiled wild area of windswept ridges, sheltered valleys, and deserted beaches, once used as a military defense post and now part of the vast Golden Gate National Recreation Area. From several vantage points there are spectacular views of San Francisco and the sea and, on autumn days, you can see migrating eagles and ospreys gliding past Hawk Hill.

Locator Map

Marin Headlands

SAN FRANCISCO

Barracks *house various offices, among them the Headlands District Office, the Golden Gate Raptor Observatory, and an energy and resources center.*

Barracks

MITCHELL ROAD

Wooden Footbridge

Rodeo Beach

COASTAL

From the beach, turn inland again as you approach the tip of the lagoon, crossing a wooden footbridge.

A 15-minute walk from the parking area will bring you to the sandy **Rodeo Beach**. *Fishing boats may be seen bobbing out at sea, but the beach is mostly empty of people.*

South Rodeo Beach

From Rodeo Beach there is a fine view of **Bird Island** *lying to the south.*

Bird Island

| 0 meters | | 300 | N |
| 0 yards | | 300 | ↑ |

← Rodeo Lagoon at dusk, bordered by windswept hillsides

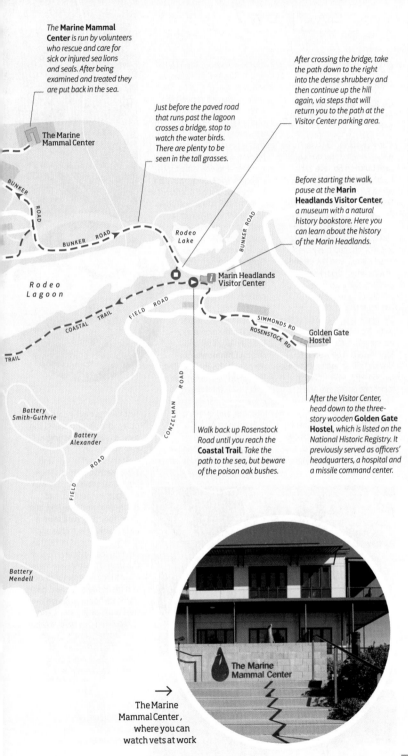

The **Marine Mammal Center** is run by volunteers who rescue and care for sick or injured sea lions and seals. After being examined and treated they are put back in the sea.

The Marine Mammal Center

Just before the paved road that runs past the lagoon crosses a bridge, stop to watch the water birds. There are plenty to be seen in the tall grasses.

After crossing the bridge, take the path down to the right into the dense shrubbery and then continue up the hill again, via steps that will return you to the path at the Visitor Center parking area.

Before starting the walk, pause at the **Marin Headlands Visitor Center**, a museum with a natural history bookstore. Here you can learn about the history of the Marin Headlands.

BUNKER ROAD

BUNKER ROAD

Rodeo Lake

BUNKER ROAD

Rodeo Lagoon

Marin Headlands Visitor Center

COASTAL TRAIL

FIELD ROAD

SIMMONDS RD

ROSENSTOCK RD

Golden Gate Hostel

TRAIL

Battery Smith-Guthrie

Battery Alexander

CONZELMAN ROAD

FIELD ROAD

Walk back up Rosenstock Road until you reach the **Coastal Trail**. Take the path to the sea, but beware of the poison oak bushes.

After the Visitor Center, head down to the three-story wooden **Golden Gate Hostel**, which is listed on the National Historic Registry. It previously served as officers' headquarters, a hospital and a missile command center.

Battery Mendell

→ The Marine Mammal Center, where you can watch vets at work

THE EAST BAY

10

Oakland

 🚊🅿🚌🚏 **ℹ 482 Water Street; www.visitoakland.com**

Many visitors to Oakland arrive by ferry and dock at **Jack London Square**. Jack London, author of *The Call of the Wild* (1903) and *White Fang* (1906), grew up in Oakland in the 1880s, and was a frequent visitor to the Oakland Estuary waterfront. It is a bright and busy promenade, lined with shops and restaurants, which have outdoor tables in fine weather. There are also pleasure boats offering trips along the estuary. Little of the waterfront that London knew remains, but the writer's footsteps can be traced to Heinold's First and Last Chance Saloon, which is located in Jack London Square and has been around since 1883.

Dating from the same era is **Old Oakland**, also known as Victorian Row: two square blocks of attractive wood-and-brick commercial buildings erected between the 1860s and 1880s, and thoroughly renovated in the 1980s. They now contain an appealing array of shops, restaurants, and art galleries. Friday mornings bring crowds of shoppers to the popular Farmers' Market, where stalls sell fresh produce and prepared foods. By night, the crowds move on to The Trappist on 8th Street. Don't miss Ratto's, located at 827 Washington Street, an Italian delicatessen which opened in 1897 and was once famed for its "Pasta Operas," in which singers serenaded the diners. The musical tradition carries on: every Saturday afternoon you can hear live jazz here.

Oakland is home to the Bay Area's second-largest **Chinatown** – or perhaps it should be called "Asiatown", as its Cantonese majority is augmented by immigrants from Korea, Vietnam, and other parts of Southeast Asia. The neighborhood receives far fewer tourists than San Francisco's Chinatown but its restaurants have good food at reasonable prices, and the area is full of interesting and colorful murals.

At the center of Oakland lies **Lake Merritt**, formed when a saltwater tidal estuary was dredged, embanked, and partly dammed. The lake and its surrounding park form a lovely oasis of rich blue and green. Designated in 1870 as the first state game refuge in the United States, Lake Merritt still attracts migrating flocks of birds. Rowers can rent boats from two boathouses on the west and north shores, and joggers and cyclists can circle the lake on a 3-mile (5-km) path. The north shore at Lakeside Park has flower gardens, an aviary, and

 ←

A contemporary art exhibit at the Oakland Museum of California

The entrance to the Oakland Zoo and a pair of patas monkeys *(inset)*

Old Oakland
🚇 12th Street ⓦ old-oakland.com

Chinatown
🚇 Lake Merritt

Lake Merritt
🚇 Lake Merritt, 19th Street ⓦ lakemerritt.org

Children's Fairyland
📍 699 Bellevue Ave 🚌 AC Transit 12 🕐 Summer: 10am-4pm daily (Winter: Fri-Sun) ⓦ fairyland.org

Oakland Museum of California
📍 1000 Oak St 🚇 Lake Merritt 🕐 11am-5pm Wed-Fri (to 10pm Fri), 10am-6pm Sat & Sun ⓦ museumca.org

Oakland Zoo
📍 9777 Golf Links Rd 🚌 AC Transit bus line 46 🕐 10am-4pm daily ⓦ oaklandzoo.org

Children's Fairyland: a whimsical storybook theme park for youngsters. The park has been a Lake Merritt fixture since 1948, and has dozens of storybook sets – such as Peter Rabbit's Garden and The Alice in Wonderland Tunnel – and a carousel, a miniature Ferris Wheel, live entertainment, and a small petting zoo of domestic animals, from guinea pigs and rabbits to ponies.

The **Oakland Museum of California** is California's only museum exclusively dedicated to documenting the state's art, history, and natural sciences. The building and the handsomely terraced gardens are features that mark this museum as an important architectural icon. The Gallery of California Natural Sciences showcases more than 2,000 native species across 7 habitats. The Gallery of California History has a large collection of artifacts from across the state, while the Gallery of California Art boasts early oil paintings of Yosemite and San Francisco. Check the museum website for details of the latest exhibitions.

On the outskirts of the city, **Oakland Zoo** is a magnificent menagerie with more than 700 native and exotic species living in naturalistic habitats. These include recreations of a tropical rainforest and African ecosystems. In 2018, the California Trail opened (doubling the size of the zoo) with eight new animal exhibits in huge, carefully recreated California habitats carved out of the forested upper slopes. They're dedicated to California's animal denizens, including black bears, grizzly bears, mountain lions, and bison. It's reached via a gondola ride.

Jack London Square
🚇 12th Street, then AC Transit 12, 72, 72M, 72R bus 🚌 Oakland

3.4 miles
The circumference of Lake Merritt (5.5 km).

EAT

Commis
Perch at the counter in this sleek restaurant to watch chefs work each seasonally led dish to perfection. The tasting menu changes daily, but favorites – including slow-poached egg yolk with onion cream – remain constant.

📍 3859 Piedmont Ave, Oakland 🕐 Mon & Tue ⓦ commisrestaurant.com

$ $ $

Oakland's impressive five-spired Mormon Temple sitting on a hill above town

Francisco now uses the top deck; eastbound traffic to Oakland, the lower.

The eastern cantilever section is raised on more than 20 piers. It climbs up from the toll plaza causeway in Oakland to 191 ft (58 m) above the bay at Yerba Buena Island. In 1989 a 50 ft (15 m) segment of the bridge collapsed during the Loma Prieta earthquake. The East Bay crossing was rebuilt between 2002 and 2013 in order to make it more earthquake resistant. The current suspension bridge features a single tower across the shipping channel, which gives way to a graceful sky-way. Boring through the island in a tunnel 76 ft (23 m) high and 58 ft (17 m) wide, the roadway emerges at the West Bay section of the bridge. Two suspension spans join at the concrete central anchorage, which is deeper in the water than that of any other bridge.

Mormon Temple Visitors' Center

🏠 4766 Lincoln Ave, Oakland 🚇 Fruitvale, then AC Transit 39 bus 🕐 9am–9pm daily 🌐 lds.org/locations/oakland-temple-visitors-center

Designed in 1963 and built on a hilltop, Oakland's Church of Jesus Christ of Latter-day Saints is one of only two Mormon temples in Northern California. The stunning building's central ziggurat is surrounded by four shorter towers, all terraced and clad with white granite and capped by gold pyramids.

Those eager to see the temple up close should first head to the Visitors' Center, which offers guided tours by missionaries, who explain the tenets of the faith with multimedia presentations.

Bay Bridge

🌐 baybridgeinfo.org

The San Francisco–Oakland Bay Bridge (known simply as the "Bay Bridge") was built from 1933–6. It consists of two distinct structures joining at Yerba Buena Island in the middle of the Bay, and reaches 4.5 miles (7.2 km) from shore to shore. Its completion heralded the end of the age of ferryboats on San Francisco Bay, by linking the peninsular city at Rincon Hill to the mainland at Oakland.

The bridge has two levels, originally housing road vehicles on the upper deck and trains and trucks below. However, the rail tracks were removed in the 1950s, leaving the bridge for use by more than 250,000 vehicles a day. Five traffic lanes wide, westbound traffic into San

⑬ 🏷️ 🖥️

Tilden Regional Park

📍 2501 Grizzly Peak Boulevard, Orinda
🚉 Downtown Berkeley, then AC Transit 67 bus
🕐 5am–10pm daily
🌐 ebparks.org/parks/tilden

Though preserved for the most part in a natural, wild condition, Tilden Park offers a variety of attractions. It is noted for the enchantingly landscaped **Botanic Garden**, specializing in California plants. Visitors can enjoy a leisurely stroll from alpine meadows to desert cactus gardens by way of a lovely redwood glen, and there are also guided nature walks. If you have children, make sure you don't miss the carousel, the miniature farmyard, and the model **steam train**.

Botanic Garden
📞 (510) 544-3169
🕐 8:30am–5pm daily (Jun–Sep: to 5:30pm)

Steam train
🏷️ 📞 (510) 548-6100
🕐 Summer: 11am–5pm daily; Winter: 11am–6pm Sat & Sun

⑭

Rockridge

🚉 Rockridge

A leafy residential area with large houses and flower gardens, Rockridge also attracts shoppers to College Avenue. The streets are lined with posh markets, boutiques, and al fresco restaurants.

⑮ 🍴 🛍️

Claremont Club and Spa

📍 41 Tunnel Rd, Berkeley
🚉 Rockridge, then AC Transit 79 bus 🌐 fairmont.com/claremont-berkeley

The Berkeley Hills form a backdrop to this chic, palatial hotel built in 1915. When Prohibition ended in 1933, the hotel failed to prosper like other similar establishments, due partly to a law that forbade the sale of alcohol within a 1-mile (1.6-km) radius of the Berkeley campus. After a change in the law in 1937, an enterprising student actually measured the distance, and found that the radius line passed through the center of the building, and so a hotel bar was built just beyond it.

As well as being one of the Bay Area's plushest hotels, this is a good place to have a drink and enjoy the views.

DRINK

The East Bay has a vibrant craft beer scene, with plenty of microbreweries and warehouse spaces with gardens.

Triple Rock Brewing
📍 1920 Shattuck Ave, Berkeley 🌐 triplerock.com

Jupiter
📍 2181 Shattuck Ave, Berkeley 🌐 jupiterbeer.com

Westbrae Biergarten
📍 1280 Gilman St, Berkeley
🌐 westbraebiergarten.com

⬅
Bay Bridge lit up at night with the stunning San Francisco skyline in the background

Shops and cafés on
Telegraph Avenue,
popular with students ↑

Berkeley

 **2030 Addison St;
www.visitberkeley.com**

Berkeley is renowned for
its university, **UC Berkeley**,
though some would argue
that its reputation for counter-
cultural movements some-
times eclipses its reputation
for academic excellence. For
all that, it remains one of the
most prestigious universities
in the world.

Founded as a utopian
"Athens of the Pacific" in 1868,
Berkeley has more than ten
Nobel Laureates among its
fellows and staff.

The campus (p228) was laid
out by landscape architect
Frederick Law Olmsted on
the twin forks of Strawberry
Creek; changes by San

Francisco architect David
Farquharson were later
adopted. Today there are over
41,000 students and a wide
range of museums, cultural
amenities, and a number of
buildings of note. These
include the **Phoebe A. Hearst
Museum of Anthropology**,
the **Berkeley Art Museum
and Pacific Film Archive**, and
Sather Tower, which is also
known as the Campanile.

At Berkeley's Strawberry
Canyon lies the **University
Botanical Garden**, where
more than 10,000 species
of plant from all over the
world thrive. Collections are
arranged in thematic gardens
linked by paths. Particularly
noteworthy are the Asian,
African, South American,
European, and California
gardens. The Chinese medicinal herb garden and the
carnivorous plants are also
well worth a visit.

Running from Downtown
Oakland to UC Berkeley is
arguably the most stimulating street in the East Bay:
Telegraph Avenue. The
blocks near UC Berkeley have
one of the highest concent-
rations of bookstores in the
country, in addition to which
there are plenty of coffee
houses and eateries. This
district was the center of

student protest in the 1960s.
Today it swarms with students
from dawn to dusk, along with
numerous street vendors,
musicians, protesters, artists,
and eccentrics.

If you are traveling with
children, don't miss the
Lawrence Hall of Science,
UC Berkeley's museum, which
makes science great fun for
all the family. The changing
interactive exhibits encourage
visitors of all ages to explore,
investigate, discover, and
invent, from plotting the
stars in the planetarium to
learning about animals, such
as pythons, geckos, lizards,
and rabbits, in the Animal
Discovery Room. You can
design your own rocket and
build a city with Lego bricks.
And in the National Geo-
graphic 3D Theater you can
experience science on the
big screen.

One of California's largest
collections of historical
artifacts pertaining to Jewish
culture, from ancient times
to today, is housed at the
**Magnes Collection of Jewish
Art and Life**. Among them are

→

The striking Cubist-style
Berkeley Art Museum and
Pacific Film Archive

> 💬 INSIDER TIP
> ### Take the Train
>
> Berkeley can be easily
> reached in around 30
> minutes from down-
> town San Francisco.
> The Downtown
> Berkeley BART station
> on Shattuck Avenue
> is within walking
> distance of the campus.

fine art treasures from Europe and India, paintings by Marc Chagall and Max Liebermann, and poignant reminders of Nazi Germany, such as a burned Torah scroll rescued from a synagogue. Lectures, films, and traveling exhibits enliven the halls.

When you are ready for something to eat, head for "**Gourmet Ghetto**", a north Berkeley neighborhood, which acquired fame as something of a foodie destination when American chef Alice Waters opened Chez Panisse here in 1971. The restaurant on 1517 Shattuck Ave is acclaimed for its use of fresh local ingredients in a French-inspired style that gave rise to what is known as California cuisine. In its original house on Shattuck Avenue, Chez Panisse has influenced many worthy imitators. There is also an abundance of specialty markets and coffee houses in the neighborhood.

Another rewarding neighborhood is **Fourth Street**, a gentrified enclave north of University Avenue, characteristic of Berkeley's climate of fine craftsmanship and exquisite taste. Here you can buy everything from handmade paper and stained-glass windows to organically grown lettuce and designer garden tools. It is also known for its restaurants *(p229)*.

UC Berkeley
Visitor Center: 2227 Piedmont Ave 🚇Downtown Berkeley

Phoebe A. Hearst Museum of Anthropology
103 Kroeber Hall 🕐11am-5pm Wed-Sun (to 8pm Thu) 🌐hearstmuseum. berkeley.edu

Berkeley Art Museum and Pacific Film Archive
2155 Center St 🚇Downtown Berkeley 🕐11am-7pm Wed-Sun (to 9pm Fri & Sat) 🌐bampfa.org

University Botanical Garden
200 Centennial Dr 🚌H 🕐9am-5pm daily 🌐botanicalgarden. berkeley.edu

Telegraph Avenue
🚌AC Transit 800 🚇Downtown Berkeley

Lawrence Hall of Science
Centennial Dr 🚌From Mining Circle, UC Berkeley (except Sat, Sun & hols) 🚇Downtown Berkeley, then AC Transit 65 bus 🕐10am-5pm Wed-Sun (Summer: daily) 🌐lawrencehall ofscience.org

Magnes Collection of Jewish Art and Life
Bancroft Library, UC Berkeley, 2121 Allston Way 🚇Downtown Berkeley, 🚌AC Transit 6, 7, 18, 51B, 52, 65, 67, 79, 88, F 🕐11am-4pm Tue-Fri (during the academic year only) 🌐magnes. berkeley.edu

Gourmet Ghetto
Upper Shattuck Ave 🚇Downtown Berkeley, then AC Transit 7, 18, 67 bus 🌐gourmetghetto.org

Fourth Street
🚌AC Transit Z 🚇Ashby, then AC Transit 51B, Z bus

A LONG WALK
THE UNIVERSITY OF CALIFORNIA CAMPUS IN BERKELEY

Distance 2.5 miles (4 km) **Time** 50 minutes
Terrain Some sloping paths and hills, which provide beautiful views **Nearest BART station** Downtown Berkeley

This walk concentrates on a distinct area of Berkeley: the campus of the distinguished University of California *(p226)*. A stroll around the area offers a stimulating glimpse into the intellectual, cultural, and social life of this vibrant university town. Its days as "Berzerkeley" – when student protestors and tear-gas clouds filled the streets in the 1960s – are only a fading memory now, and the campus is a lovely place for a walk, full of natural spaces, interesting architecture to admire, and museums to explore.

Follow University Drive past the **Valley Life Sciences Building**, *which contains natural history, zoology, and paleontology museums.*

Head into campus via **The Crescent**.

Cross over Strawberry Creek at Bay Tree Bridge, and bear left for the nature area, with its eucalyptus trees, some of the tallest in the world.

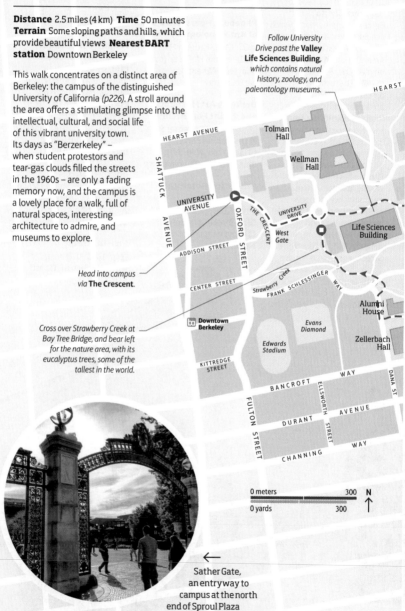

HEARST AVENUE
HEARST
Tolman Hall
Wellman Hall
SHATTUCK AVENUE
UNIVERSITY AVENUE
OXFORD STREET
THE CRESCENT
UNIVERSITY DRIVE
West Gate
Life Sciences Building
ADDISON STREET
CENTER STREET
Strawberry Creek
FRANK SCHLESSINGER WAY
Alumni House
Downtown Berkeley
Evans Diamond
Edwards Stadium
Zellerbach Hall
KITTREDGE STREET
BANCROFT WAY
DANA ST
FULTON STREET
ELLSWORTH STREET
DURANT AVENUE
CHANNING WAY

0 meters   300
0 yards   300
N ↑

← Sather Gate, an entryway to campus at the north end of Sproul Plaza

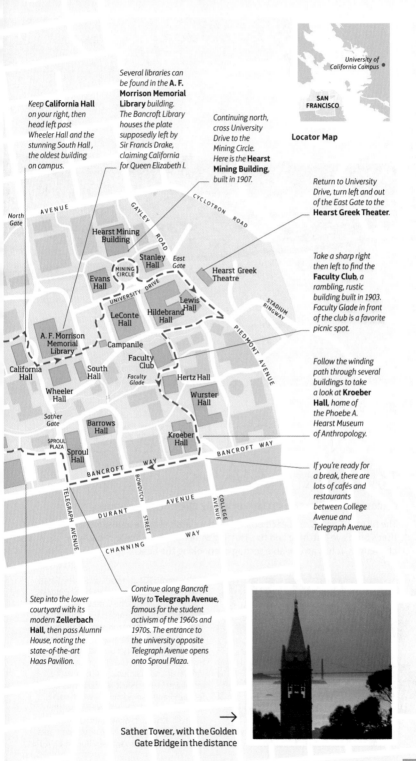

Keep **California Hall** on your right, then head left past Wheeler Hall and the stunning South Hall , the oldest building on campus.

Several libraries can be found in the **A. F. Morrison Memorial Library** building. The Bancroft Library houses the plate supposedly left by Sir Francis Drake, claiming California for Queen Elizabeth I.

Continuing north, cross University Drive to the Mining Circle. Here is the **Hearst Mining Building**, built in 1907.

Return to University Drive, turn left and out of the East Gate to the **Hearst Greek Theater**.

Take a sharp right then left to find the **Faculty Club**, a rambling, rustic building built in 1903. Faculty Glade in front of the club is a favorite picnic spot.

Follow the winding path through several buildings to take a look at **Kroeber Hall**, home of the Phoebe A. Hearst Museum of Anthropology.

If you're ready for a break, there are lots of cafés and restaurants between College Avenue and Telegraph Avenue.

Step into the lower courtyard with its modern **Zellerbach Hall**, then pass Alumni House, noting the state-of-the-art Haas Pavilion.

Continue along Bancroft Way to **Telegraph Avenue**, famous for the student activism of the 1960s and 1970s. The entrance to the university opposite Telegraph Avenue opens onto Sproul Plaza.

University of California Campus

SAN FRANCISCO

Locator Map

North Gate

AVENUE

GAYLEY ROAD

CYCLOTRON ROAD

Hearst Mining Building

Stanley Hall

East Gate

MINING CIRCLE

Evans Hall

UNIVERSITY DRIVE

Hearst Greek Theatre

STADIUM RINGWAY

LeConte Hall

Hildebrand Hall

Lewis Hall

A. F. Morrison Memorial Library

Campanile

PIEDMONT AVENUE

California Hall

South Hall

Faculty Glade

Faculty Club

Hertz Hall

Wheeler Hall

Sather Gate

Wurster Hall

Barrows Hall

Kroeber Hall

BANCROFT WAY

SPROUL PLAZA

Sproul Hall

BANCROFT WAY

BOWDITCH STREET

AVENUE

COLLEGE AVENUE

TELEGRAPH AVENUE

DURANT AVENUE

WAY

CHANNING

→ Sather Tower, with the Golden Gate Bridge in the distance

Did You Know?

The Giant Dipper reaches a height of 70 ft (21 m) and speeds of 55 mph (89 km/h).

17 ⊘ ▭ 🛍

SANTA CRUZ BEACH BOARDWALK

⌂ 400 Beach St, Santa Cruz ⏰ 11am – 8pm daily 🌐 beachboardwalk.com

The historic Santa Cruz Beach Boardwalk is a classic seaside amusement park that's both eye-catching and fun. Hosting thrill rides and family-friendly attractions, it has an enviable setting overlooking the beach.

↑ Visitors swarming between the brightly colored rides along the Boardwalk

Dating from 1907 and dominating the Santa Cruz waterfront, the Boardwalk is the oldest amusement park on the West Coast. The entire Boardwalk is a California Historic Landmark, and although most of the original amusements have been replaced by modern rides, two still-functioning centenary rides are National Historic Landmarks. The first of these is the classic Looff carousel; one of only five remaining in the USA, it was built in 1911 and features hand-carved horses, which spin to music from a 19th-century pipe organ. But the main attraction is undoubtedly the Giant Dipper roller-coaster, whose wave-like tracks soar up above the Boardwalk. Built in 1924, this

↑ Skyline of the Boardwalk's amusement park, dominated by the Giant Dipper

← Visitors enjoying a sunset ride on the Sky Glider

TOP 4 BOARDWALK HIGHLIGHTS

Wild Rides
There are over two dozen rides for thrill-seekers to enjoy.

Sweet Snacks
From cotton candy and churros to fish and chips, you'll be spoilt for choice come snack time.

Sea Lions
Head to the Santa Cruz Wharf to watch the sea lions relax in the sun.

Main Beach
A sandy stretch with volleyball nets and gentle waves, and movies screened in summer.

red-and-white landmark still provides riders with a swooping, heart-pounding adrenaline rush. The apogee of the Giant Dipper, along with those of other thrill rides along the Boardwalk, offers a postcard view of sand, sea, and the Santa Cruz Pier. Slightly more low-key attractions in the area include a video arcade, a laser tag arena and laser maze challenge, and even an ice-skating rink in winter. There are also plenty of gentler rides that aim to delight toddlers. If the crowds become too much, head to the Santa Cruz Wharf for a leisurely stroll or a quiet coffee break, and stunning views from the pier.

⑱ 🍴 🥤 🛍️

HALF MOON BAY

📍 ℹ️ 235 Main Street; www.visithalfmoonbay.org

A perfect weekend getaway, the small town of Half Moon Bay – located between San Francisco and Santa Cruz – is home to great beaches and some of the world's most epic waves and surfing contests. It also falls along the gray whale coastal migration path, offering front-row seats to this magnificent spectacle.

Founded in the 1840s as a small fishing and agricultural community, Half Moon Bay later developed as a beach resort. Its Main Street still displays renovated Victorian buildings that house quaint art galleries, shops and restaurants. Inland, the Pilarcitos Creek watershed protects many rare wildlife species. Half Moon Bay's State Beach is comprised of four contiguous beaches (Francis, Venice, Dunes, and Roosevelt) that unfurl for 4 miles (6 km). While it's ideal for long, leisurely walks, swimming is not advised due to rip currents. At the north end of the bay is Mirada Surf Beach, at the lively resort of El Granada. Sheltered within its harbor – once a whaling station – are three lovely beaches that are safe for swimming, including Princeton Beach and Pillar Point Harbor Beach. Outside the harbor, white-sand Mavericks Beach has panoramic bay views and is a great place for experienced surfers to tackle the region's legendary waves.

Another good spot in the Half Moon Bay area is the photogenic Montara Lighthouse. It was transferred from Cape Cod in 1928, and from

here gray whales may be glimpsed migrating close to shore during winter. To its south, scimitar-shaped Moss Beach is popular for the Fitzgerald Marine Reserve; its tidepools teem with starfish, anemones, and crabs at low tide.

Pumpkins are a major crop around Half Moon Bay, and the annual Art & Pumpkin Festival is a highlight of the local calendar. In late October, 250,000 visitors pour in for the weekend-long festival featuring costume and pie-eating contests, and a parade of gargantuan gourds (which often exceed 1,000 kg/2,200 lbs in weight). The festival also includes arts and crafts, music concerts, and tasty pumpkin-based treats.

1 The patio at the Half Moon Bay Brewing Company is a popular spot in summer.

2 Many species of wildlife may be found in the region, including pelicans.

3 The gentle curve of the bay's coastline is also home to a links golf course.

← Stretches of beach in Half Moon Bay, which may offer either gentle surf or giant waves *(inset)*

EAT

Sam's Chowder House

A waterfront favorite known for its signature New England-style chowder. Head outside for firepits on the patio.

⌂ 42010 N. Cabrillo Hwy
ⓦ samschowder house.com

⑤⑤⑤

Half Moon Bay Brewing Company

Hearty dishes such as fish and chips washed down by choice brews, from a light pilsner to a creamy dark stout.

⌂ 390 Capistrano Rd
ⓦ hmbbrewingco.com

⑤⑤⑤

THE PENINSULA

19

San Jose

📧🏠🚍🚕 ℹ️ **408 Almaden Blvd; www.sanjose.org**

The original capital city of California, San Jose is now the nation's capital for innovation and industry, home to major companies like Adobe, Samsung, and eBay, with headquarters for Apple Inc, Facebook, and Google also located nearby. As the tenth largest city in the US with many residents being professionals in hi-tech industries, San Jose citizens enjoy high disposable income, although this is slightly offset by its astronomical rents.

In contrast to the modern atmosphere of downtown San Jose, **The Winchester Mystery House®** is one of the city's oldest and most unique attractions. In 1884 Sarah Winchester, heiress of the rifle fortune, was grieving over the loss of her child and husband. She consulted a medium who advised her to build a house that would never be completed, in order to silence the evil spirits that haunted her. She employed carpenters for 38 years and built 160 rooms set amidst beautiful gardens. The stairways that lead nowhere and windows set into the floor are just a few of the oddities within. Book a Flashlight Tour to see it at its creepiest.

For more standard – but no less fascinating – attractions, San Jose also has its fair share

of museums. Inspired by the Temple of Amon at Karnak, Egypt, the **Rosicrucian Egyptian Museum** houses ancient Egyptian, Babylonian, Assyrian, and Sumerian artifacts. Funerary boats, mummies, Coptic textiles, pottery, jewelry, and a full-size tomb are on display. The museum's accompanying planetarium – one of the oldest in the country – also has daily and special weekend shows. The **Tech Museum of Innovation** is a colorful technological museum divided into several themed galleries, including exploration, biodesign and virtual reality. Many of the exhibits have a "hands-on" element, such as designing robots or measuring your moods with wearable technology. The Body Worlds Decoded exhibition uses augmented reality to examine what is going on inside the human body. The **Children's Discovery Museum** is great for families and kids of all ages. Children can play in a real red fire engine or in an

 ←

The weird and wonderful Winchester Mystery House® set in beautiful gardens

ambulance with flashing lights, and the more adventurous can climb trees connected by sky bridges in the outdoor Tree Climber. At the Waterways exhibit, kids will enjoy discovering the special properties of water by creating unique fountains from magnetic half-pipes. There's even a hands-on, early-learning exhibit for children aged 0–4.

For a museum with a twist, **History Park** is a charming attraction in Kelley Park that re-creates San Jose as it was in the early 20th century. More than 21 original houses and businesses have been restored and set around a town square. They include a fire station, an ice-cream parlor with a working soda fountain, a gas station, and a vintage trolley that travels around the grounds.

The Winchester Mystery House®

⊛⊛⊝⊕ 🏠525 South Winchester Blvd ⏰9am-5pm daily 🌐winchester mysteryhouse.com

Rosicrucian Egyptian Museum

⊛ 🏠1660 Park Ave ⏰9am-5pm Wed-Fri, 10am-6pm Sat & Sun 🌐egyptian museum.org

Tech Museum of Innovation

⊛⊝⊕ 🏠201 South Market St (at Park Ave) ⏰10am-5pm daily 🌐thetech.org

Children's Discovery Museum

⊛⊝⊕ 🏠180 Woz Way ⏰10am-4pm Tue-Sat (to 5pm Sat), noon-5pm Sun; Summer: also 10am-4pm Mon 🌐cdm.org

History Park

⊛ 🏠1650 Senter Rd ⏰Noon-5pm Mon-Fri, 11am-5pm Sat & Sun 🌐historysan jose.org

EAT

Outdoor dining is a way of life in sunny California, and San Jose offers lots of options for those who want to join in the tradition.

SP2 Communal Bar + Restaurant
🏠72 N Almaden Ave ⏰Mon 🌐sp2sanjose. com.

$$⑤

Scott's Seafood
🏠185 Park Ave 🌐scottsseafoodsj.com

$$$

Siena Bistro
🏠1359 Lincoln Ave ⏰Sun & Mon 🌐sienabistro.com

$$⑤

↑ Families exploring a fire engine at the Children's Discovery Museum, San Jose

←
The Romanesque-style arches of the Memorial Church, Stanford University

Stanford University

🚩 Palo Alto 🚉 Caltrain to Palo Alto station
🌐 stanford.edu

One of the country's most prestigious private universities, with over 16,000 students, Stanford was built by railroad mogul Leland Stanford in memory of his son, and opened in 1891. The heart of the campus is the Main Quad, designed mainly in Romanesque style. The main landmarks are the Hoover Tower, the Memorial Church, and the Stanford University Museum of Art, where you can see the Golden Spike that completed the transcontinental railroad in 1869. The Cantor Arts Center owns an impressive collection of Rodin sculptures. For guided tours of the college phone 650-723-2560.

STAY

Stanford Park Hotel
This colonial-style building oozes grandeur, from the antiques in the lobby to the elegant grounds.

🚩 100 El Camino Real, Menlo Park
🌐 stanfordpark hotel.com

$$$

Pescadero Creek Inn
A quiet and charming spot for those who want to get out of the busy cities of the Bay Area and back to nature.

🚩 393 Stage Rd, Pescadero
🌐 pescadero creekinn.com

$$$

Año Nuevo

🚩 Take Cabrillo Hwy, then New Years Creek Rd
⏰ 8am–6pm daily
🌐 parks.ca.gov

In the 19th-century, northern elephant seals were hunted almost to extinction for their oil-rich blubber. They disappeared from many traditional habitats along the Pacific Coast, including Año Nuevo. Descendants of the survivors began showing up here in the 1950s. Today, a year-round population is protected within this State Park, 20 miles (32 km) north of Santa Cruz. The site is a traditional breeding ground for the world's largest seals, which leave the sea to mate, give birth, and laze in the sun. In winter months, males (which are typically five times bigger than females) engage in bloody battles for harem dominance. Visits are limited to guided naturalist walks during mating season. Stellar sea lions also breed here, and sea otters can be seen foraging in the kelp. In addition, Año Nuevo Point is a great birding spot. Viewing the seals requires a 3-mile (5-km) hike along sandy trails.

Did you know?

The Pescadero State Beach is a long swath of sand backed by rocky cliffs.

→
Remote and beautiful Pigeon Point Lighthouse near Pescadero

22

Pescadero

 Daly City, then SamTrans 118 to Linda Mar park and ride, then 17 bus

Only an hour's drive from San Francisco to the north and Silicon Valley to the east, the picturesque town of Pescadero is a pleasant escape from the fast-paced world around it. Athough it contains little more than a white-washed church (the oldest in the county), a general store, a post office, and the popular Duarte's Tavern along its two main streets, the town has the charming and photogenic appearance of an old movie set. Its many white-washed buildings follow a tradition that goes back to the 19th century, when a cargo of white paint was rescued from a nearby shipwreck.

Eight miles (12 km) south is **Pigeon Point Light Station State Historic Park**, where visitors can enjoy the scenery and views. Tours of the area are offered by volunteers at 1pm from Thursday through Monday (call 650-879-2120 to check availability or book).

About 20 minutes south, families can enjoy Swanton Berry Farm's **Coastways Ranch U-Pick** for an afternoon of fruit-picking.

Pigeon Point Light Station State Historic Park

⊛ ⊜ 210 Pigeon Point Rd 8am-sunset parks.ca. gov

Coastways Ranch U-Pick

⊛ 640 Hwy 1 May-Oct: 8am-5pm swantonberry farm.com

23

Filoli

86 Cañada Rd, near Edgewood Rd, Woodside 10am-5pm Tue-Sun filoli.org

The lavish 43-room Filoli mansion was built in 1915 for William Bourne II, owner of the Empire Gold Mine. Gold from the mine was used in its opulent decoration. The elegant house is surrounded by a large, enchanting garden, with many English garden-style features, and an estate where guided nature walks, as well as tours of the orchard can be arranged. "Filoli" stands for "Fight, love, live," which refers to Bourne's love for the Irish and their struggle. You can either visit the house on your own or take a guided tour, which costs a little extra.

24

NAPA VALLEY WINE COUNTRY

 🅸 600 Main St, Napa; www.visitnapavalley.com

Since the legendary Judgment of Paris in 1976 – when the Napa Valley wines beat Burgundy to top honours in both the red and white categories – this region has been firmly on every wine-lover's radar. People also come for the experience; to tour grand chateaux, dine at world-renowned restaurants, and sip small-batch wines in tiny, boutique tasting rooms.

①

Charles Krug Winery

🄰 2800 Main St, St. Helena
🕒 10:30am–5pm daily
🅦 charleskrug.com

Many firsts can be attributed to Napa Valley's oldest winery. Charles Krug, who founded the estate in 1861, was a pioneer of varietal labelling. It was also the first to import French oak barrels for wine aging. The tasting room, yet another first in California when it opened to the public in 1882, is the crowning glory, with a soft peach, Tuscan-style

exterior leading to a sleek space with daily tastings of limited-release wines.

②

V. Sattui

🄰 1111 White Lane, St. Helena
🕒 9am–6pm daily (Winter: to 5pm) 🅦 vsattui.com

With tasting room staff pouring everything from estate cabernet to champagne-method bubbles, you can't really go wrong at V. Sattui. Even those who aren't wine lovers can delight in exploring

the vast grounds, with vine-combed slopes and shaded picnic areas. Book in advance to take a tour through the cellars and listen to the fascinating history of this family-run winery, which was started in San Francisco in the 19th century, destroyed by Prohibition and, finally, resurrected here in 1976.

③

The French Laundry

🄰 6640 Washington St, Yountville 🚌 10 🕒 Times vary, see website
🅦 thomaskeller.com

Possibly the most coveted tables in Napa Valley are those that fill the chic dining room of Thomas Keller's venerable restaurant.

↑ A glass of Twin Oaks wine being served at Robert Mondavi winery

↑ The rolling hills and stunning golden vineyards of Napa Valley

Its unlikely location in the rural village of Yountville, and the cozy atmosphere inside, belie the intense work that goes into the ever-changing daily menu. Each of the nine courses is underpinned by classical French cooking and Keller's formidable imagination, which has earned his restaurant the top Michelin rating of three stars.

④ 🎨 🍴 🏛

Robert Mondavi Winery

🏠 7801 St. Helena Hwy, Oakville 🚌 10 🕐 Times vary, see website 🌐 robert mondaviwinery.com

The flagship estate of one of Napa's pioneering vineyard owners is styled to resemble California's Spanish missions, with graceful arches and a vast, elegant courtyard. A passionate ambassador for Napa Valley wines until his death in 2008, Robert Mondavi is credited with helping to elevate the area to one of the world's most recognised wine regions. Still family-run, the winery continues to pour its

renowned cabernets and signature fumé blanc, fermented with sauvignon blanc grapes. Visitors can join tasting flights, cellar tastings with reserve wines, and barrel room tours.

⑤ 🎨 🍴 🏛

Domaine Chandon

🏠 1 California Dr, Yountville 🚌 29 🕐 10am–5pm daily 🌐 chandon.com

From classic brut to blushing rosé, it's all about the bubbles at Domaine Chandon, a lavish estate founded by Moët & Chandon in 1973. While it exudes a certain French elegance, there's nothing stuffy about the atmosphere. As befits a spot specializing in fizz, a visit here is all about having a good time.

Experiences range from tasting flights, including the estate's still varieties, to weekend mixology classes, when participants can make and sip cocktails using the signature sparkling wine.

⑥ 🎨 🏛

Opus One Winery

🏠 7900 St. Helena Hwy, Oakville 🚌 10 🕐 10am–4pm daily 🌐 opusone winery.com

Opus One was founded in 1979 as an unprecedented joint venture between two wine legends – Napa Valley's Robert Mondavi and Baron Philippe de Rothschild, founder of Château Mouton Rothschild in Bordeaux, France. Their plan was to create a single, world-class Bordeaux blend based on California cabernet, and their legacy is a wine that is consistently considered one of Napa's best.

The striking stone building of the winery, tucked low against the hillside, hosts intimate, appointment-only tastings of the current vintage, or you can book a tour to explore the vast grounds and production areas.

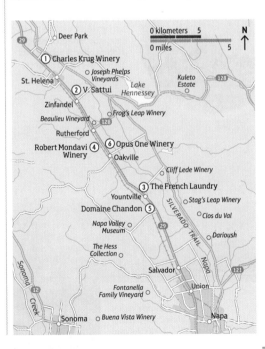

NAPA VALLEY

 25

St. Helena

 1320 Main St; www.sthelena.com

Perhaps the most polished of Napa Valley's towns, St. Helena overflows with the temptation to shop, sip, and eat. The charming and quaint Main Street is packed with cocktail bars and restaurants firmly focused on vibrant local and seasonal ingredients. You can delve deeper into the scene at the **Culinary Institute of America at Greystone**; responsible for training many a star chef, the institute also offers cooking classes, demonstrations and tastings. Or you can enjoy a more leisurely experience with a meal cooked by the next generation of cooking talent at the onsite restaurant. You'll discover some of the area's most revered wine estates, including Charles Krug (p238) and **Beringer**, in the surrounding vine-clad hillsides.

Culinary Institute of America at Greystone
2555 Main St, St. Helena ciachef.edu

Beringer
10am–5:30pm daily beringer.com

26

Calistoga

1133 Washington St; www.visitcalistoga.com

At the northern tip of the Napa Valley, the laid-back town of Calistoga is renowned for its geothermal waters and mud baths. The resorts here take full advantage of both, offering indulgent spa treatments and pools fed by hot springs. Typical of the town's retro-cool vibe is **Calistoga Motor Lodge & Spa**, with its tucked-away garden, where guests can slather on mud before drying out in the sun. The main drag of Lincoln Avenue is dotted with quirky gift stores, bookshops, and galleries. The hillsides are dominated by grand wineries, including **Castello di**

TOP 3 LUXURY EXPERIENCES IN NAPA VALLEY

Napa Valley Aloft
Hot-air balloons launch daily at sunrise for peaceful voyages over the vineyards, with distant views of San Francisco's skyline (www.nvaloft.com).

Spa Terra at Meritage Resort
Nestled in a wine cave, this resort offers treatments, mineral pools and heat rooms (www.meritagecollection.com).

Napa Valley Wine Train
Pullman carriages chug through the landscape for tasting tours or fine-dining experiences (www.winetrain.com).

→ The Napa Valley Wine Train passing by a vineyard

Amorosa, housed in a medieval-style castle. And, with direct access to the famed routes of Highway 29 and the Silverado Trail, there are plenty more wine-tasting opportunities nearby.

Calistoga Motor Lodge & Spa
⌂ 1880 Lincoln Ave
ⓦ calistogamotorlodge andspa.com

Castello di Amorosa
⊛ ⊛ ⌂ 4045 St. Helena Hwy
ⓦ castellodiamorosa.com

㉗ ⊛ ⌨ ⌂

Old Faithful Geyser

⌂ 1299 Tubbs Ln, Calistoga
🚌 10, 29 ⏰ 8:30am–7pm daily (Oct–Feb: to 5pm)
ⓦ oldfaithfulgeyser.com

Though not as famous as the bigger "Old Faithful" in Wyoming, California's smaller version is still one of the few geysers in the world erupting at predictable intervals (every 20–30 minutes). Its occasional failure to erupt has been linked to imminent earthquakes. Casting a light mist through the air and often creating a hazy rainbow, the eruptions make for a

↑ An eruption of boiling water and steam at Old Faithful Geyser

particularly picturesque picnic backdrop. The grounds around the geyser contain a geology museum, gardens, and a farm. Try not to frighten the goats here: these black-and-white creatures are Tennessee Fainting Goats, which stiffen and topple over when they sense danger. Other weird and wonderful animals occupying a section of the site's grounds include four-horn sheep and guard llamas.

㉘

Napa

🚌 🛈 1331 1st St, Napa;
www.napatouristinfo.com

There's an undeniable air of sophistication to downtown Napa, from Michelin-starred dining to the excellent **Blue Note** jazz club, and First Street Napa – an open-air shopping mall with boutiques and galleries – all clustered within a few blocks. There are

plenty of opportunities for wine sampling at tasting rooms and bonded wineries; at **Vintner's Collective** you can try small-batch wines not available anywhere else.

Blue Note
⊛ ⌂ 1030 Main St ⏰ Times vary, check website
ⓦ bluenotenapa.com

Vintner's Collective
⊛ ⌂ 1245 Main St
⏰ 11am–7pm daily
ⓦ vintnerscollective.com

> 💬 INSIDER TIP
> ### Microclimate
> Napa Valley has several microclimates that can cause the temperature to vary considerably from north to south, and by as much as 30 °F (15 °C) from morning to night. Pack carefully so you don't get caught out by a sudden chill.

29

HEALDSBURG

🚋 🈯 217 Healdsburg Ave; www.healdsburg.com

Nestled in the Alexander Valley and surrounded by the nation's top wine regions, Healdsburg is a beautiful town with a small-village feel. Its tree-shaded streets are lined with Victorian mansions that house boutiques, restaurants, and wine-tasting rooms.

EXPERIENCE Sonoma County

Today this lively and progressive river-front town combines old-fashioned charm with hip eateries. At its heart is a classic 19th-century Spanish plaza, shaded by soaring coast redwoods and surrounded by excellent antiques stores. The Russian River runs through town, and visitors can enjoy canoeing and kayaking at various points along its length. On one bend of the river in the south side of town lies Veterans Memorial Beach, a silvery swath of sand beside the historic steel-truss Memorial Bridge. This popular stretch is staffed with lifeguards, and offers calm swimming in summer.

Healdsburg Museum

This regional museum is a hidden gem housed in the neo-Classical Healdsburg Library, which is located on Matheson Street. Entry is free, and inside it profiles the history of Sonoma County with fascinating exhibits that include Native American Pomo and Wapo basketry, and an eclectic miscellany of historical artifacts. A touch-screen computer station also offers an animated 3D tour of the plaza.

↑ Diners sitting beneath wide canopies at one of Healdsburg's many restaurants

→ The meticulously tended vines and fruit *(inset)* of a vineyard in Healdsburg

Did You Know?

Smithsonian magazine placed Healdsburg second in its 2014 list of "America's 20 Best Small Towns."

EAT & DRINK

SingleThread

The 11-course tasting menu uses ingredients fresh from the restaurant's own farm. You'll need to book well in advance to enjoy this popular Michelin-starred spot.

🏠 **131 North St** ⓦ **single threadfarms.com**

$$$

SHED Café

Located in a stylish, airy space, this hip restaurant serves a fusion menu using fresh, locally sourced organic produce.

🏠 **25 North Street** ⓦ **healdsburgshed.com**

$$⑤

The Brass Rabbit

Bare brick walls and a wooden floor comple-ment a menu of American classics, served alongside cocktails such as Mint Juleps and Manhattans.

🏠 **109 Plaza St** ⓦ **thebrassrabbit healdsburg.com**

$$⑤

Wineries

Located at the junction of three major wine-growing regions, Healdsburg is surrounded by dozens of wineries, most of which are open to visit. South of town, Rodney Strong Vineyards offers complimentary tours and year-round events, many hosted in an outdoor amphi-theater. Nearby, the ruggedly beautiful Chalk Hill Estate has a renowned culinary program. And at Ferrari-Carano, a gorgeous Italianate winery in Dry Creek Valley, paths meander through a 5 acre (2-ha) garden that boasts a kaleidoscope of color throughout the year.

SONOMA COUNTY

 30

Francis Ford Coppola Winery

🏠 **300 Via Archimedes, Geyserville** 🚌 **60** 🕐 **11am–9pm daily** 🌐 **francisford coppolawinery.com**

This resort winery produces award-winning wines and is famous as the quasi Hollywood of Wine Country estates. Movie producer (and winery owner) Francis Ford Coppola has stamped his legacy throughout the French-style stone château. Sampling wines here is secondary to admiring the displays of iconic memorabilia from Coppola's movies, including Don Corleone's desk from *The Godfather* and Colonel Kurtz's uniform from *Apocalypse Now*. Scenes from the movies are screened and Coppola's Oscars are on display. Don't miss the Bottling Ballet Mécanique Tour, a behind-the-scenes tour of the bottling plant. Coppola's personal Italian passion for fine food is reflected in a gourmet restaurant with gorgeous views from the terrace over the Alexander Valley. Plus,

there are Bocce ball courts, swimming pool, and a Performing Arts Pavilion, the venue for free live entertainment every weekend from April through October.

31

Bodega Bay

🚌 ℹ️ **913 Hwy 1; www. bodegabay.com**

In 1963 the coastal town of Bodega Bay appeared in Alfred Hitchcock's *The Birds*. In the tiny neighboring town of Boedga, visitors can still see the Potter Schoolhouse, which was used in the film. The area is now a very popular resort destination known for its sea-weathered clapboard homes, golf courses, and nearby beaches. It also boasts a thriving deep-sea fishing community, and visitors can watch the fishing fleets unload their day's catch at Tides Wharf dock on Highway 1.

Bodega Head, the rugged hook-like peninsula that shelters Bodega Bay, is one of California's best whale-watching points. The northern end of the bay marks the start

10 miles

The length of coast designated as Sonoma Coast State Park (16 km).

of **Sonoma Coast State Park**, which is scalloped with miles of sandy coves separated by surging headlands and rocky bluffs. Swimming is generally not safe owing to strong waves and undertows, but the area offers fabulous clifftop hiking and sublime vistas.

Sonoma Coast State Park
🌐 parks.ca.gov

32

Guerneville

🚌 ℹ️ **16200 First St; www. guerneville-online.com**

Surrounded by towering redwoods, this charmingly rustic town spans the wide, lazy Russian River in the heart of the Russian River Valley Wine Region. It's known for its famously laid-back attitudes and for its riverside resorts, many popular with a gay clientele. Main Street is lined with trendy art galleries, boutiques, and cafés, many housed in quaint Victorian buildings,

↑ Patrons enjoying food on the terrace at Francis Ford Coppola Winery

↑ One of the sandy coves that characterizes Sonoma Coast State Park, near Bodega Bay

gaily colored as if by Crayola. In summer, you can rent a chair and umbrella and spend a few hours lazing on the riverside gray-sand Johnson's Beach; float in a rented inner-tube; or get some exercise on a paddle boat or kayak. The beach has a roped-off "kiddy pool" and is open on week-ends from May through September. Camping in nearby Armstrong Redwoods State Park is serenely satisfying any time of year. And you'll want to visit some of the more than 50 local wineries, such as **Korbel Champagne Cellars**, famous for its California Champagnes.

Korbel Champagne Cellars

 13250 River Rd, Guerneville ⓦ korbel.com

㉝
Santa Rosa

🖷 🛈 9 Fourth St; www. visitsantarosa.com

At the northern end of the Sonoma Valley, Santa Rosa is the largest city in wine country. This peaceful town is a lively center for the arts and has many sites of interest. A good place to start is Railroad Square Historic District, a hip enclave of fine-dining, galleries and boutiques, built in the early 20th century by Italian stonemasons. Don't miss the Church of the One Tree, built in 1873 from the wood of a single redwood tree; and the Sonoma County Museum, dedicated to the arts and history of the Wine Region. Cartoon-lovers will appreciate the Charles M. Schultz Museum, honoring Snoopy and his creator. On the edge of downtown, the Luther Burbank Home & Gardens preserves a modest Greek Revival house where horticulturalist Luther Burbank lived and conducted plant-breeding experiments. For a bucolic escape, Shiloh Ranch Regional Park is laced with trails and rich in wildlife,.

㉞
Armstrong Redwoods State Park

🏠 17000 Armstrong Woods Rd, Guerneville 🚌 20, 28 🕗 8am to 1 hour after sunset daily ⓦ parks.ca.gov

Only a five-minute drive from Guerneville, but a whole world away from urbanity, this 1.3 sq mile (3.3 sq km) grove of majestic coast redwoods provides a cool summer escape amid the world's tallest living things. The tallest tree in the grove, Parson's Tree, soars to 310 feet (95 m). Hiking beneath the soaring canopy – or better still, camping – is a sublime experience. Several inter-linked self-guided nature trails total 6 miles (9 km).

STAY

Farmhouse Inn

Wine on arrival, a Michelin-starred restaurant, and suites with enormous double-sided fireplaces all contribute to the sense of understated luxury at this secluded hotel. Rooms are arranged around the outdoor pool and surrounded by quiet woodlands.

🏠 7871 River Rd, Forestville ⓦ farmhouseinn.com

ⓢⓢⓢ

35 Fort Ross State Historic Park

📍 19005 Coast Hwy 1
🚌 95 🕐 Sunrise-sunset daily; buildings: 10am-4:30pm 🌐 parks.ca.gov

Occupying a breezy oceanfront perch, Fort Ross State Historic Park preserves a wooden stockade community that flourished as the southernmost Russian settlement in North America from 1821 to 1841. Named for Rossia (Russia), it was established by the Russian–American Company as an agricultural colony and base for hunting sea otters.

The reconstructed and restored buildings offer a fascinating insight into life for Russians in the contested world of early 19th-century California. A scenic trail leads from the Visitor Center and Museum to the wooden stockade. The only original Russian structure is Rotcher House, which belonged to the company manager, decorated with homely furnishings. The Kuskov House displays weapons and agricultural tools, while another building is devoted to the crafts – including tanning, carpentry, and blacksmithing – which sustained the Russians. A tiny Russian Orthodox chapel is adorned with religious icons. Don't miss the nearby Russian Cemetery, with its weatherbeaten wooden crosses.

36 Gloria Ferrer Champagne Caves

📍 23555 Arnold Dr, Sonoma
🚌 32 🕐 10am-5pm daily
🌐 gloriaferrer.com

This beautiful Spanish Mission-style winery and large estate, 5 miles (8 km) south of Sonoma, is renowned for its distinctive sparkling wines using Méthode Champenoise blends. Located in the Los Carneros AVA (American Viticultural Area) at the southern end of the Sonoma Valley, the winery's distinct *terroir* is influenced by the cool air and creeping fogs of the Pacific Ocean: perfect conditions for growing Chardonnay and Pinot Noir grapes that are used for Gloria Ferrer's famous "blanc de noirs" – sparkling wine made from red grape varieties. The tasting room is open for tours for a fee. You can sit on the outside terrace, where you can enjoy picnics and specialty culinary experiences, such as Spanish tapas pairings. Chocoholics might like to sample the chocolate-covered Blanc de Noirs – a bottle of sparkling wine dipped in melted chocolate, then chilled; you break the "zip tab" to nibble on bite-size chunks of chocolate between sips. Each summer, the winery hosts the Catalan Festival of Food, Wine & Music.

GREAT VIEW Mission Trail

The Mission San Francisco Solano is the last of the 21 missions on the Historic Mission Trail that you come to, traveling north from San Diego. All are located on or near Hwy 101 and most still operate as Catholic parishes.

37 Sonoma

 453 1st St East; www.sonomacity.org

One of California's most picturesque towns, Sonoma is graced with quaint buildings recalling its Spanish-Mexican heritage. The compact town dates back to 1823 and is of immense historic importance. It was here on June 14, 1846, that American farmers seized the Mexican governor, General Mariano Vallejo, and declared an independent republic. Twenty-five days later, the United States annexed California. The bronze monument at the northeast corner of grassy Sonoma Plaza, recalls the "Bear Flag Rebellion." Sites of historic significance surround the plaza, including the 1823 Mission San Francisco Solano. It's flanked by the Sonoma Barracks, headquarters of the Mexican Army; and La Casa Grande, an adobe building

→

The alluring Russian River lazily winding its way past lushly forested banks

that was Vallejo's first home. A ten-minute stroll brings you to Vallejo's later home, the Gothic Revival Lachryma Montis. Other treats include the former Toscano Hotel, furnished in turn-of-the-20th century decor and, next door, the Sonoma Cheese Factory. Sonoma is bursting with trendy art galleries, boutiques, restaurants, and wine-tasting rooms, tempting you wisely to linger.

East of Sonoma's plaza is the restored **Mission San Francisco Solano de Sonoma**, the last of California's 21 historic Franciscan missions. Father José Altimira of Spain founded the mission in 1823 at a time when California was under Mexican rule. Today, all that survives of the original building is the corridor of Father Altimira's quarters.

Mission San Francisco Solano de Sonoma

 114 E Spain St
🕐 10am–5pm daily
🌐 parks.ca.gov

←

Fine historic buildings in Sonoma, recalling its Spanish-Mexican past

38

Jack London State Historic Park

🏠 2400 London Ranch Rd, Glen Ellen 🕐 Mar–Nov: 9:30am–5pm daily
🌐 jacklondonpark.com

A short drive north of Sonoma leads to the Jack London State Historic Park. In the early 1900s, London, author of *The Call of the Wild* (1903) and *The Sea-Wolf* (1904), abandoned his hectic life-style to live in this 1-sq-mile (3-sq-km) expanse of oaks, madrones, and redwoods. The park retains eerie ruins of London's dream home, the Wolf House, which was mysteriously destroyed by fire just before completion.

After London's death in 1916, his widow, Charmian Kittredge, built a magnificent home on the ranch, called the House of Happy Walls. Today it is a museum, well worth a visit for its display of Jack London memorabilia,

including his writing desk and early copies of his works.

___

39

Russian River

ℹ️ 16200 First St, Guerneville; www. russianriver.com

The second largest river in the Bay Area – after the Sacramento River – Russian River starts in the Laughlin Range in Mendocino County and flows south for 110 miles (177 km). All along the river are campgrounds, beaches, redwood forests, wineries, day spas, and charming towns, making it a great trip whether you're after action and adventure or simply some peace and tranquility. The river spills into the Pacific Ocean near the hamlet of Jenner. Here hundreds of grey harbour seals bask in the sun on Goat Rock Beach, which was used as a location in the film *The Goonies*.

> **The park retains eerie ruins of London's dream home, the Wolf House, which was mysteriously destroyed by fire just before completion.**

↑ Monterey's historic
Cannery Row, a six-block
street on the harbor

40

MONTEREY

 i 401 Camino El Estero; www.seemonterey.com

Monterey was established by the Spanish in 1770, and served as the capital of northern California under Spanish and later Mexican rule. During the Mexican–American War (1846–8), the US flag was raised over the town and northern California became part of the United States. Today Monterey has several prestigious universities, and is a popular resort town renowned for its spectacular setting, world-class aquarium, historic attractions, and great seafood.

①

Monterey Bay Aquarium

⌂ 886 Cannery Row
🚋 MST Trolley ⏰ 10am–5pm daily 🌐 montereybay aquarium.org

This fascinating venue is one of the world's best aquariums. It exhibits more than 550 species and some 35,000 live specimens. Highlights include the peaceful Kelp Forest and the Open Sea Gallery, full of sea creatures including giant tuna, sharks, green sea turtles, and shoaling sardines. Daily feedings and educational shows are must-sees, as are the playful sea otters (the aquarium's mascot) and inter-active exhibits such as the Splash Zone and touch pool.

②

Cannery Row

⌂ Cannery Row 🚋 MST Trolley 🌐 canneryrow.com

This popular waterfront street spanning four blocks was formerly occupied by sardine canning factories. It was the setting for John Steinbeck's novel, *Cannery Row* (1945); the title came from the nickname for Ocean View Avenue, as the name "Cannery Row" was formalized in 1958. The last cannery closed in 1973 following the collapse of the industry due to over-fishing, and the area fell into decay. Today the canneries have been converted into hotels, eclectic shops, wine-tasting rooms, and restaurants, including the Sardine Factory, which opened in 1968 and signaled the renaissance of Cannery Row.

③

Old Fisherman's Wharf

⌂ 1 Old Fisherman's Wharf
🚋 MST Trolley 🌐 monterey wharf.com

This historic wharf in Monterey harbor was an active fishing pier into the 1970s. Today

Did You Know?

The Monterey Jazz Festival is a major annual event that dates back to 1958.

it's a lively commercial venue with a medley of candy and souvenir stores, and seafood restaurants with wonderful views. As you explore, keep an eye out for sea otters drifting on the surface and sea lions frolicking in the harbor. For close-ups with the local marine life, Old Fisherman's Wharf offers glass-bottom boats, whale-watching tours and deep-sea fishing trips.

National Steinbeck Center

🏠 1 Main St, Salinas 🚌 Buses to Salinas Transit Center ⏰ 10am–5pm daily 🌐 steinbeck.org

Monterey and neighboring Salinas are synonymous with novelist John Steinbeck (1902–68), who set many of his stories here. The Nobel Prize-winning author's life, literature, and legacy are the theme of the National Steinbeck Center, two blocks from his birthplace in downtown Salinas. The museum brings Steinbeck's works to life with movie clips and dioramas that recreate scenes from novels.

An adjoining section celebrates the heritage of the local Japanese community (the first of whom immigrated in the 1890s). Another section explores the history of farming in Salinas Valley.

Del Monte Beach

🏠 123 Tide Ave 🚌 12, 20, 67

This gorgeous scimitar of dune-backed, golden-white sand curls north from Old Fisherman's Wharf and merges into other beaches that run unbroken for almost 20 miles (32 km). The lovely Monterey Bay Recreational Trail snakes alongside the beach, and is a delight for walking, skating or cycling. There are fire pits for chilly evenings, and picnic benches at the west end.

The waters are usually calm enough to make for a pleasant kayak ride, and to allow waders to spy sand dollars in the shallows. Offshore, a large reef encrusted with clams tempts divers with its large population of octopi, sponges, and fish. Spawning halibut can even be seen close to shore in spring.

Monterey State Historic Park

🏠 20 Custom House Plaza 🚊 MST Trolley ⏰ Times vary, check website 🌐 parks.ca.gov

Monterey's well preserved historic core features many notable 19th-century buildings. You can explore the area and a few museums on a self-guided walk, but those wishing to get a better look inside the historic buildings should book a tour.

EAT

Monterey's Fish House

A seafood restaurant with a casual yet lively atmosphere. The huge range of dishes - from ahi tuna to cioppino - use fish and shellfish fresh from the bay.

🏠 2114 Del Monte Ave 🌐 montereyfish house.com

💲💲💲

Ghiradelli's

This gourmet ice cream and chocolate shop also serves classic American drinks such as malts and shakes. The terrace overlooking the bay is the perfect place to enjoy a sundae.

🏠 660 Cannery Row 🌐 ghirardelli.com

💲💲💲

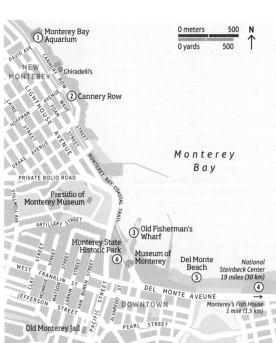

① Monterey Bay Aquarium

DAVID AVE

NEW MONTEREY

○ Ghiradelli's

CANNERY ROW

LIGHTHOUSE AVENUE

② Cannery Row

FOAM STREET

WAVE STREET

LAINE STREET

HOFFMAN AVENUE

DRAKE AVENUE

PRIVATE BOLIO ROAD

Presidio of Monterey Museum

STILLWELL AVE

ARTILLERY STREET

WEST STREET

CLAY STREET

FRANKLIN STREET

MONROE STREET

WATSON STREET

LARKIN ST

VAN BUREN STREET

JEFFERSON STREET

PACIFIC STREET

ALVARADO ST

Old Monterey Jail

PEARL STREET

Monterey State Historic Park ⑥

Museum of Monterey

③ Old Fisherman's Wharf

MONTEREY BAY COASTAL TRAIL

Monterey Bay

DEL MONTE AVEUNE

Del Monte Beach ⑤

DOWNTOWN

National Steinbeck Center 19 miles (30 km) ④

→
Monterey's Fish House 1 mile (1.5 km)

0 meters 500
0 yards 500

N ↑

BEYOND THE BAY

41

Sacramento

 1002 2nd St; www.visitsacramento.com

Founded by John Sutter in 1839, California's capital city has many historic buildings along the waterfront in Old Sacramento. Some of the structures here were built to serve the gold miners of 1849, but most date from 1860–70, when Sacramento sealed its positon as the link between rural California and the commercial centers along the coast. The Pony Express and transcontinental railroad both had their western terminus here, with paddle-wheel riverboats providing the connection to San Francisco. A handful of museums trace the area's historic importance, including the **California State Railroad Museum**, which houses some fine old locomotives and operates excursions on an old steam-train from April through September.

A short distance from the old town is the **California State Capitol**, Sacramento's primary landmark and one of the handsomest buildings in the state. It was designed in 1860 by Reuben Clark and Miner F. Butler in grand Greek Revival style, with Corinthian porticos and a tall central dome. Along with the chambers of the state legislature, which are open to visitors even when they are in session, the Capital houses a museum of the state's history.

California State Railroad Museum
125 I St ◘10am–5pm daily ⓦcsrmf.org

California State Capitol
1315 10th St ◘7:30am–6pm Mon-Fri, 9am–5pm Sat & Sun ⓦcapitolmuseum.ca.gov

---

42

Mendocino

 345 N Franklin St, Fort Bragg; www.visitmendocino.com

The settlers of this village came to California from New England in 1852, and built their new homes to resemble those they had left behind on the East Coast. Perched on a rocky promontory high above the Pacific Ocean, Mendocino has retained the picturesque charm of its days as a major fishing and logging center, and has been declared an historical monument. While tourism is now its main industry, the town remains

→

Elegant Bixby Bridge, part of the stunning Pacific Coast Highway

Fine historic buildings on the waterfront in Old Sacramento

virtually untarnished by commercialism. Visitors can stroll around the many boutiques, bookshops, galleries, and cafes, while those who prefer the attractions of nature can look out for migrating gray whales and admire the stunning ocean vistas.

43
Carmel-by-the-Sea

🚌 **ℹ** Ocean Ave; www.carmelcalifornia.com

The charming seaside town of Carmel-by-the-Sea ("Carmel," for short), has been a haven for artists and writers since the early 20th century. Ocean

Did You Know?

Bixby Bridge was constructed using concrete partly due to its aesthetic similarity to sea cliffs.

Avenue is lined with art galleries, boutiques and cafés, and beautiful homes border the steep hillsides down to the ocean, where Carmel Beach provides a 1 mile (1.5 km) stretch of white sand.

###
Big Sur

ℹ 47555 CA-1, Big Sur; www.bigsurcalifornia.org

California's coastal beauty is nowhere more awe-inspiring than along Big Sur: the rugged shoreline south of Monterey (p248). The Pacific Coast Highway snakes past surging headlands, leaps across plunging canyons, and weaves above remote beaches pounded by crashing surf. The 65-mile (105-km) route between Carmel and San Simeon is one of the world's most magnificent coastal drives – but make sure you drive carefully, as the route has many clifftop switchbacks and is often fog-bound, especially in summer.

Make sure you stop to photograph Bixby Bridge,

a classic landmark and single-arch engineering marvel with a stunning setting. It's also worth making a reservation to visit **Hearst Castle**, an ostentatious fantasy in stone perched atop a mountain at San Simeon.

Hearst Castle
 ⌂750 Hearst Castle Rd, San Simeon **W** hearst castle.org

STAY

Pine Inn
Just a few blocks from the beach, this iconic inn – the oldest in town – offers elegant rooms and a great on-site restaurant that's popular with locals.

⌂ Ocean Ave & Monte Verde, Carmel
W pineinn.com

$$$

NEED TO KNOW

A crowded cable car on Nob Hill

BEFORE
YOU GO

Forward planning is essential to any successful trip. Be prepared for all eventualities by considering the following points before you travel.

AT A GLANCE

CURRENCY
US dollar (USD)

AVERAGE DAILY SPEND

ON A BUDGET
$100

MODERATE SPENDER
$200

SPLASH OUT
$300+

BOTTLED WATER
$2.00

COFFEE
$2.50

BEER
$8.00

DINNER FOR TWO
$80

CLIMATE

The months of Apr to Aug see around 14 hours of sunlight, dropping to under 10 hours from Nov to Feb.

Temperatures can change by the hour, averaging 18°C/65°F in summer and 10°C/50°F in winter.

The city is officially in drought, and rain rarely occurs from Feb to Nov.

ELECTRICITY SUPPLY

Plug sockets are type A and B, fitting two- and three-pronged plugs. Standard voltage is 100–120 volts AC.

Passports and Visas

Holders of a European Union, Australian, or New Zealand passport with a return ticket do not require visas if staying in the US for 90 days or less, but must apply for an Electronic System for Travel Authorisation (**ESTA**) at least 72 hours before travel. There is a small charge. All other visitors need a visa before traveling. Contact your local US embassy for current requirements.
ESTA
W esta.cbp.dhs.gov/esta
US Department of State
W travel.state.gov

Travel Safety Advice

Visitors can get up-to-date travel safety information from the **Department of State** in the US, the **Foreign and Commonwealth Office** in the UK, and the **Department of Foreign Affairs and Trade** in Australia.

Certain neighbourhoods have a reputation for being less safe: the Tenderloin, Civic Center, Western Addition, the Lower Haight, the Mission south of 24th Street, South of Market above 5th Street, and the Bayview district. Take the usual precautions against petty crime and avoid walking around at night.

San Francisco is at risk of earthquakes. Should you experience a quake, there are simple safety guidelines to follow. If indoors, stand under a doorway or table, away from windows and wall hangings and hold on until the shaking stops. If outdoors, stay away from power cables and trees. Pull over, away from power lines and bridges, if driving, and remain in the car. If on the beach, move to higher ground. The Federal Emergency Management Agency (**FEMA**) has a useful website for safety precautions.
UK
W gov.uk/foreign-travel-advice
US
W state.gov
Australia
W smartraveller.gov.au
FEMA
W fema.gov/earthquake-safety-home

Customs Information

Nonresidents will need to fill in a Customs and Border Protection Agency form upon arrival to the US. Customs allowances for visiting nonresidents over the age of 21 are: 200 cigarettes (1 carton), 100 cigars (except from Cuba); 1 litre (2 pints) of alcohol; and gifts to the value of $100. Meat products, cheese, seeds, live plants, and fresh fruit all carry restrictions. Foreign visitors to the US may bring in or take out up to $10,000 in US or foreign currency. Amounts higher than this will need to be declared.

US Customs and Border Protection
W cbp.gov

Language

The official language of San Francisco is English, although more than one hundred languages are spoken across this cosmopolitan city. Spanish and Chinese are well established as second and third languages, and you are increasingly likely to overhear Tagalog (the official language of the Philippines) around the Bay Area.

Insurance

Check that your coverage includes emergency medical and dental care, lost or stolen baggage and travel documents, accidental death, and trip-cancellation fees.

Vaccinations

No inoculations are required for visiting the United States.

Booking Accommodations

Booking a package deal is often the most inexpensive way of visiting San Francisco. Websites offer airfares, hotels, and sometimes car rentals. Make sure you book in advance to get the best deals, especially if visiting from June through August. Prices also spike around holidays and local festivals, so check your dates before you book. As well as luxury hotels, you can also find a range of good-value hostels and B&Bs. San Fransisco Travel have a range of suggestions.

San Francisco Travel
W sftravel.com

Money

Most retailers will accept card or cash. It is common to sign for your purchases rather than entering a pin. You're never far from an ATM in the city. Check your bank's withdrawal fees before traveling; the ATM may also charge $2.50 to $3.50 per transaction. You will be able to exchange currency in the larger branches of Bank of America, Wells Fargo, and Chase, as well as at bureaux de change. Prepaid currency cards can be used to withdraw money, and can act like debit cards in shops and restaurants.

Travelers with Specific Needs

San Francisco is famous for its steep hills, particularly around Russian Hill and Nob Hill, which may prove challenging for those with mobility issues. Aside from this, most places in the city are equipped to welcome disabled visitors. Public transportation is largely accessible for those with specific needs, and prices are usually discounted.

Closures

Businesses, restaurants, museums, and shops close earlier during the winter season, from November to March. Most banks are closed on Sundays. Some museums close on Mondays or Tuesdays, and on public holidays.

PUBLIC HOLIDAYS	
Jan 1	New Year's Day
Jan 21	Martin Luther King Jr. Day
Feb 18	Presidents' Day
May 27	Memorial Day
Jul 4	Independence Day
Sep 2	Labor Day
Oct 14	Columbus Day
Nov 11	Veterans Day
Nov 28	Thanksgiving Day
Dec 25	Christmas Day

GETTING AROUND

Whether navigating the hills by cable car, or taking a ferry across the bay, San Francisco's public transportation options are well worth exploring.

AT A GLANCE

PUBLIC TRANSPORT FARES

SINGLE TICKET

$2.75

120 mins
First use transfers

1-DAY PASSPORT

$12.00

Unlimited travel on Muni-operated transport

7-DAY PASSPORT

$39.00

Unlimited travel on Muni-operated transport

TOP TIP
Download the 511 SF Bay Transit Trip Planner app for routes and times.

SPEED LIMIT

RURAL FREEWAYS

70 mph
(113km/h)

URBAN FREEWAYS

65 mph
(105km/h)

NEIGHBORHOOD SLOW ZONE

25 mph
(40km/h)

URBAN AREAS

35 mph
(55km/h)

Arriving by Air

San Francisco International Airport (SFO) is one of the busiest airports in the world, receiving flights from all major international airlines, but is very user-friendly. Other nearby airports include San Jose International Airport (SJC), which is about 1 hour away from San Francisco, and Oakland International Airport (OAK), which is 30 minutes away.

SFO is 14 miles (23 km) south of the city center. The airport offers international connections to and from the Pacific Rim, Latin America, and Europe. For a list of transportation options, approximate journey times, and travel costs for transportation between San Francisco International Airport and downtown San Francisco, see the table opposite. The Bay Area Rapid Transport (BART) station is connected to the terminal by a light-rail shuttle.

Visitors will arrive at the airport on the lower level. The top level provides services for those departing the city. All car rentals, parking shuttles, public buses, and door-to-door shuttle minibuses deliver and pick up passengers at this level.

Train Travel

Amtrak trains link most major US cities and are a great way to see parts of the country you would not otherwise experience. Advance booking is recommended for travel during peak periods. Those visiting San Francisco by train will arrive at the Amtrak station in Emeryville, to the north of Oakland. From here, take a free 45-minute shuttle to the Ferry Building in the city center. Amtrak offers special discounts and packages, including 15-, 30-, and 45-day travel passes.

Alternatively, you can arrive by **Amtrak** to San Jose, then transfer via the CalTrain commuter rail system to San Francisco. A separate ticket is required for this journey. The **CalTrain** stops near several Muni bus and Metro stops.

Amtrak
w amtrak.com
CalTrain
w caltrain.org

GETTING TO AND FROM THE AIRPORT

Transportation	Journey time	Fare
Taxi	25–45 minutes	$45
SuperShuttle shared ride	40–60 minutes	$19–$40
American Airporter Shuttle	60–75 minutes	$17
Bay Area Rapid Transit (BART)	30 minutes	$9.65

Public Transportation

San Francisco has a reliable and easy-to-use public transportation system, but there are a few different options to choose from. The Municipal Railway (Muni) runs the public transport system. You can use an interchangeable pass – the Muni passport – to travel on Muni buses, Muni Metro streetcars (electric trams), and cable cars. The San Francisco Peninsula and the East Bay are linked by the Bay Area Rapid Transit (BART). This is an efficient way to get to both SFO and Oakland International airport. The San Francisco Municipal Transportation Agency (**SFMTA**) website features lots of useful information and maps.

SFMTA
W sfmta.com

Long-Distance Bus Travel
For travelers on a budget with more time, buses are a great way to travel. **The Greyhound Bus Line** takes passengers from Los Angeles to San Francisco in around 9 hours from $27. Discounts are offered for online purchases, 14-day advance purchases, students, seniors, children, and large groups. **The Green Tortoise** bus company offers a friendly and adventurous way to see California, with passengers sharing meals among the group along the way, and often stopping at tourist sites.

Greyhound
W greyhound.com
Green Tortoise
W greentortoise.com

Planning Your Journey
Public transportation is busiest from 7am–9am and 4pm–7pm from Monday through Friday. This may be the best time to explore the city by foot. The cable cars are a popular tourist activity, so are busy during the summer months.

The Muni Metro runs from around 5am to 1am on weekdays, from 7am on Saturdays and 8am on Sundays. There are ten Muni Owl services that run 24 hours a day, 7 days a week. Schedules are modified for public holidays, so check the SFMTA website before travelling.

Tickets
You can purchase a reusable Clipper card from Muni metro stations, online, or from Walgreens stores for just $3. Top up the card with money and hold it against the reader when boarding a vehicle. You can use it to travel on the Muni, BART, and the cable cars.

Buses and streetcars both cost $2.50 per ride, or $2.75 by cash. You can request a fare transfer that will allow you to transfer to another bus or streetcar for free within 120 minutes.

Muni passports are available for 1, 3, or 7 days, allowing unlimited travel on buses, streetcars, and cable cars. These can be purchased from the Visitor Information Center, the kiosk at San Francisco airport, and at other stores throughout the city.

Buses
There are bus stops every two or three blocks. Bus shelters list the route number of the buses that stop there, as well as maps and service frequency information. Most have digital signs showing when the next bus will arrive.

The route number and name of the destination are shown on the front and side of every bus. Route numbers followed by a letter are either express services or make limited stops. Either pay with exact change, or show your Muni Passport.

Streetcars
Streetcars, also known as Light Rail Vehicles (LRVs), operate both above and below ground, and are another great way to see the city.

Streetcar lines J (Church), K (Ingleside), L (Taraval), M (Ocean View), N (Judah), and T (Third) share the same tracks, so check the letter and name of the streetcar when boarding from Market Street. To go west, follow station signposts for "Outbound" streetcars; to go east, chooose "Downtown." The F line streetcar runs along Market Street only, and features vintage streetcars from all over the world.

BART

BART trains run from 4am on weekdays, from 6am on Saturdays, and from 8am on Sundays, until around midnight. Tickets are issued by machines in BART stations, which take cards or cash. You must present your ticket at the turnstile both when you board and leave the train. You can also use a Clipper card. The final destination of the train will be displayed on the front of the train itself, and the direction of travel will be marked on the platform.

BART
ⓦ bart.gov

Taxis

Taxis in San Francisco operate 24 hours a day. They are licensed and regulated, so expect efficient service, expert local knowledge, and a set price. A taxi will have its rooftop sign illuminated if vacant. It will also display the company name and telephone number, plus the cab number. Make a note of this, and if you leave anything in the cab, call the company and quote the cab number.

To catch a cab, wait at a taxi stand, call and request a pick-up, or hail a vacant cab. Tell your driver your exact destination. The meter will be on the dashboard, and expect to add a 15 to 20 percent tip to the final amount. Fares are often posted inside the cab. There is usually a flat fee of around $3.50 for the first mile (1.6 km). This increases by about $2.75 for each additional mile, or 55 cents per minute while waiting. Fares from the Ferry Building to the west coast beaches are about $35, and the average fare from San Francisco airport to the city center is $45. The driver will write you a receipt on request. If you travel 15 miles (24 km) or more beyond the city limits, the fare will be 150 percent of the metered rate.

All taxi-cabs are now non-smoking. If you have a complaint about a taxi driver, call the Police Department Taxicab Complaint Line (415-701-4400).

The taxi companies Uber and Lyft are very cost-effective and reliable in San Francisco. Download the apps on your smartphone. Payment is handled through the apps and you can track your journey, split fares with other users, and report complaints through the app.

It is advisable not to take a limousine from a taxi stand or from the street. Legally, limousines are only available for prearranged trips.

Uber
ⓦ uber.com
Lyft
ⓦ lyft.com
Yellow Cabs
ⓦ yellowcabsf.com

Driving

Congestion, a shortage of parking spaces, and strictly enforced laws discourage many visitors from driving in San Francisco, but possibly the best way to experience the twists and turns of Lombard Street is on four wheels.

Car Rental

To rent a car, you must be at least 25 years old with a valid driving license. Most agencies require a large deposit. Always return the car with a full tank of gas to avoid inflated gas prices charged by the agency. It is slightly cheaper to rent a car from San Francisco airport. Additional rental taxes can drive up the price, especially if you hire from within the city. It is also more cost-effective to do a round trip, to avoid large drop-off costs. Check your existing insurance policy before signing up to car insurance, as you may already be partially covered.

Rules of the Road

The maximum speed limit is 35 mph (55 km/h) in the city. Many streets are one-way, with traffic lights at most corners. In the US, if there is no oncoming traffic, drivers may turn right at a red light, always giving pedestrians the right of way. Otherwise, a red light means stop, and an amber light means proceed with caution.

Parking

Parking meters operate 9am to 6pm Monday through Saturday, except on national holidays, when parking is free. Meters in some tourist areas operate on Sundays, including at Fisherman's Wharf and the Embarcadero. Most meters have two-hour time limits, some have four-hour limits, and others no time limit at all. You can prepay from 4:30am online. Costs range from $2 to $6 per hour. City-center parking garages are also available from $16 per day.

Curbs here are color-coded. A red curb means no stopping; yellow denotes a commercial loading zone; green allows 10 to 30 minutes of parking; and white allows you to park for five minutes during business hours, with the driver remaining in the vehicle. Blue curb areas are reserved for the disabled. By law, you must curb your wheels when parking on steep hills. Turn your wheels into the road when your car is parked facing uphill, and toward the curb when facing downhill. Check signs for tow warnings and follow all instructions.

Penalties

If you park your car at an out-of-order meter, expect to get a parking ticket. Blocking bus stops, fire hydrants, driveways, garages, and wheelchair ramps will also incur a fine, as will running a red light or a stop sign, or driving while texting. Traffic fines in San Francisco can exceed $100. If your car has been towed away, contact the City and County of San Francisco Impound. Expect to pay a towing and storage fee when retrieving your car.

City and County of San Francisco Impound
📞 415-865-8200

Driving Outside the City

No toll payment is required to leave the city, but you will need to pay between $4 and $7 to re-enter. During rush hour, cars with three or more occupants can use the carpool lane, avoiding both traffic and tolls. In other parts of the city, only two occupants are required. It is legal to drive in the carpool lane when it's not rush hour, but not to avoid the bridge tolls. Those caught using the carpool lane illegally face steep fines.

Cycling

Cycling is popular in San Francisco. There are many bicycle lanes and all Muni buses are equipped to carry bikes on the outside. Bikes can also be taken on the light-rail Muni cars and on BART, although not at rush hour. There are two marked scenic bicycle routes. One goes from Golden Gate park south to Lake Merced; the other starts at the southern end of Golden Gate Bridge and crosses to Marin County.

Bicycles, equipment, and tours are available from Bay City Bike and Blazing Saddles. They rent out bikes from $8 per hour, $32 ($20 for children) per day, or $105 for seven days. Bay Area Bike Share stations, which are spread across the city, also hire bikes, charging $9 a day and $22 for 3 days.

Bay City Bike
🅦 baycitybike.com
Blazing Saddles
🅦 blazingsaddles.com

Boats and Ferries

Ferries are one of the best ways to appreciate the beauty of the Bay Area. They shuttle to and from the cities of San Francisco, Oakland, and Larkspur, as well as the smaller towns of Tiburon and Sausalito, and nearby Angel Island. Viewing the coastline from the ferry is less expensive than a sightseeing cruise. The trip from San

Francisco to Sausalito is $12.50 each way and food and drink are available on board. These ferries only carry foot passengers and bicycles, not motor vehicles. Golden Gate Ferry and San Francisco Bay Ferry services depart from the Ferry Building, and the Blue and Gold Fleet and Red and White Fleet dock at Fisherman's Wharf.

Several companies also offer sightseeing cruises of the Bay. Destinations include Angel Island and towns on the north shore of the Bay. Many of these boat trips pass near Alcatraz, but only Alcatraz Cruises stops there. Hornblower Dining Yachts offer weekend brunches and dinners from Thursdays to Sundays. Oceanic Society Expeditions arranges nautical environmental safaris to the Farallon Islands, 27 miles (43 km) off shore, for $128 per person for a full day, where whales, sea lions, seals and dolphins are often spotted. Shorter whale-watching expeditions also depart from Pier 39 for $45 per person ($35 for children) from March to October.

Alcatraz Cruises
🅦 alcarazcruises.com
Blue and Gold Fleet
🅦 blueandgoldfleet.com
Red and White Fleet
🅦 redandwhite.com
Golden Gate Ferry
🅦 goldengateferry.org
San Francisco Bay Ferry
🅦 sanfranciscobayferry.com
Horn Blower
🅦 hornblower.com
Ocean Society
🅦 oceanicsociety.org/expeditions
SF Bay Whale Watching
🅦 sfbaywhalewatching.com

Cable Cars in San Francisco

San Francisco's cable cars are world-famous, and even classed as a "moving national monument". You're likely to hear their distinctive bells all over the city center.

Service runs every ten minutes from 6am to midnight daily. The fare is $7 per journey, with a discount for seniors and the disabled after 9pm and before 7am. There are three routes: the Powell-Hyde line, which passes Union Square and climbs Nob Hill, providing good views of Chinatown. The Powell-Mason line begins in the same place and branches off to pass North Beach, ending at Bay Street. Sit facing east on the Powell lines for the best views. The California line runs from the base of Market Street at the Embarcadero, through the Financial District and Chinatown, over Nob Hill, ending at Van Ness Avenue. You are more likely to get a seat if you board the cable car at the end of the line, but you may prefer to hang onto a pole while standing on a side running board.

PRACTICAL
INFORMATION

Forward planning is essential for any successful trip. Prepare yourself for any eventuality by brushing up on the following points before you set off.

AT A GLANCE

EMERGENCY NUMBERS

GENERAL EMERGENCY	AMBULANCE
911	**911**

FIRE SERVICE	POLICE
911	**911**

TIME ZONE
PST/DST. Daylight Saving Time (DST) from the second Sunday in March till the first Sunday in Nov.

TAP WATER
Safe to drink, but bottled water is widely available.

TIPPING

Waiter	20%
Hotel Porter	$1.50 per bag
Housekeeping	$2 per day
Concierge	€1–2
Cab Driver	15–20%

Personal Security

San Francisco is one of the safest large cities in the US. Police patrol tourist areas frequently, and few visitors are victims of street crime.

San Francisco has a high population of homeless people, and can be quite unsafe in some areas at night. Plan your routes in advance, look at maps discreetly, and walk with confidence. If you need directions, ask hotel or shop staff, or the police. If you use common sense, your stay should be safe and pleasant.

Health

Healthcare in the US is high quality but costly. Ensure you have full medical cover prior to your visit, and keep receipts to claim on your insurance if needed.

Walgreens pharmacies can be found all over the city, and branches at 498 Castro Street, 135 Powell Street, 459 Powell Street, Divisadero Street, and Westborough Square are open 24 hours. Certain medications available over the counter in the UK require a prescription in the US. There are several emergency rooms open 24 hours, including the following:
California Pacific Medical Center
W cpmc.org
Saint Francis Memorial Hospital
W saintfrancismemorial.org

Smoking, Alcohol and Drugs

You must be over 21 to buy and drink alcohol, and to buy tobacco products. It is legal for over 21s to smoke marijuana in the home or in a building licensed for its consumption. Drinking alcohol is not allowed in most public areas, especially from open containers. Driving while under the influence of alcohol or any drug is prohibited. It is illegal to smoke in public buildings, workplaces, restaurants, and bars. It is also illegal to smoke anywhere that exposes others to second-hand smoke, including parks, beaches, queues, and bus stops. These laws extend to e-cigarettes.

ID

Take some form of photo identification when buying alcohol, tobacco, or marijuana, as bars, clubs, restaurants, and shops are required by law to check it.

Local Customs

San Francisco is a very laid-back city. Casual clothing such as jeans, T-shirts, and trainers is quite acceptable for all but the most upmarket restaurants and nightclubs.

LGBT Safety

San Francisco has an incredibly diverse LGBT+ community, with a history spanning back to the Gold Rush. The Castro district is the most welcoming area for the LGBT+ community, and information on events can be found across the city.

Visiting Churches and Cathedrals

Always dress respectfully when visiting places of worship: cover your torso and upper arms. Ensure shorts and skirts cover your knees.

Mobile Phones and Wi-Fi

Cellphone service in San Francisco is strong. The main US network providers are AT&T, Sprint, T-Mobile US, and Verizon. Most of these offer prepaid, pay-as-you-go phones and US SIM cards, starting at around $30 (plus tax), which you can purchase upon arrival. Calls within the US are cheap, but making international calls may be pricey.

Triband or multiband cell phones from around the world should work in the US, but your service provider may have to unlock international roaming. The Three UK network offers a competitive SIM-only deal from £10 a month, including data and calls to the UK. If you are planning to use your mobile phone for Wi-Fi only, switch off data roaming.

Free Wi-Fi is widely available throughout the city and the Bay Area. Service can be accessed on trains, in the subway tunnel linking San Francisco and Oakland, and in many cafes and hotels.

Post

Stamps can be purchased at post offices, hotel reception desks, and some grocery stores. Check current postal rates at post offices or online. Letters can be mailed from post offices, your hotel, and street mailboxes. Express mail can also be arranged through private delivery companies, such as DHL, FedEx, and UPS.
US Postal Services
w usps.com

Taxes and Tipping

Sales tax in San Francisco is 8.5 percent. Tax is charged on everything except groceries, plants used for food, and prescription drugs, with a few other exemptions. A useful trick to figure out a restaurant tip is to double the tax. Always remember to sign your receipt, and avoid leaving cash on the table.

Discount Cards

Several websites offer discounts and passes, often grouping together attractions and public transportation. Visitors with proof of student status receive discounts at many museums and theaters. You can apply for an International Student Identity Card (ISIC) prior to traveling.
Sightseeing Pass
w sightseeingpass.com
City Pass
w citypass.com

WEBSITES AND APPS

www.sfchronicle.com
Search under "Datebook" for listings and events.
www.sftravel.com
Full of information and ideas for trips and activities throughout the city.
Moovit
This app tells you the best way to your destination via public transportation.
Parknow
Book parking spaces in advance, or find open parking spaces in the city. and listings, including festival dates.
Routesy
App showing live transportation times.

INDEX

Page numbers in **bold** refer to main entries.

ACKNOWLEDGMENTS

The publisher would like to thank the following for their kind permission to reproduce their photographs:

Key: a-above; b-below/bottom; c-centre; f-far; l-left; r-right; t-top

123RF.com: Mariusz Blach 14-5b; Maciej Błędowski 8clb; Lucy Clark 123tl; Coralimages 162bl; Frank Fennema 38tl; Filip Fuxa 14clb,; Nick Kontostavlakis 64-5t; Pius Lee 17t; Wasin Pummarin 94-5t.

Alamy Stock Photo: Aflo Co. Ltd. 79cr; AGE Fotostock 86-7t, 118crb, 178-9t; Arcaid Images 148-9bl; Archive Farms Inc 53cla; Archive PL 83tl; Gonzalo Azumendi 179cl, 183t; Sergio Torres Baus 106bl; Nancy Hoyt Belcher 222-3t; Bildagentur-online / Schickert 125t; Jon Bilous 180-1b; Bob Masters 109br; Phillip Bond 37tr, 221br; Kanwarjit Singh Boparai 192-3t; Dembinsky Photo Associates / Dominique Braud 24br; Paul Brown 151b; Jan Butchofsky 198-9t; California Dreamin 101tr; Cannon Photography LLC 34-5bl, 112bl, 139cb, 242-3c; Scott Chernis 43t; Felix Choo 47br, 88bl, 102tr, 170cr, 171cl; Chronicle 66crb; Ronnie Chua 40-1b, 152b; Citizen of the Planet 235br; Patrick Civello 36t; Classic Image 94cb, 118cb; Robert Clay 39cl; Directphoto Collection 80t, 106crb; Curved Light USA 123cr; Ian G Dagnall 42bl, 126-7b, 226t, 240clb; Ethan Daniels 37cl; Danita Delimont Creative 233tr; David Sanger Photography 203cr; Joe Decker 232-3b; Danita Delimont 41crb, 45bl, 118-9t, 204bl; Design Pics Inc 31bl; Don Douglas 205br; Randy Duchaine 118c; Daniel Duenser 50br; Everett Collection Inc 56cr, 57crb, 67crb; Eye35 Stock 171cr; F8grapher 198bl; Michele Falzone 78-9c, 130bl; Stephen Finn 187tl; Tim Fleming 185br; Zachary Frank 205t; Neil Fraser 156bl; Robert Fried 244bl, 246b; Gado Images 99tr; GL Archive 95bc, 97ca, 97br; Paul Christian Gordon 194bl; Granger Historical Picture Archive 118clb; Michael Halberstadt 30bl; Yuval Helfman 202bl, 220bl; Bill Helsel 18cb, 132-3; Hemis 104b; Hero Images Inc. 42tl; Heyengel 26tl; History and Art Collection 53c, 162bc; The History Collection 118fclb; The Hollywood Archive / PictureLux / Phil Bray 57cr; Peter Horree 81b, 125cr; Dave G. Houser 242bl, 247t; Robert Huberman 169tr; Della Huff 78bl, 155br, 229br, 242cra; imageBROKER 206bl, 241tr; Interfoto 97tr; Anton Ivanov 193crb; Rich Iwasaki 79cra; Jejim120 170br; Mark A. Johnson 111br; Mariusz Jurgielewicz 51tl; Ei Katsumata 41cla; Matthew Kiernan 113br; Art Kowalsky 18tl, 36bl, 40-1t, 114-5, 193cb; Kimberly Kradel 202-3tl; Bob Kreisel 70b; Chris LaBasco 153cra; Lebrecht Music & Arts 54tl; Chon Kit Leong 165t; Michael Lingberg 177cra; Andrew Lloyd 37crb; Lucky-Photographer 236-7b; Ilene MacDonald 166-7b; Stefano Politi Markovina 22t, 24clb, 105tl, 149tr; Mauritius Images Gmbh 27cla; Brian McGuire 94bc; Mike Kipling Photography 67bc; Mikle15 224tl; Geoffrey Morgan 76-7t; Luciano Mortula 22bl, 54bl; Moviestore collection Ltd 56crb, 56bl; MShieldsPhotos 22cl; Ilpo Musto 104cl; Naeblys 146t; Jonathan Nguyen 82b, 150tl; Ron Niebrugge 55tl, 152-3t; Nikreates 19, 110cra, 158-9, 162cra, / *Shaking Man statue* © Terry Allen/VAGA at ARS, NY and DACS, London 2018 142bl;

1NiKreative 129tl; Sérgio Nogueira 55tr; Novarc Images 131br; Oldtime 94clb; George Ostertag 84-5b; Efrain Padro 12-3b, 119br; @Painet Inc. 51tr; David Parker 95crb; Susan Pease 130-1t; Photo.zoommer.ru 218tl; Aurora Photos 233tl; Pictorial Press Ltd 179br; The Picture Pantry 13br; Chuck Place 233cra; Prisma by Dukas Presseagentur GmbH 79crb; Oleksandr Prokopenko 26cra; Ed Rhodes 184br, 248t; Cheryl Rinzler 228bl; Robertharding 54cr; Clive Sawyer 84t; R Scapinello 186-7b; Peter Schickert 30-1t; Ian Shaw 136crb; SiliconValleyStock 98-9b, 235tl; Entertainment Pictures / Snap 57bl; Jo Ann Snover 216-7t; Stars and Stripes 51bl, 51br, 164b; Stephen Saks Photography 38-9b, 250t; Stockimo / Leelocke 21tl, 188-9, / jonathan bailey 12c; Rohan Van Twest 177tl, 201tr; UrbanTexture 144br, 227b; Michael Urmann 207tl; Martin Valigursky 236tl; David Wall 128bl; Michael Warwick 4; Scott Wilson 67cr, 89br, 224-5b; World History Archive 94crb; Zoonar GmbH 113tr; ZUMA Press, Inc. 156tr, 165br, 167tl, 232cl, / Jerome Brunet 42-3b.

AWL Images: Walter Bibikow 14t, 136-7b; Danita Delimont Stock 48-9b; Sabine Lubenow 212.

Bridgeman Images: SZ Photo / Scherl / Bridgeman Images 53br.

Charles Zukow Associates: 15cr.

Chinese Historical Society: 126tl.

Coi: 34-5t.

Depositphotos Inc: Bertl123 68-9b; dell640 6-7; srongkrod481 234bl.

Disney: 69tr.

Dorling Kindersley: Neil Lukas 97crb; Andrew McKinney 170cl; Robert Vente 87bl.

Dreamstime.com: Ahfotobox 214t; Annalevan 200-1b; Coralimages2020 162cr, 163, 195; Debsta75 95bl; F11photo 103b; Giovanni Gagliardi 71t; S Gibson 214bl; Enrique Gomez / *Frieda and Diego* © Banco de México Diego Rivera Frida Kahlo Museums Trust, Mexico, D.F. / DACS 2018 141cla; Karin Hildebrand Lau 231clb; Pius Lee 72-3; Legacy1995 197br; Miniimpressions 222cra; Randy Miramontez 143t; Fergal Moran 51cl; Olgashuster 44-5t; Photopictures Project 33crb; Radkol 193br; Sborisov 13cr; Siempreverde22 53tr; Simathers 184-5t; Tifonimages 29br; TobySophie 218br; Hakan Can Yalcin 144-5t.

Gallery of California Art, Oakland Museum of California, 2012: 222bl.

Geburtshaus Levi Strauss Museum: 183br.

Getty Images: 500px / Josh Beam 2-3; Al Greene

Contributors Kat Rosa, Karen Misuraca, Nick Edwards, Ella Buchan, Christopher P. Baker, Gabrielle Innes, Sophie Blackman, Jamie Jensen, Barry Parr, Dawn Douglas, Shirley Streshinsky, Rachel Everett

Senior Editor Alison McGill

Senior Designer Laura O'Brien

Project Editor Robin Moul

Project Art Editors Bess Daly, Bharti Karakoti, Priyanka Thakur

Factchecker Emma Gibbs

Editors Ruth Reisenberger, Rachel Thompson

Proofreader Samantha Cook

Indexer Zoe Ross

Senior Picture Researcher Ellen Root

Picture Research Ashwin Adimari, Ruchi Bansal, Susie Peachey, Jane Smith, Sumita Khatwani

Illustrators Arcana Studios, Dean Entwhistle, Nick Lipscombe

Senior Cartographic Editor Casper Morris

Cartography Rajesh Chhibber, Mohammad Hassan, Jane Hugill, Jennifer Skelley

Jacket Designers Maxine Pedliham, Bess Daly, Simon Thompson

Jacket Picture Research Susie Peachey

Senior DTP Designer Jason Little

DTP Azeem Siddiqui, George Nimmo

Producer Igrain Roberts

Managing Editor Rachel Fox

Art Director Maxine Pedliham

Publishing Director Georgina Dee

MIX
Paper from responsible sources
FSC™ C018179
www.fsc.org

The information in this DK Eyewitness Travel Guide is checked regularly.

Every effort has been made to ensure that this book is as up-to-date as possible at the time of going to press. Some details, however, such as telephone numbers, opening hours, prices, gallery hanging arrangements and travel information, are liable to change. The publishers cannot accept responsibility for any consequences arising from the use of this book, nor for any material on third party websites, and cannot guarantee that any website address in this book will be a suitable source of travel information. We value the views and suggestions of our readers very highly. Please write to: Publisher, DK Eyewitness Travel Guides, Dorling Kindersley, 80 Strand, London, WC2R 0RL, UK, or email: travelguides@dk.com

First edition 1994

Published in Great Britain by Dorling Kindersley Limited, 80 Strand, London, WC2R 0RL

Published in the United States by DK Publishing, 1450 Broadway, 8th Floor, New York, NY 10018

A CIP catalog record for this book is available from the British Library.

A catalog record for this book is available from the Library of Congress.

ISSN: 1542 1554
ISBN: 978 0 2413 6007 1

Printed and bound in China.

www.dk.com